ON A WING AND A CHAIR

An Epic Solo Flight Around Australia

DAVE JACKA

Published by Dirt Track Publishing
PO Box 208
Fairfield Vic 3078
Australia

Copyright © Dave Jacka 2022
Dave Jacka asserts his right to be known as the author of this work.

ALL RIGHTS RESERVED.
No part of this book may be reproduced, stored in a retrieval system, transmitted in any form by any means electronic, mechanical, photocopying, recording or otherwise without prior written consent of the publishers. All inquiries should be made to the author.

 A catalogue record for this book is available from the National Library of Australia

9780648582625 (paperback)
9780648582632 (ebook)

Cover design by Peter Long
Text design by Libby Austen
Cover photo: Dave Jacka photo by Linda Sands
Cover photo: Jabiru plane flying by Rudy Van Donkelaar
Map by Karen Rumley

Every effort has been made to acknowledge and contact the owners of copyright for permission to reproduce material. Any copyright owners who have inadvertently been omitted from acknowledgements and credits should contact the publisher and omissions will be rectified in future editions.

To Linda, who offered me her love and support to follow my passions.

And to those who dare to dream.

CONTENTS

Introduction		1
Prologue		3
1	A New Beginning	5
2	Out of My Comfort Zone	13
3	Back to the Drawing Board	23
4	Modifications	27
5	Training	31
6	On a Wing & a Chair	35
7	A New Direction	39
8	Out of the Blue	45
9	Falling into Place	49
10	The Why	53
11	Up and Down	57
12	Thailand	61
13	The Trial Flight	67
14	Ramp Up	75
15	One Week to Go	81
16	One Day to Go	89
17	D-Day	93
18	First Milestone: South East Cape	105
19	Sick as a Dog	117
20	The Airlie Beach Incident	135

21	This is No Paradise	143
22	Gotta Get Outta This Place	157
23	Third Down, One to Go	163
24	Burketown Schoolkids	169
25	Days 16 and 17 Nhulunbuy NT	175
26	Darwin Here We Come	181
27	Stage Two: Kununurra	191
28	Change of Plan and Happy Birthday	199
29	Homeward Bound	213
30	We're Going Coastal	219
31	The Great Australian Bight	223
32	Stuck Again	237
33	Party, Fog and Frustrations	243
34	Worth the Fish 'n' Chips	251
35	Welcome Home Dave and Team	257
36	After the Flight	267

| Epilogue | 271 |
| Acknowledgements | 273 |

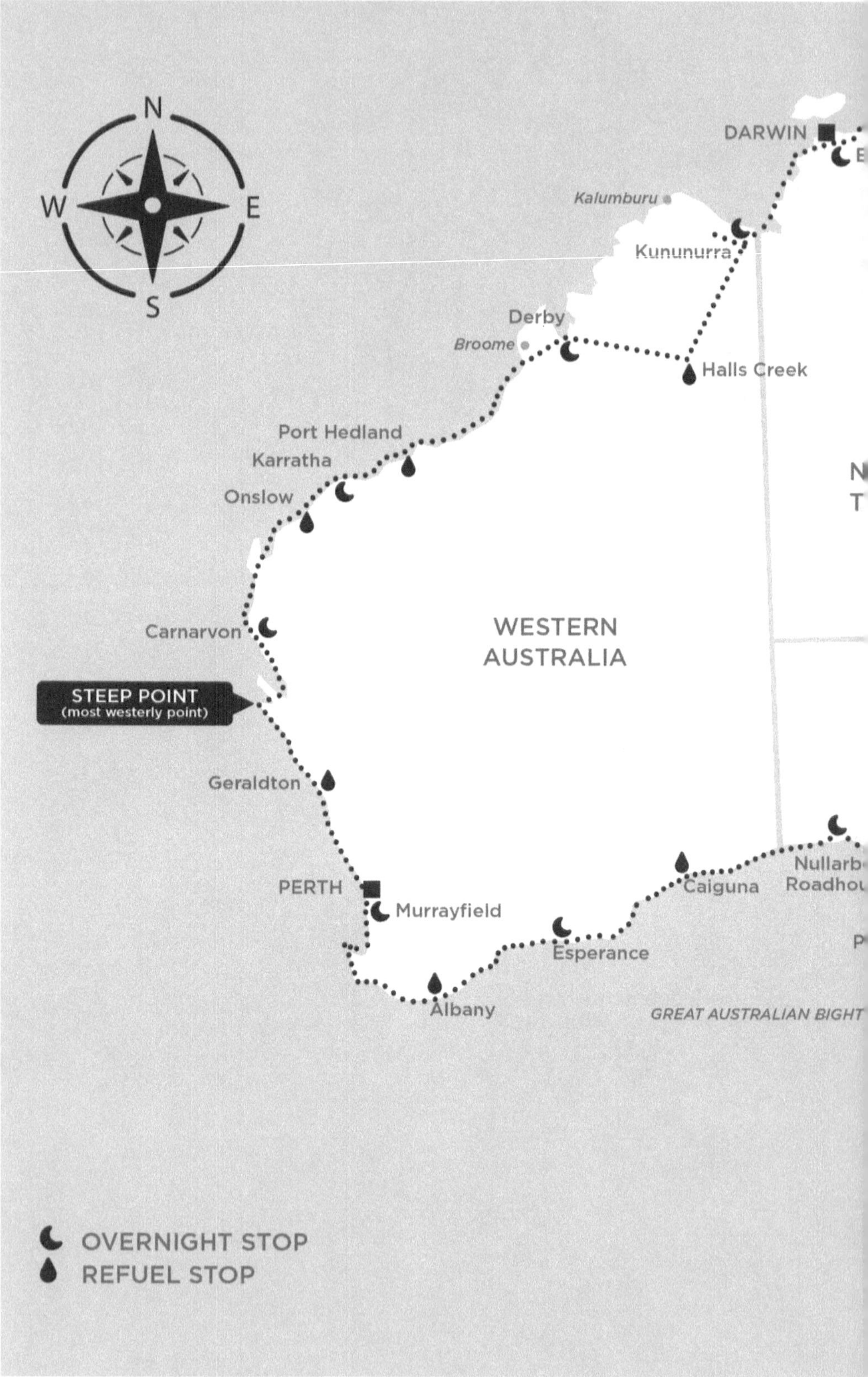
N
S
E
W
DARWIN
Kalumburu
Kununurra
Derby
Broome
Halls Creek
Port Hedland
Karratha
Onslow
Carnarvon
WESTERN AUSTRALIA
STEEP POINT
(most westerly point)
Geraldton
PERTH
Murrayfield
Esperance
Albany
Caiguna
GREAT AUSTRALIAN BIGHT
OVERNIGHT STOP
REFUEL STOP

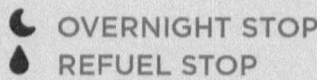

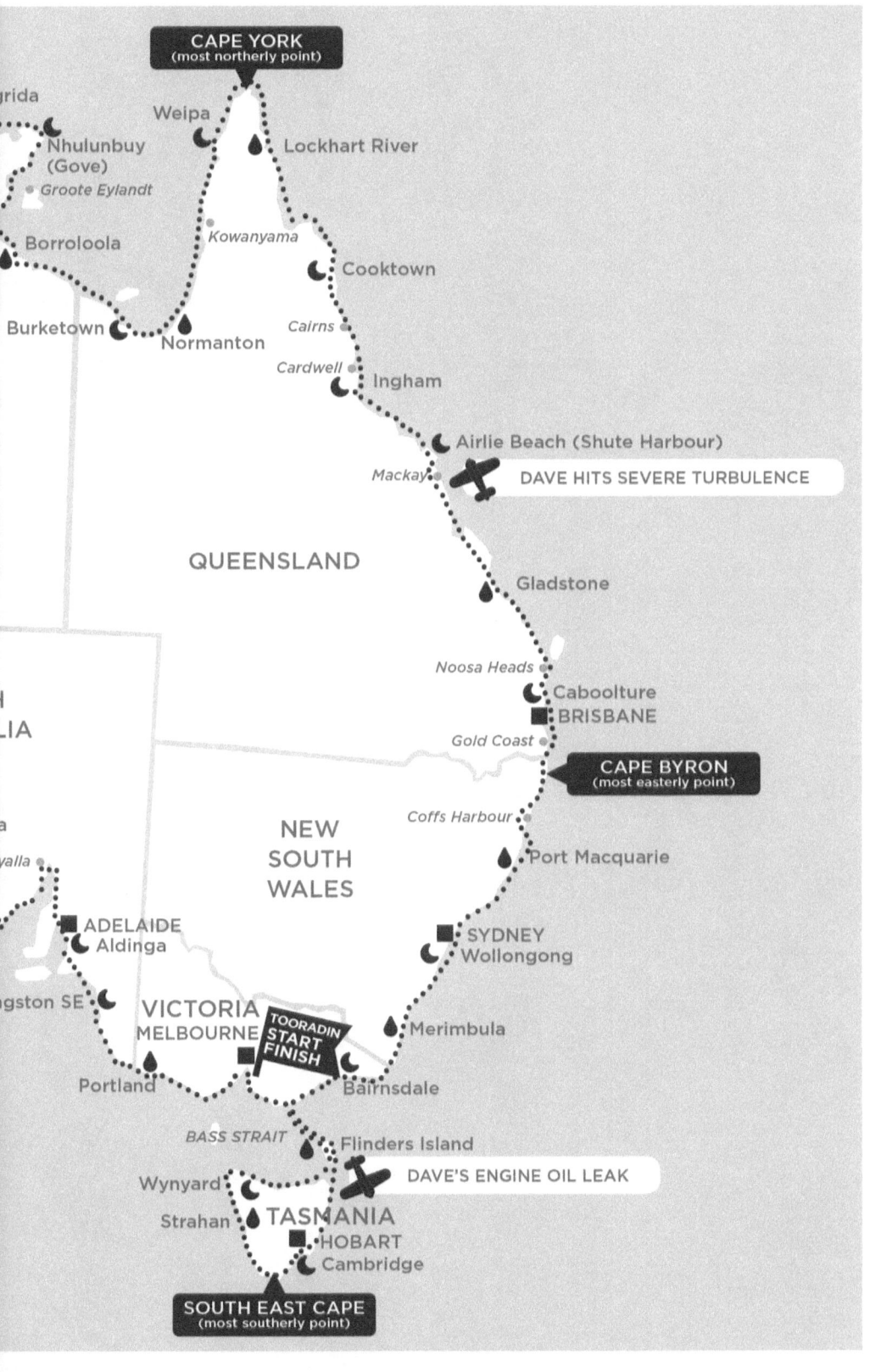

INTRODUCTION

On a Wing and a Chair is my second book following on from *Six Percent*, an account of my motorbike accident that left me with quadriplegia and only six percent physical function.

Six Percent traces the change in my perspective over time, showing what became possible when I began to think outside the square and 'do it differently.'

On a Wing and a Chair is the story of my epic adventure flying solo around Australia, daring to test the limits of my six percent—and in so doing, achieving a world first.

I set this goal because I wanted a challenge; I wanted to push myself beyond my comfort zone and test my limits. But also, having dealt with negative social attitudes towards disability, I wanted to raise the public's expectations of what people with disabilities can achieve.

I hope that by sharing my experiences I may give the public greater insight into the challenges faced by people with disabilities, and of their need to adapt constantly to the physical world. In turn, I also hope this will lead to a greater appreciation of the resourcefulness and capabilities of people with disabilities—people who are capable of achieving much more than what many others may think. Hopefully, this deeper understanding will lead to greater equity, respect, and equality of opportunity for such individuals—as one might expect in an inclusive society.

In writing this book, I have referred to my blogs, videos, personal diary and recalled many details, including characters' dialogue, from memory, so please forgive any inaccuracies.

I've aimed to provide an open and honest account, sharing my experiences as I perceived them. I have also tried to highlight what I learned from my successes, mistakes and struggles, which I hope readers find relevant and applicable to their own lives.

The *On a Wing & a Chair Around Australia Flight* was a tremendous adventure for me and the team. I hope you are inspired to drag a dusty dream out of the closet, dust it off and have a go at making it happen. Why put off what is important to us until tomorrow and miss the opportunity today?

PROLOGUE

For a split second I felt like I was floating—like the coyote in the Road Runner cartoon who runs off a cliff, then hangs in the air momentarily with an *Oh bugger!* expression on his face.

The look on my face—if anyone could have seen it—was of serious consternation as I was jolted by an enormous *thump!* Suddenly, my head hit the roof of the aircraft as it dropped from beneath me like a rock with a bulldozer strapped to it. Following the peculiar feeling of weightlessness, I crashed down into the pilot's seat, falling to the right. *Fuck!* I thought, as I feared I might end up in the passenger seat beside me, my heart rate and adrenalin kicking into overdrive.

The small, single-engine, two-seater Jabiru aircraft I was piloting felt like a tiny cork on a stormy sea as I flew through the churning turbulence coming off a nearby mountain. For a person with quadriplegia—only six percent physical function and no balance—this was not a good situation to be in.

Thankfully, my left wrist was still locked into the hand-support on the rudder-lever handle beside me so I could pull myself back up. It was a taxing effort to hold my limp body upright in the seat with my left arm while steering the plane with my right, all the while being constantly knocked around like a pinball.

My pilot training immediately kicked in as I instinctively sipped on the small plastic tube in my mouth, throttling down the revs of the engine to slow my airspeed so I didn't overstress the wings while also making it a slightly less uncomfortable ride.

I sipped on the plastic tube again to further slow the aircraft, but before I could reach forward with my left hand and adjust the elevator trim control toggle switch on the instrument panel to raise the nose of the plane—*bang!*—another sledgehammer belted down from above. *Shit, shit, shit!* the primal being within me yelled as I felt I was being finished off like a dead tree toppling in the wind.

My left hand came out of the rudder-lever hand-support, and like a limp sausage I fell to the right onto my survival kit in the passenger seat. My reflexes instinctively propelled my left arm out as I frantically tried to grab something, but there was nothing to lock my paralysed fingers onto as I desperately struggled to raise my twisted body.

Everything seemed to be in slow motion and when I looked up, to my dismay, the Perspex windscreen showed the grey choppy ocean of Pioneer Bay as the plane banked over and nosed down. Shit, this is it!

It was Day 9 of the *On a Wing & a Chair Around Australia Flight*, my greatest challenge and one I'd worked towards for six years. My support team and Linda, my wife, had already landed at Shute Harbour in Airlie Beach and were waiting for me to arrive, unaware of my predicament. I was alone in the cockpit on this solo flight and it had been my choice to be there. So many decisions I had made had led me to this point and it was sobering to realise that now, more than ever, my life was in my hands.

1
A NEW BEGINNING

My journey began on 10 July 1988, the night I came off a motorbike, four days before my twentieth birthday. I was thrown headfirst into a tree and shattered the fifth vertebra in my neck, leaving me with quadriplegia. This was the moment my world came crashing down: my life as I knew it, with all my dreams, was over.

Up until that night, my life—or at least the next ten years or so—was mapped out. I would finish my carpentry apprenticeship, start my own business, travel and pursue my boyhood dream of learning to fly. Until the accident, my whole sense of self was linked to my physicality; it was the foundation of my identity.

I enjoyed and excelled at my job as an apprentice carpenter building houses and, at the time of my accident, fitting out an office building. On weekends in summer, with a few mates and girlfriends, I would drive down to the beach to surf all day until we were contentedly tired and starving; then feed our faces with fried dim-sims, chips and cans of Coke for the drive home. With the arrival of winter, I indulged in my real passion: snow-skiing. Hurtling down a mountainside like a 'bat out of hell' was so exhilarating, as was riding my motorbike.

When I broke my neck, I smashed the fifth cervical vertebra (C5) into three pieces. Despite this, I have retained some movement down to the next level, C6. My tactile sense—that is, what I can feel—is also closer to C6. I'm classified as C5/6 complete. The little bit of C6 that works makes a difference in what I can do.

My injury left me with no finger function; I have wrist extension, which means when my palm is facing down, I can raise the back of my hand towards my forearm. But I have no wrist flexion, which means that when my palm is facing up, I can't raise my hand towards my forearm. I also have no movement below my armpits. My arm function is also limited; my biceps work but my triceps don't. If I lift my arm above my head it falls back down—which makes it hard to pick my nose when I'm lying on my back!

I have relatively normal feeling around my shoulders and on the top sides of my arms down to my thumbs, but no feeling on the underside of my arms or hands. Unless you fully sever your spinal cord, some patches of sensation may remain; in my case, I have dull sensations on my bum and feet.

One of the most difficult things to manage is temperature control, as my body no longer automatically regulates it. Rather, it takes on the temperature of the environment: when it's hot I overheat, when it's cold I freeze. I'm like a reptile.

After my accident, a specialist who assessed my level of function said I was 94 percent impaired. The question of what I would be able to do or experience with six percent function became ever-present in my mind. Would I achieve only six percent of my potential? Did it mean my life would be six percent fulfilling? Or did it mean something else? I became obsessed with finding out.

I spent my first two months at the Austin Hospital Spinal Unit lying in bed with head-tongs screwed into the sides of my skull. An attached rope that held around three kilograms of weight hung over the end of the bed. This medieval-looking device was to pull my neck straight to allow the broken vertebrae to heal. Once the head-tongs were removed, I was mobilised into a wheelchair, to start rehabilitation.

Rehab was like being reborn into a second life—but with a man-sized floppy body that I couldn't control. Like a baby, I had to relearn all the basic everyday tasks that I once took for granted. My first big challenge, attempting to feed myself, initially left me with more food on me than in my mouth. But with constant practice, carefully taking one mouthful at a time while using a Palm Pocket, a special device strapped to my hand to hold a fork or spoon that I could use without finger function, I eventually mastered it.

During my seven months of rehab, my days were spent at physio and occupational therapy, building my strength with the few muscles that still functioned and relearning the last twenty years of living skills. In the beginning it was how to pick up a polystyrene cup for a drink, use a microwave to make a cup of coffee (I could no longer lift a kettle), do up and undo a shirt button to dress my top half (the bottom half was too difficult), brush my hair and clean my teeth.

There were also new challenges: how to transfer independently from my wheelchair into bed; managing the side effects of my medication; avoiding pressure sores, especially on my bum; and understanding how my body worked, such as peeing. I had to wear a special latex condom with an adhesive on the inside so it would stick to my penis, which was then connected to a tube that fed into a leg-bag.

And let's not forget the most personal of bodily functions: having a poo. It was now a lot more involved and, to be honest, no longer enjoyable. Now it was a drawn-out process every second day. I had to take Senokot (a laxative) the night before, and the following morning an enema was inserted to get things moving. This was followed by an hour or so of sitting on a commode waiting for my bowel to expel its load. Finally, to make sure I was completely pooped out—as I couldn't tell due to lack of sensation—my carer would whip on a latex glove, liberally smear K-Y Jelly over a preferred finger and insert it up my bum. This was to ensure there was no biohazard up high in the bowel, removing the risk of shitting my pants throughout the day.

These were only a few of the many everyday processes I had to come to terms with, relearn and remaster.

After nine long months of hospital recovery, I finally went home to pick up my life where I had left it—although it was never going to be the same, no matter how much I wanted it to be.

My greatest loss was my independence. I had to rely on carers to get me up in the morning and help me with everything such as showering, dressing, going to the toilet, putting on the leg-bag that I'd pee into during the day; then I'd need someone to empty it for me periodically, help me prepare meals and even cut up my food.

But the most difficult and frustrating aspect of losing my independence was having to rely on my mum, dad and sisters in the evenings to help me out of my wheelchair onto the bed and then to undress. If I could have had one wish (apart from a new spinal cord), it would have been to be able to transfer out of my wheelchair independently—just to get a fraction of independence, a tiny bit of relief, from my physical imprisonment.

Out of desperation, I reached a crossroads: I could either resign myself to depending on my family or carers, thereby limiting my choices and opportunities for the rest of my life, or I could give it my absolute best shot and try to work out a way to transfer, no matter how long and how much effort it took.

To be honest, I was very doubtful that I would ever be able to transfer out of my wheelchair and onto my bed independently; it was like trying to imagine myself climbing Mount Everest. But I knew that if I didn't try, I would be left wondering, *What if?* I had to have a go; only then could I accept reliance on others for the rest of my life.

The only way I could even consider this impossible goal was to break it down into smaller achievable goals: small steps I could get my head around and attempt.

At the Austin, I was shown how to transfer: put my feet on the ground, move my body forward in the wheelchair seat, then move my bum across onto the bed, and finally lift up my legs. It sounds easy, but even if I managed to get onto the bed, I could never lift my legs; they were like lead weights and I didn't have the strength.

The way I was shown didn't work for me. If I was to have even a slight chance, I had to do it differently. I had to work out a way that suited my physical capabilities.

During rehab at the Austin I had met another quad with years of experience in a wheelchair who had worked out another way. He put his legs up first, which was easier and gave him better balance. I decided to give it a go.

Now my new process was: lift my legs onto the bed, move my bum forward and then slide across. Sounds simple.

Every day I practised getting my legs onto the bed. With the chair parallel to the bed, brakes on, I had to first lift my left leg up, then the right. They were so heavy, I struggled to lift my left leg even halfway up. Time and time again I tried. As soon as the leg was at 45 degrees or so, it felt like a rubber band was attached and it sprung back, no matter how hard I tried. For the next month I worked at it, over and over again, changing my technique to use the frame of the chair as a pivot point for my elbow to lever my leg up.

Then, unexpectedly, one day it seemed as if an invisible force grabbed my leg as I lifted, and with a quick flick it was up on the bed. Getting the right one up proved to be not as difficult due to the position and my right arm being stronger. Within days I had both legs up. My first big victory! I suddenly felt light, a sparkle of excitement mixed with a glimmer of hope that motivated me to keep going. I was a little closer to achieving my 'impossible' goal.

My next goal was getting my bum forward in the wheelchair. Putting my legs up first solved one problem but caused another: the rubber soles of my shoes prevented my feet from sliding on the sheets, which made it much more difficult to slide my body forward. However, after a fair bit of yoga-like twisting of my legs, I eventually managed to work out a way to remove my shoes.

To move my bum forward I had to throw the top half of my body forward while pushing off the right wheel and the bed for leverage. Gathering my strength like a wild cat ready to pounce on its prey, I pushed with all my might.

'Faaark!' I yelped as the front of the chair spun away, my bum slid off the seat and I landed hard on the floor, my upper body falling backwards and my head hitting the bedside table. 'This is fuckin' impossible,' I moaned and gave my carer a roasting for not stopping the chair in time.

Positioning the back of the wheels against the bedside table helped a little, but the front kept moving out. It was no use. I didn't have enough bodily function, or enough strength, to hold the chair and move forward, let alone slide across.

By asking my carer to hold the chair, I eventually managed to move my bum forward, which required a lot of heaving, swearing and throwing myself forward like a pendulum. Although the cavernous four-inch gap between my chair and bed remained, with my carer holding my chair, I surprised myself by being able to straddle it and drag myself to the other side. I felt stable enough that I wasn't going to fall but, more importantly, I began to think that maybe, just maybe, I might be able to do it. If I could just work out a way.

The hurdle that I couldn't overcome was stopping the front of the chair from moving away from the bed. I just didn't have the strength to hold it in place. I practised and practised over many months, trying different techniques, hoping that over time I might develop enough strength.

My motivation and sanity fluctuated like a roller coaster. My swearing and yelling didn't help my transfer, but it made me feel better. Each week I felt like giving up, especially when I couldn't see any progress; it was so disheartening. I was so close but no matter what I did, I just couldn't do it.

Frustrated and pissed off with trying and getting nowhere, I'd leave it for a day or even a week if necessary to recharge my mental energy, then have another go when I felt a little more positive.

I tried various ideas such as caster locks which held the front casters of the wheelchair in place; they worked a little but not enough. My ideas got a little more elaborate, like devising an electric locking mechanism on the floor to hold the front of the chair.

Working out a way to stop the chair from moving was consuming my waking thoughts. It was my last obstacle; I was so close.

As I sat next to my bed looking at the floor in a daze from my last failed try and consequential disappointment, thoughts trickled through my mind as to how I could stop the front from moving. I suddenly experienced what could only be described as an epiphany.

The Holy Grail I had been looking for was so simple. A hook! *A simple hook!* I scolded myself for not thinking of it sooner; it was so obvious.

By bolting a hook to my bed, I could clip it onto the frame to hold my chair secure. It was brilliant! My heart raced with excitement; I was now sure I could do it.

Dad found some scrap steel rod, bent it into shape, attached a strap made from an old seat belt and nailed it to the wooden bedframe.

I was impatient, ordering Dad to hurry up and move out of the way so I could try it.

Parking my chair next to the bed on a slight angle to minimise the gap between the chair and bed, I clipped the hook on easily. With my legs up, I threw myself forward—whack, whack—and pushed off the chair and bed, sliding my whole body forward. It held perfectly! Steadying myself, Dad ready to catch me if I fell, leaning forward, I dragged my bum a little to test it. With the hook still holding, I pushed off with two short slides, dragging one bum cheek, then the other from the chair onto the bed.

'I did it!' I said, panting, with the biggest grin from ear to ear.

'Well done, David, that was really great,' Dad said, as happy as I was with the thought of no more late nights putting me to bed.

I needed my slide-board and some help to get back onto the wheelchair, but with some experimentation I managed to work it out and do it myself within a few weeks.

The hook idea was transferrable to the car. With a few modifications, I was soon getting myself in and out. My challenge then was dismantling my wheelchair and getting it in and out of the car. Initially it took me half an hour, but motivated by the possibilities and lots of practice, I got it down to under ten minutes.

Achieving this seemingly impossible goal was a turning point in my life. It gave me independence and, more importantly, it changed my perspective. The experience altered the way I viewed challenges. It opened my mind to the possibilities inherent in challenges, instead of the obstacles.

This new perspective redefined how I saw my potential. I realised that six percent was only a number. It did not define what I was capable of.

Six percent enabled me to go back to study and start a new career in engineering, progress into project management, compete at the 1996 Paralympics in wheelchair rugby, buy a house and move out of my parents' place to live independently. But most important of all, six percent allowed me to follow my dream to fly.

2

OUT OF MY COMFORT ZONE

In 2006, I was living my dream of flying; I couldn't get enough of it. I'd regularly drive the four and a half hours from Melbourne to Porepunkah on a Friday evening, fly all day Saturday and Sunday morning, then drive back home in the afternoon. However, the novelty started to lose its gloss as I was spending far more time in the car than in the air. With the approach of winter in 2006, I moved my aircraft to Benalla airport, located on the flat plains of northern Victoria, which was a more manageable two-and-a-half-hour drive from where I lived.

Tony Dennis, a past weight-shift microlight trike instructor at the airfield, leased out a section of the dilapidated WWII hanger and for a small fee, I and a few others stored our trikes. Barry and Mike, whom I had initially met at the Avalon Airshow in 2005, were also there; they were indirectly responsible for reigniting my dream to fly when I saw one of their trikes on display.

Until that airshow in 2005, I had never imagined I'd be able to fly with my disability, given my limited arm strength and non-functioning fingers, amongst other physical limitations. But when I saw their trike, I immediately envisioned the possibilities.

A weight-shift microlight trike is essentially a powered hang-glider, constructed of a large hang-glider wing with a pod hanging below the wing where the pilot and passenger sit (the pilot at the front between the passenger's legs). There is a motor at the back and it has a front and two rear wheels. It takes off and lands like a regular plane.

In flight it is controlled by a horizontal bar called the base-bar which hangs in front of the pilot and is connected to the wing. To steer, the base-bar is pushed left or right, which shifts the weight of the pod, causing the aircraft to turn. To make it climb and descend, the pilot powers the engine up and down.

I'd found the perfect aircraft, but to my surprise the greatest obstacle I came up against was trying to find someone to teach me to fly. 'I don't think you will be able to fly a trike, you don't have enough strength,' said one instructor as he unclipped himself from the back seat. 'Maybe you should try something else.' Those words devastated me and I almost gave up on my dream.

It wasn't until sometime later when I contacted Steve Ruffels, chief flying instructor at the Eagle School of Microlighting, that my luck changed. He was one of the few people who could see beyond my disability and was willing to give me a go.

After a successful Trial Instructional Flight (TIF) with Steve in November 2005, and his confidence that I was capable of flying solo with a modified aircraft, I immediately bought a second-hand trike from him and adapted it so I could fly it independently. I installed a fibreglass go-cart seat and harness to give me good lateral support as I have zero trunk balance. As I don't have finger function, I developed a base-bar adaptation that locked my hands on the base-bar so I could control the wing and steer in the air. I also had push buttons installed on the base-bar adaptation so I could throttle the speed of the engine up and down without needing to use a foot. Also, on my left side I had a hand-lever added so I could steer the front nose-wheel for taxiing on the ground instead of using my feet. These adaptations, as well as Steve's continuous support and encouragement, enabled me to become a fledgling eagle and soar the skies.

My first solo flight on Valentine's Day in 2006 was one of the scariest and most exciting experiences of my life, one that opened my mind to possibilities far greater than I could ever have imagined. I felt that I could do almost anything.

At the culmination of my training and having completed my cross-country endorsement, Steve asked, 'So Dave, what's next?'

I thought about it for a moment. I wanted to do something bigger, something that would test me, something that would push me to the absolute limits of my six percent.

'Flying solo around Australia would be good!' I said.

Steve laughed, patting me on the back. 'Oh man … that'll be some trip!'

Barry and Mike came up to Benalla most weekends, which made it that much more enjoyable to have others to fly and chat with. Most mornings, not long after sunrise, they would be out prepping their aircraft, with me not far behind (if my carer didn't sleep in). We'd be taking off as the glowing golden ball slowly rose above the horizon, our trikes soaring through the cool, smooth air before the thermals or wind picked up in the late morning.

Being a novice to the world of flying, I listened with interest to their flying stories as they tinkered with their planes and, like most pilots, they willingly shared their knowledge and advice. Barry was easygoing; Mike was quite the opposite, being somewhat cautious, which was probably a good thing for me given I had a lot to learn about the challenges of flying.

During my flight training and thereafter, I flew mainly in the early morning and late afternoon when the conditions were generally benign. It was very enjoyable flying, but on the downside,

I was not increasing my experience in more windy and turbulent conditions. Although somewhat naïve about the physical effort and skills required to tackle tougher conditions on longer cross-country flights, I couldn't wait to get stuck into it.

Flying for me wasn't just about doing 'touch and go' circuits around the airport, with occasional local flights to nearby towns, although this was fun; it was about Adventure—having the freedom to go places I hadn't been before.

A few people at the microlight club I was involved in discussed organising some flying trips, but nothing ever eventuated. However, in March 2007, with limited experience and less than sixty flying hours under my belt, I got my first taste of cross-country flying when I joined Peter McLean's Navex flying trip.

Peter was an ex-navy pilot turned microlight trike instructor at Yarrawonga Airport. Twice a year he organised flying trips, the Navex being the shorter one for slower aircraft, and a longer one for faster aircraft in May called the Megafauna. The trips were very well organised, with booked hotel accommodation and a bus that carried our gear and fuel, and also my carer, Sam, who met us along the route.

On Day 1, around ten aircraft and twenty people left at 10.00 a.m. to fly our first leg to Deniliquin. Taxiing my trike to Runway 23 at Yarrawonga, with only my right hand locked in the base-bar adaptation, I struggled to hold the wing down into the light wind; it was like hanging on to a huge beach umbrella. With my left hand on the steering lever, I tried with all my might to steer the front wheel against the force of the wind, but it was impossible. I ended up taxiing into a stormwater ditch.

Feeling embarrassed and like a dickhead, I was glad to see Peter arrive on his quad-bike to help push me out. Taking off, I just kept thinking, *Don't stuff up now, don't stuff up now,* as all eyes watched me accelerate down the runway into the air.

I had an easy landing at Deniliquin with the wind straight down the runway, and with the memory of Yarrawonga still fresh in my mind, I was very careful to keep the wing down into the wind as I turned off the runway. But suddenly the wind grabbed the wing again, pushing me towards the landing lights that marked the edge of the runway. *Shit!* I thought, realising I couldn't steer against it, so I aimed between the lights, just missing them, and stopped the trike on the grass at the side of the runway. Shane, another pilot, came taxiing past in his Drifter Ultralight. Realising my problem, he came over and gave me a hand to wing-walk (holding the wing tip) to the parking area.

I was pissed off with myself and again embarrassed about requiring help for the second time that day.

Taxiing the tike wasn't working out well, so Peter suggested that he and a couple of the guys wing-walk me to the runway and point me into the wind for takeoff, which was fine by me.

But Murphy's Law—what can go wrong will go wrong—prevailed. As Peter and Shane walked me out to the runway my brake-cable snapped, so now I had no brakes. What else could happen? As I pointed into the wind, I gunned the machine. Peter and Shane ran beside me, holding on to the wing for as long as they could, then let it go. I lifted into the air towards Hay, our final leg for the day.

On my approach, Hay and the surrounding area was desolate and dry: empty dams dotted the landscape like craters on the moon, and barbed-wire fences divided dust-filled paddocks. Except for the occasional scraggy-looking tree, the countryside was bare of vegetation.

Peter radioed me. 'Dave, land long and we'll grab your wing.'

'Affirmative, Peter,' I replied.

I landed too short. As I rolled down the runway the wind gusted, lifting the wing. 'Shit, not again!' I swore at myself as I tried pulling it back to level, but it was impossible with my right arm wrenched across to my left side. Reacting instinctively, I pulled hard on the steering lever to try and avoid a two-foot-high bank some metres off to the side of the runway, but it was already in full lock. There was nothing I could do except grit my teeth and wait for the imminent impact, hoping it wouldn't hurt too much.

Smack! My body jolted forward, the front wheel bounced on top of the bank, the trike tipped over to the left side, balancing on the wing tip and stopped. *That wasn't so bad.*

With my right hand jammed in the base-bar adaptation, I couldn't reach the kill switches to shut off the engine. Looking to my left, I could see fuel leaking from the top of the tank. Trying again to violently wrench my hand free, I realised it was well and truly jammed. I just hoped I wouldn't catch fire, otherwise I'd be one cooked quad.

It seemed like an eternity as I watched the stream of fuel, but within seconds Ian Willis, another pilot, rushed up with Peter. They quickly shut down the engine and freed me. There was no damage to the trike, but my confidence, as well as my right hand, had taken a battering.

With Day 2 being a rest day, we saw the sights around Hay. Most notable was the Shearers Hall of Fame, although with the drought there were no sheep. I was glad to have the day off as it gave my swollen right hand some time to recover. Shane, a paramedic in his day job, fixed me up with a compression bandage and I bought some anti-inflammatory tablets in the hope they would reduce the swelling.

At the Day 3 morning team briefing, I waited for Peter to pull me aside to tell me that I couldn't go further, and to spend the rest of the trip on the bus. After the briefing we had a quick chat. 'You're the pilot in command,' he said, 'it's up to you.' He was right: it was my responsibility to decide if I should fly or not, not his. I was going to fly.

My right hand was still very swollen and wouldn't fit into the hand-support on the base-bar adaptation, so with Sam pushing down I gave it a bash with my left hand, eventually forcing it in. It wasn't going anywhere now. By twisting my wrist, I could still press the button to throttle the engine; I was all set.

The horizontal wind-sock made me nervous; I wished the wind would die off a little until I got into the air, but it kept blowing around 15–20 knots. Peter and Shane again wing-walked me to the runway and pointed me into the wind. I powered up the engine and within a few metres I was up, climbing above the airfield. With a quick circle of the airfield to make sure the aircraft was operating correctly after the previous incident, I headed to Moulamein, a dirt airstrip with a rusted tin lean-to as a terminal building, to refuel. Then on to Swan Hill for our overnight stop. It was a pleasant surprise once I was up, with the air so smooth I could relax a little and enjoy flying.

Approaching Swan Hill the weather changed to low cloud and patches of rain. I could go around the smaller patches but 10 nautical miles (NM) from the aerodrome, I had no choice but to go through a thin band of rain. Descending to 500 feet so I could still see the ground, in less than a minute I burst out the other side, soaked through, with the aerodrome dead ahead.

My Day 4 log says it all: flying from Swan Hill to Boort for lunch, then on to Bridgewater for the overnight stop.

Logbook Entry
29/3/07
Weather – Shit, cloudy, moderate/fresh wind
Swan Hill – Boort – Bridgewater
Very strong wind at Swan Hill almost pulled out as I was very nervous of conditions.

Not a bad flight to Boort. Took off at Boort into 25-knot winds, wing-walked take-off. Very rough flight to Bridgewater & crap landing. Was tired and glad to get on ground.
It was a good experience, realised I can handle rough conditions.
Flight Duration: 2.5 hours solo.

Reaching Bridgewater, I was cold, physically tired and mentally drained. I would have prayed for good weather if I'd believed it would do any good.

'Sam, what's the weather like?' I asked my carer as I lay in bed at five in the morning on the fifth and final day, Ian snoring on the bunk next to me.

'I can't really see, but it looks windy,' she said.

I felt uneasy again. I hadn't slept much on the trip, and last night was the worst. I lay there wondering if I could do it.

As Sam packed my gear, I looked up at the swaying trees. It was at least 15–20 knots, which made me feel even more apprehensive. I watched Ian take off for a joy flight, his craft bouncing around as it hit turbulence.

I couldn't go on. I might have been able to battle through my physical tiredness, but not my mental exhaustion. I knew it was time to quit.

Looking out the bus window watching everyone else take off, I felt like a failure. I'd had one day to go; maybe I should have tried; maybe it would have been all right. The scenarios flicked through my head and my emotions cascaded from feelings of failure, to relief, then to doubt, over and over again.

In my heart, though, I knew I'd made the right decision. I had achieved far more than I could have imagined by stepping way beyond my comfort zone, putting myself in situations I would normally have avoided. I had pushed myself to my absolute limits both physically and mentally. I had done my best; I had no more to give.

Arriving at Yarrawonga on the bus that afternoon, the wind was blowing 30 knots, further validating my decision.

My idea of flying around Australia now seemed so out of reach. I needed another plan.

3

BACK TO THE DRAWING BOARD

Although I felt like a failure at the time, the trip was a fantastic learning experience and actually a huge success. Experiences like these are part of the learning and creative process—trying different options, doing things differently, ruling out what doesn't work, and getting closer to discovering what does. It's all trial and error. This was, and still is, my life.

The support and encouragement from Peter and the other pilots enabled me to see how far I could go. No one ever suggested that I quit. Instead they helped me find ways to continue, allowing me to achieve so much.

My biggest lesson was that I didn't want to be in the same position again. If I wanted to fly around Australia, I needed a new game plan.

Since telling Steve my goal of flying around Australia, I was constantly thinking about how I could do it. I had been slowly working out a plan with dozens of maps of the Australian coastline. The enormity of the task wasn't apparent until I plotted how long it would take to travel from one point to another in good conditions, then realising that what appeared to be a few days was actually one week of flying. Australia is one hell of a big country!

My lessons following that first cross-country flight in 2007 were that I needed a faster trike and a better method for ground steering. With my new Airborne XT-912 fitted with a faster Cruze wing, I implemented my biggest innovation and game-changer—the development of a sip/puff system to steer the front nose-wheel on the ground. By sipping (sucking in) on a tube in my mouth the front wheel steered left, while puffing steered it right; it was brilliant. This now allowed me to control the wing with both hands and steer with my mouth—in all conditions.

On one of the Megafauna trips, I landed in 30-knot winds and with Laura, my carer, sitting in the back seat helping me to hold the wing, we managed to get the trike to a hanger without any problems. These changes opened up the world of flying to me.

However, the trike was very limited in what it could carry—essentially one passenger or my wheelchair in the back seat. To fly around Australia, I would need carers and other support during the flight. A ground crew would then be necessary to meet up at each landing spot. But the logistics of transporting a ground crew into remote areas—the time and costs alone for support vehicles—made this option impractical.

Also, the memory of flying to Broken Hill on the 2008 Megafauna trip was still fresh in my mind. In the open cockpit I was miserably cold. Trying to solve this problem, I wore a heated vest to keep me warm; but unable to feel the heat, I ended up with a burn the size of a fifty-cent piece in the middle of my back. Again, I realised I needed another plan.

John Kidon, a trike pilot and good friend, had just gone to the 'dark side' and bought a new Jabiru J230 fixed-wing aircraft. It was a high-wing two-seater, quite fast at 120-knot cruise speed with room in the back for gear. Also, with the wing strut and undercarriage behind the pilot's door, it provided good access to park a wheelchair alongside, so I could get in. The control column to steer was in the centre console out of the way of your legs, but the best thing was: it had a heater! I started to think this might be my solution.

From my experience, the more goals you achieve, the bigger they get. Your comfort zone expands, and so does your mindset and self-belief. Similarly, the way I viewed problems had also changed since I'd started to fly. Initially I saw my hands as a limitation: without finger dexterity I couldn't use small knobs or buttons on the instruments of more complex aircraft. However, I now saw this as a challenge, an obstacle that could be overcome with the right solution. I realised there was a solution to every problem—it was just a matter of finding it.

As with my car and the trike, I couldn't fully try before I bought. All I could do was go up in a Jabiru with an instructor where I flew using only the control column, while he did everything else. Instantly, I could tell it required much less strength to fly than the trike, and it could handle tougher weather conditions. However, on the downside, it was far more complicated to fly and adapt than the trike.

For cross-country flying it would give me much more independence. I could take a passenger and carry all my gear, including my wheelchair, to avoid getting stuck without it, as had happened on the trip to Broken Hill. On that trip, another pilot took my wheelchair in his Cessna 172, but he forgot to meet me at our lunch spot at a remote airfield in Pooncarie, NSW. Fortunately, a council worker at the airfield went home and got a plastic chair for me so I didn't have to be in the trike all day. I only got my wheelchair back at our overnight stop at the end of the day in Mildura. I was a little annoyed!

Without my wheelchair, I'm like a turtle on its back. The wheelchair is my legs, my independence; without it I can't get around. It's frustrating enough to be limited to the mobility of the wheelchair, but when it's taken away, I feel totally helpless. At home, I prefer to stay in my chair instead of sitting on the couch to watch a film because I would then have to rely on someone to get me a drink or empty my leg-bag. Even for brief periods, I hate losing my freedom.

The Jabiru ticked all the boxes with great range and speed to easily cover large distances but, more importantly, I could use another support aircraft to follow me with a support crew instead of requiring a ground crew. I had found my solution—I had a plan!

4

MODIFICATIONS

Flying a fixed-wing aircraft is completely different from flying a weight shift microlight trike.

To turn a trike when flying, you shift the weight of the pod by pushing the base-bar connected to the wing left and right, and to climb and descend it's a matter of throttling the speed of the engine up and down. Very simple.

The Jabiru is a fixed-wing three axis control aircraft, where the pilot controls all three axes. The rudder, operated by foot-pedals, controls the yaw of the plane (moves the nose left/right), which keeps the nose pointed in the direction of flight. The control column, which is like a big joystick, operates the elevator which adjusts the pitch (nose up/down), as well as the ailerons which alters the roll (roll wings left/right) of the aircraft. Then there is the engine: adjustment of the power settings (engine speed up/down) is done by pulling a rod in and out on the dash.

Fortunately, Jabiru was an Australian company, owned by Rod Stiff at the time, who was open to innovative ideas and agreed to approve my adaptations—providing he deemed them sound and that I bought an aircraft from him.

I spent the next four months designing the adaptations and finally got Jabiru's approval, ready for installation.

In December 2008 my new Jabiru J230D arrived from Bundaberg and Geoff Higgins, highly skilled with Level 2 aircraft accreditation and a fitter/engineer/motorbike builder in his earlier life, started work on my adaptations, taking six frustrating months to build and test them.

I had to extensively adapt the controls of the aircraft to suit my functional ability. There were no hand controls on the market that I could use, and no one had ever modified the Jabiru or developed any adaptations that would suit this aircraft. I was starting with a blank piece of paper.

My designs were only the starting point; each adaptation evolved from there. It was a methodical process of continuous improvement. Build an adaptation, test it, assess it, modify it, test it and so on, as many times as was needed until it worked the way I wanted.

Having proven myself by flying trikes made it much easier to find a willing instructor and Ian Loveridge, the Chief Flying Instructor (CFI) from Tooradin Flying School, was happy to take me on. He was open-minded, highly experienced, calm and easygoing, willing to let me make mistakes from which I could learn, but also not letting me get into dangerous situations. After completing each adaptation, I'd try it out and see how it performed; then, if needed, I would modify it and try it out again. I had to do a lot of ground tests to make certain the adaptations worked correctly, and lastly undertake a flight test with Ian to confirm the adaptations worked just right. There was never any risk of losing control or crashing as the right-hand seat, where the instructor sat, had full working controls and everything I installed could be overridden. It was a slow process and often became frustrating; fix one thing, then another problem arose.

Not everything worked out the way I had intended. I had originally planned to install a pneumatic system to operate the throttle, elevator trim and brakes. But after hours of trials, with

Geoff pulling his hair out in frustration almost to the point of a nervous breakdown, we couldn't get it to work properly. In the end we scrapped the idea, keeping the pneumatic system only to operate the brakes.

The adaptations were extensive. The rudder-pedals were removed and converted to a hand-lever on my left side, operated by push/pull (push forward the nose yaws right, pull back the nose yaws left). The control column (controlling pitch/roll) was modified so that my wrist was supported and my hand locked in place by two vertical posts—one either side of my wrist—as with the rudder-lever. In the end, I returned to my original idea to operate the throttle of the engine, using a small electric motor with a clutch. But with both hands busy on the rudder-lever and control column, I decided to control the throttle using a sip/puff system—sip (suck) on the plastic tube in my mouth to throttle the engine down, puff (blow) on the tube to throttle the engine up.

The brake, normally a hand-lever that I couldn't use as my fingers don't work, was converted to a toggle switch that activated the pneumatic system, which in turn operated the brake. By flicking the toggle up and down at different speeds the brake was operated from soft to hard, while to lock the wheels I held the toggle switch fully on. I also converted the elevator trim control to a toggle switch that activated a linear actuator to move the trim forward/backwards, instead of manual operation using a lever. The control of the electric flaps was converted to a push button on the rudder-lever handle. Lastly, I installed little levers on the knobs of the instruments so I could flick them around with my gummy fingers to adjust the settings.

The aircraft sat high off the ground, so Geoff built a compact scissor-lift that plugged into the power outlet in the plane. With it positioned under my wheelchair, it would elevate me and my wheelchair to the height of the door so I could get in and out with assistance. It was a great little unit that was stored and transported in the back of the plane.

After six months, the adaptations were finally finished but, as with anything, a few tweaks were needed during my training with Ian. One time while doing circuits, the throttle control stopped working. Ian took over as it could be operated manually and I landed the plane. It ended up being nothing more than a loose wire.

5

TRAINING

Other pilots who had converted from flying a trike to three axes warned me that as the controls are in reverse I might unconsciously do the wrong movement, in particular push forward instead of back on the control column when flaring on landing. This type of error could result in a broken plane.

I never had that problem. The challenge for me was my coordination, using my left hand on the rudder-lever to go one way while doing a totally different movement with my right hand on the control column, as well as sipping or puffing on the throttle tube. Doing all three movements at the same time was like tapping your head, rubbing your stomach and hopping on one foot. A couple of times coming in on 'final' (when the aircraft is lined up with the runway and descending to land), I'd push on my left instead of pull, my right doing the opposite, with the plane weaving left and right until I worked out where each hand needed to be. Ian was always relaxed and simply asked, 'Are you right?' I didn't answer.

Everything happens much faster in the Jabiru than the trike. Initially, it was brain overload. Throttle down, pull this, push that, adjust throttle, pull back further, flaps, trim … I struggled just to remember the sequence. As with driving a car, flying takes a lot of practice; you have to learn to think ahead of the machine, to anticipate two or three steps ahead of what's happening.

Initially, I was a little overconfident, given my previous flying experience. I was impatient and thought I'd be able to pick it up quickly. I knew how to fly, knew the theory and what to do, but putting it into practice wasn't as easy.

I was flying both Saturdays and Sundays, getting in around 2.5 hours a day in two sessions, which is a lot of flying while training. Being switched on, constantly forming an ever-changing mental picture of where other aircraft were in the circuit, doing radio calls, and managing what was happening inside the cockpit as well as flying the machine were all mentally draining,

I thought I would be doing my solo by August; however, my frustration intensified as I could not find my groove and be consistent with my landings. My own self-analysis and the advice from Ian didn't help. I knew what I needed to do, but I couldn't translate the thoughts in my head to the aircraft's operation quick enough. I was a passenger, not the pilot.

One Friday afternoon, the blanket of thick, dark clouds hanging heavy in the sky mirrored my feelings. I'd had an ordinary morning; I couldn't get anything right, missing my timing with a few rough landings in the first session. Feeling dejected from my crap effort, I drowned my sorrows in my favourite shepherd's pie with a lot of tomato sauce from the Tooradin bakery.

'Come on, the plane won't fly itself,' Ian said, giving me a rev up as I downed the last mouthful of pie. At least I felt a little happier with food in my belly.

I went for a quick fly over French Island to relax and get my mind into the flying groove. Coming in on final, I suddenly felt like Neo when he realised he could control the Matrix. Everything slowed, as if I'd stepped outside of myself, able to anticipate what was about to happen, to counteract it. I was at one with my aircraft; it was now an extension of me. I made a perfect landing, then again, and then again.

'Stop here,' Ian said.

I pulled up.

'OK, you can do your solo. Do a couple of circuits. I'll be on the radio,' Ian said as he got out.

'Oh … OK, see ya later,' I said, a little surprised as he hadn't mentioned it before, but I knew I was ready.

It wasn't like my first solo in the trike where I had nerves of excited anticipation; this time I felt comfortable. Maybe I was a little more seasoned, knowing what to expect, or that I knew I could do it. In a word, I was confident. On 7 August 2009, I completed my solo.

'So, what are you going to do now that you have your endorsement?' Ian asked as he signed me off as fully competent in my J230 two weeks later.

Reprising my conversation with Steve three years ago, I said, 'I'm going to fly solo around Australia.'

6

ON A WING & A CHAIR

The plan for the around Australia flight was simple: follow the coast and keep the land on my left. But truly, I had no idea what the next three and a half years had in store for me. I had no concept of how hard it would be, the times I'd wonder whether the stress, time and effort were worth it.

Starting from Tooradin airfield in Victoria, I planned to head down the west coast of Tasmania first, then back up the east coast travelling in an anti-clockwise direction to ride the favourable southeast trade winds up north, then across the top end, down the west coast and back along the southern coastline to Tooradin. I had planned for 21 flying days, with additional rest days. All up it was around 18,000 kilometres, equivalent to flying from Melbourne to London.

The goal was to cross the four furthest points of the country: South East Cape, Tasmania; Cape Byron, New South Wales; Cape York, Queensland; and Steep Point, Western Australia. Strangely, some people asked me, 'Why Tasmania? It can get pretty nasty down there.' But how could I claim I'd flown around Australia if I missed one state? Also, Tasmania would be a big challenge, in particular the west coast with its remoteness and changeable weather, with few places to land. It was this part of the challenge I found most appealing.

I'd planned to do the flight in June 2010, but the project evolved into something bigger and more complicated, consuming most of my time just to get it off the ground. And I was working full time as a project manager at Melbourne Water.

I couldn't do the flight alone; I needed a support team to help with every aspect of mobility—getting me in and out of the plane and prepping it, travelling to accommodation and so on. But once I was in the plane and set up, I'd be fine and could fly it independently. The risk, of course, was if my plane went down; then I'd have a problem getting out. I'd simply have to deal with the situation until help arrived.

My grand plan was to get sponsorship, find a GA8 Airvan (an eight-seater high-wing aircraft, the 'station wagon of the sky,' able to carry lots of gear), enlist a volunteer pilot for it, a personal support (carer), a project coordinator to help manage the day-to-day operations and a filmmaker. I planned to get the media involved to help spread the message, as well as use social media so that individuals and communities could follow the flight.

You only know what you know, and I didn't know much at the time. I knew how to fly but I had little idea about sponsorship or media, learning as I went. In 2009, Louise Alexander, a colleague from work in her late twenties, approached me. 'Hey Dave, I hear you're doing a big trip,' she said with a cheeky smile.

'Ah, yeah, I'm planning to fly around Australia next year.'

'How's it all coming along?' she asked, leaning over my low cubicle partition.

'Ha, slowly!' I said with a chuckle. 'Well, the planning is coming along. I'm trying to get some sponsorship to cover the costs of a support crew and plane, and media to get the word out, but that's about as far as I've got,' I said, a little deflated at the thought of it.

'I helped out a guy at a not-for-profit with sponsorship proposals a few years ago and I know the media, so if you need help, I'd be happy to be involved,' she said.

'Yeah? Sure, that'd be great, really appreciate any help you can give, Louise. Welcome aboard!' I said, a little surprised.

'What you're doing is really inspiring, and it gives me something positive to be involved in.'

I was so grateful to have someone to help with the mounting workload, and her experience in attracting sponsorship would be invaluable.

A few weeks later, at one of our lunchtime planning meetings, Louise asked, 'Do you have anyone for the project coordinator role yet?'

'No, not yet.'

'I'd be willing to take time off work to do it.'

I thought for a moment, trying to read her face as she chewed on a mouthful of sushi. 'It's a big job, and you'd be flying in the support plane,' I said.

'Yeah, I know.'

'Have you flown in a small plane before?' I queried.

'Nothing as small as yours, but I'm fine in planes.'

I considered her offer for a moment and as there was no one else with their hand up, I said, 'OK, it's yours. Congratulations!'

I had initially planned to find a charity to support during the flight, but I couldn't find an organisation whose message was in line with what I wanted to promote. Certainly, there are some fantastic organisations doing amazing work, but it was important to share my particular message.

So, in what seemed like a simple idea at the time, I ventured a not-for-profit in February 2010. On a Wing & a Chair (OWC) was born.

I had no idea how to run a charity; my plan was to get a few people involved who knew more than I did and who could help me along. Nick Fenwick, who had set up and was running the not-for-profit Able Management Group (AMG), agreed to come on board as a director; as did my good friend, Arlee Hatfield, whom I first met when I moved into my home in 1998. She was initially one of my carers, doing some evening shifts for me while studying physiotherapy, then she moved into health management. Louise took on the role of secretary, while I was the executive director and a director.

In hindsight, had I known what I do now, I would never have started a charity as most of the work fell on my shoulders, consuming so much of my time. Further, it pulled me away from my primary purpose—to fly around Australia with the mission: *To raise the public's expectation of what people with disabilities can achieve and inspire others with or without disabilities to achieve their dreams.*

7

A NEW DIRECTION

Every facet of my life was dominated by the flight; it was all I could think of. Setting up and running OWC, planning the flight and working full time was running me into the ground. I'd wake up during the night, my mind racing with endless lists of what I needed to do, unable to see how I could get it all done.

The months raced by; the 2010 deadline passed, and I hoped for an attempt in 2011. But no matter how much time and effort I invested, there was always so much more to do. I desperately needed help. The board helped with the management of OWC; however, most of the administration fell to me. Various people volunteered to work on the project at different times: some were fantastic, doing their bit to help out, while others loved the idea of being involved but when it came to doing the work, their lack of commitment and empty promises made it a struggle to meet deadlines.

Missing one deadline snowballed into missing another, then another, ultimately pushing out the date for the flight past 2011. There was no choice but to delay it again until 2012.

I felt the full weight of everything on my shoulders, and this constant battle slowly drained my energy and spirit. I even regretted telling anyone that I was going to do this flight.

At times I can be my own worst enemy, putting pressure on

myself. Each time the flight was delayed I felt responsible to those who had given their support; I didn't want to let them down and I didn't want to look like a 'gunna' (gunna do this, gunna do that).

Many people were interested and wanted to know when it was going to happen. A guy at work said, 'Have you done it yet?'

'I've had to delay it again,' I said.

'You've been talking about it for years. Are you ever going to do it?'

I was starting to feel like a failure.

Disappointment came when the prospect of getting an Airvan and fuel donated for the flight fell through. The final let-down came after talking with Recreational Aviation Australia (RAA) and the Civil Aviation Safety Authority (CASA), aviation's controlling body. I was looking into ways to raise money to cover some costs of the flight, so I contacted RAA and CASA to see if there would be an issue with running a raffle, with one of the prizes being a flight in my plane with me. However, I was duly informed that offering my services as a prize or having any form of sponsorship related to flying wasn't allowed, as this was considered payment. It was permissible if you were a commercial operation, but we weren't. I hadn't realised this would be an issue, and because the Airvan and fuel were the main costs, I was screwed.

On top of everything, I was losing my battle with a ten-year reoccurring urinary tract infection that was seriously debilitating me. When I was stressed or run-down it would flare up, hitting me hard—which was by then, most of the time. It was making my life a misery as I was constantly sick and exhausted; some mornings I could barely get out of bed.

One morning, driving to work at the Melbourne Water office in East Melbourne, my stomach was in knots and I felt as though I was suffocating. Tears filled my eyes, no matter how much I tried to stop them. The road ahead blurred as the drip turned to a stream;

my emotions gave way like a crumbling dam, unable to withstand the wall of water.

I pulled the car over and leaned my head against the steering wheel, allowing the built-up stress to release from my body. I felt as if I were drowning. I wanted to give up. I wanted it to be over.

It wasn't one thing that had pushed me over the edge; it was the accumulation of many things in my life, both to do with the flight and other factors. I realised I couldn't go on this way.

I admitted myself into hospital to have a course of intravenous antibiotics as the years of oral antibiotics had made the urinary tract infection bug resistant. It took two stays in hospital and then two months of oral antibiotics to finally knock the bastard of a UTI on its head.

I delayed the flight for a third time until April 2013. If it didn't happen then, I knew it never would.

Although I wished the flight was over, I didn't want to quit. I had to be true to myself and do the best I could; only then could I call it a day. I had wanted to do this flight for so long and had put so much of myself into it, I had to make it work. I just needed to find another way—to do it differently.

I knew why I was struggling with my anxiety; my perfectionistic traits could be a blessing, but they could also be a curse.

My sisters EJ (Elizabeth) and Madeleine had been practising meditation for years and they reckoned it helped them to relax and deal with stress. I was willing to try anything.

After reading a few books and participating in a meditation course I realised it takes a lot of practice to reap the benefits. It's all about training your mind to be in the present moment. When we are present, we are not ruminating on the past or future, which is when worry, stress and anxiety arise.

Over time I got better at meditating, becoming more relaxed, and when I was feeling stressed or anxious, I could meditate, even for a few seconds, to help settle my mind. It was subtle, but it worked.

I don't follow any religion and I don't believe in a god in the traditional sense, even though I was brought up Catholic. But through meditation I came to appreciate aspects of Buddhist philosophy. I like the idea that each person is responsible for their actions. I also found powerful the concept that the way we experience our environment is determined by our outlook. Changing our mindset changes the way we perceive and experience the world. We have the power to choose.

This concept resonates with me because it's about attitude, which is what helped me learn to transfer into my bed. Taking responsibility for yourself and being receptive frees your mind and removes barriers, allowing you to see the possibilities instead of the obstacles, all of which opens up opportunities for a fulfilling life.

In realising that my thoughts determined how I experienced my life, I began to better understand myself and how my traits could be positive, with beneficial outcomes—but also negative, with detrimental effects on me and those around me.

I had become so focused on the end goal that if we didn't meet a deadline, or if something didn't work out the way I wanted, I felt I had failed. This threatening cloud of potential failure hanging over my head was not real; it was only my unrealistic expectations of myself.

I also had to adjust my expectations of my team; except for the rare few, most would never be as driven or have the same level of commitment as me, and I had to accept that reality and manage around it.

Being so single-minded about the end goal also prevented me from realising what was important: the journey itself. The ups and downs, the achievement of little milestones along the way—these are the things that shape who we are. The goal at the end is just the icing on the cake.

Just because it doesn't work the first time doesn't mean you have failed; it simply means that it didn't work this time. Each time it doesn't work, you are one step closer to finding the solution.

I had gone down a few paths trying to get this project off the ground, enlisting various people and organisations, seeking sponsorship, and so on. I had no idea how it would pan out. As with everything else in my life—learning to transfer, adapting my aircraft—it was all trial and error until I found a way to make it work. Each path became a learning experience, and although I occasionally felt dispirited, I took time to reflect on why the option didn't work. Through this trial-and-error approach, I gradually came to understand what worked for me, and each time I inched closer to the solution.

In September 2011, driving to Tooradin where my plane was hangared, I had an epiphany. Through the various paths I had taken, the road narrowed to one final option. It was so simple, like the idea of the hook for transferring; I couldn't believe I hadn't thought of it sooner. I would find people who were interested in an adventure, who wanted to be part of something that would make a positive impact on others' lives.

I planned to pay for all my plane costs, and hopefully enlist other pilots who would agree to cover their own aircraft costs when flying the various legs, and be willing to transport my personal support (carer) and the project coordinator. The best part was that many pilots were looking for an excuse to fly, so I figured it wouldn't be too hard to find a few willing participants.

My parents, Brian and Roberta Jacka, were, as always, ever supportive and offered to help the project by taking on one of the biggest tasks—soliciting donated accommodation and transport at each overnight stop around Australia for the team. This would relieve me of a huge pressure, allowing me to concentrate on pushing everything else forward.

The solution was so clear, so simple but, most importantly, it felt right. I knew it would happen. Now, I just had to find the right people.

8

OUT OF THE BLUE

With the OWC project delayed until April 2013 it was time to have a break, and in the latter part of the year I decided to roll the dice again to see if my luck might change with the online dating site, eHarmony.

I had been on eHarmony for a year or so but I was losing interest—the dating process was more time-consuming than going for a job. Searching the candidates, eventually finding a person who had similar interests, and who looked and sounded nice was only the beginning. Then came the myriad of obscure questions that had to be answered online. If you both liked the answers, many hours were then spent corresponding by email to determine if the person at the other end was who they said they were. And if everything squared up and you hadn't been put off by some weird comment, you finally got the interview you'd been fantasising about—which usually ended in disappointment, with no desire to see the person again.

No matter how good the person appeared on paper, without the initial spark of attraction face-to-face, it was a complete waste of time.

Admittedly, I was a little apprehensive about going online at first after hearing a few 'chair chaser' stories (a person taking advantage of a wheelchair user). But also, I was clueless as to what to expect:

would anyone even be interested in dating me? I figured honesty was the best approach and I didn't want to shock my date by rolling up in a wheelchair. On my profile, I posted pictures of me in my wheelchair and even had one of me holding a little fish with my gummy (non-functioning) hands to test the more discerning ones.

To my surprise, many women didn't seem to care much about the wheelchair and, fortunately, all those I met were really nice: they were who they said they were and resembled their photos. They were attractive and interesting people—an artist, a coroner, a lawyer, to mention a few. But after a couple of fun dates, the spark that was necessary to draw me in, to want to be with the person, was absent.

In October 2011, a message came through from a cute blonde called Linda, along with the dreaded questions. I had had enough of the online dating scene by that point, plus I was busy organising a flying trip to Birdsville in Queensland for a beer at the iconic Birdsville pub. In addition, the flight was to test out the blogging and photo-uploading process in a remote area, and also to assess whether Louise could keep her lunch down on a long flight in a small plane.

Three other planes with flying friends were coming and I was really looking forward to the trip. I love flying in the outback; it is relatively easy, with more stable weather than the coast, and without high hills to get over, low cloud is less of an issue. In the heat, however, it gets very thermic, which results in a bumpy ride. The vastness, the changeable and unique scenery, and the novelty of flying into a town a long way from anywhere is pretty cool.

Linda smiled with her whole face, which caught me instantly. Even the photo of her holding her cat didn't put me off (I'm a dog person). On paper, she was different from many of the other women, which intrigued me. She had been an Australian champion in karate in her teens, a scientist, and was into meditation, which immediately sparked my interest; plus the photo was very attractive.

I answered her questions with a final comment, 'I hope you like my answers.' She responded, 'They are perfect.'

The day before I was due to leave on the Birdsville flight, she called me. I was distracted and in such a rush that I couldn't focus on talking. I said, 'I'll call you when I get back,' and hung up.

The trip didn't exactly go as planned. Greg, in his Jabiru J230, crashed on take-off at Cameron's Corner due to windy conditions. Coming home I was delayed in Ballarat with Lida, my carer, when the weather closed in very quickly—it was a very sobering experience. And Louise threw up in my plane, which made me wonder whether she'd handle 21 days flying around Australia.

Earlier, as I flew over Lake Eyre, the white salt lake stretching into the distance, I thought about Linda and decided to give her a call when I got back, but this would be my last online dating attempt. I was content to be on my own and I really didn't need anyone.

My expectations were low for our first date. I assumed it would be no more than a coffee, like the rest of my dates, which rarely developed further.

I arrived at a trendy café in Camberwell half an hour early to scout out the best position. I found a table outside to sit in the warm November sun and as she approached, I was relieved that she resembled her photos.

She talks a lot, was my first impression, although she admitted she was nervous. When I lifted my coffee cup, she glanced at my hands. I could tell she suspected something was wrong with my fingers but couldn't quite pick it, and wasn't game to ask.

She was smart, which I found sexy: a doctor of philosophy (PhD) in heart research. She was interesting, attractive with a great smile, but it was her motivation and passion that grabbed me. The qualities I'd been searching for in a person were right in front of me—that little spark I'd been looking for.

Time went quickly, and I managed to get a few words in. After an hour she suddenly said, 'I have to go. I have someone coming to buy my bike.'

Was this her 'get out of jail' card? I wondered.

As she left I said, 'Would you like to have dinner, lunch or something?' trying to appear casually confident.

She paused for quite a long time; it felt like one of those uncomfortable *How do I get rid of this bleeding-heart type* pauses.

'Ah, I don't know, I'll think about it,' she said, and left.

Dejected, I wheeled back to my car, a P-plater hoon tooting at me to get off the road as he sped past. I wouldn't have been surprised if a solitary rain cloud had dumped its load on me in that moment. Linda was the first person I had wanted to see again, and I'd blown it.

Three hours later a text came through. 'You are really easy to talk to,' signed off with an 'XO.' Obviously, playing hard to get.

The following week we went for lunch that turned into a ten-hour date. From lunch at the Vegie Bar in Fitzroy to an ice-cream in St Kilda with a walk along the pier, and then an evening film. We got along so well, with much in common; our values and what we wanted in life seemed to align. I knew I was falling for her.

9

FALLING INTO PLACE

When you least expect something to happen, uncannily it comes out of the blue.

At the disabled pilots fly-in at Griffith in November 2011, I started chatting with Gordon McCaw. He was in his early sixties and was lucky enough to 'win the award' of paraplegia following a gliding accident in the '80s. The winch cable got caught over the wing, forcing the glider into a spin from which he was able to recover, but then landed hard, which resulted in a crushed T12 vertebrae. He was a low incomplete para with some leg movement, which left him quite able. The only thing he couldn't do was walk.

I was telling Gordon—and anyone else who would pay attention for more than a few seconds—of my plan to fly around Australia, and that I was looking for a support team. Without hesitation, Gordon said, 'I'll come!' Then turned to his mate Bob Frauenfelder. 'What are you doing April to June 2013?'

'Looks like I'll be flying around Australia,' said Bob.

At sixty-eight, Bob reminded me of an old sea dog with his neatly trimmed white beard, short hair and sun-nobbled skin. At over six foot, he was slightly stooped from the heavy work he had done most of his life.

Bob was a storyteller: I particularly liked hearing about his time in the 4th Royal Australian Regiment (RAR) from 1964–67 in Malaysia, including his adventures eating monkey and drinking rum on the beach that he claimed never ended well.

It took a good few seconds before it began to sink in that my biggest problem had suddenly been solved. The flight was now on.

Bob and Gordon agreed to supply the two support planes for the trip and cover their fuel. Each would transport a team member, Louise the project coordinator (although this would soon change) and a personal support (carer), which I still needed to find.

With the support planes sorted I was on a high, so I said to Lida Paunova, my carer, 'How would you like to come on the around Australia flight?'

'Sure!' she said.

Lida was in her late thirties, Macedonian, with a degree of abruptness, English being her second language. She had been one of my carers for a few years and had joined me on a number of flying trips around Australia. She had been fantastic on my solo trips, a very hard worker, assisting me as well as handling the tasks with the plane. She had my routine down pat and enjoyed flying. The only time I saw her nervous was when we were flying over the Channel Country from Birdsville to Noccundra Hotel, Queensland, in April 2011. When my engine started vibrating intermittently, I found that slowing it down, then throttling it back up seemed to solve the problem.

The Channel region below us, previously a dry landscape, was now an ocean of water due to the floods up north, with no place to land. The vibration returned so I sucked on the throttle tube. 'Eeeeeeh!' A high-pitched squeal from the right seat made me jump as I throttled the engine back up. 'Bloody shit, don't do that again!' Lida blurted in a panic.

I planned to have two personal support staff during the flight, each person doing one half of the trip. Lida wanted to do the first stage.

Each member of my team offered a distinctive set of skills and knowledge: a huge asset when you need to brainstorm solutions. I felt excited and energised; I was starting to believe my trip would happen.

With most of the team sorted, for the first time in so long I felt I could relax over Christmas and forget about the flight for a few months.

Linda and I were dating and spending a lot of time together. She was at my place quite a few nights where we would make love and talk into the early hours of the morning, then at five a.m. I'd have to get up and go to work … exhausted.

In all my other relationships—even one that lasted three years—I had never wanted to fully commit and move in together. Maybe it was because I was now older and had achieved my independence, but this time it was very different. I felt ready and that it was the right thing for me.

When I told my parents that Linda was moving in after a month and a half of dating, I could tell they were a little apprehensive. I certainly didn't blame them. I'm sure they were thinking, *What the hell are you doing, you idiot?*

I had been living alone for the past fifteen years so when Linda moved in, bringing a cat and small dog, I struggled for a while to adjust to my loss of space, especially my study. To this day, I haven't adjusted to the cat—it's a love-hate relationship. Linda loves it, I hate it.

For Linda, the biggest challenge in our relationship was the carers. I'd had the last twenty-four years to get used to them being around me in the mornings and afternoons. But for Linda, having a stranger knocking on the bedroom door when we were asleep or barging into the bathroom when she was in there was a little confronting and took some getting used to. It was also the constant change, with different people coming at different times of the day. But the hardest aspect was the loss of solitude, the lack of space—especially for an introvert like Linda.

Needless to say, I would've much preferred not to have carers and to be able to do everything myself, as it would have removed a big challenge in our relationship. But having the carers gave me independence and choice, and I didn't want to have to rely on Linda.

For me it was, and remains, important for Linda to be my best friend and lover—not my carer. Having her as my carer would have changed the dynamics in our relationship. From being an empowered, self-reliant person, I would have become dependent again. When we met, I was independent due to having carers, working, being a pilot, in charge of my life. It was critical for me to maintain the independence I had worked so hard to gain over the years. Of course, if a carer didn't turn up, Linda would gladly get me up and going for the day, but I was adamant that she was not to be responsible for my daily care. I wouldn't allow my life or relationship to be a compromise because of my disability.

In mid-February 2011, I proposed to Linda as we'd relaxed on the grass at the Bendigo botanical gardens. She gave me a thirty-day cooling off period, just in case.

10

THE WHY

Linda often read to me while I got into bed as it takes a while, and on this night the book was Simon Sinek's *Start with Why*.

'People don't buy what you do; they buy why you do it. And what you do simply proves what you believe,' she read.

Sinek talked about inspiring people, how Apple and other corporations became successful by giving people a reason to believe, a why for what they were doing.

You can pay a person to do a job, and they will do it to the required standard and put in the set hours. But by giving a person purpose and instilling a belief in what they are doing, they will willingly follow and go beyond, giving their all.

I realised that I had made a fundamental error in my leadership with OWC. Over the last two years I had talked about what we were doing and how we would do it, but I had not reinforced *why* we were doing it. Of course, I knew the reason I was doing the flight, but I hadn't made the *Why* front and centre. Each person had to participate for the right reasons. It couldn't be just to help me—which was the reason for some (which I greatly appreciated)—as this would do little for long-term motivation. They had to be doing it for themselves.

Without the Why—a clear purpose, something each person could relate to and believe in—I could never expect total commitment.

The flight team was as keen as Kim Kardashian's paparazzi. It promised to be a once-in-a-lifetime experience, but we had a long way to go before departure day (D-Day). There would be many challenges, and when things got tough, I wondered: would the team stick at it?

In May 2012 the flight team got together for the first time at the Tooradin bowling club.

Bob and Gordon flew down from Griffith carrying our newest team member, Michael Prince. He would fly with Bob in the support plane as second pilot.

A lean, blond-haired 21-year-old, Michael was one of the youngest chief flying instructors in Australia, teaching students to fly the Jabiru J230, the same aircraft as mine. This was really handy as he knew my type of aircraft intimately, which would help with maintenance. Michael was circumspect, thinking deeply before answering a question, and made decisions with caution. He prided himself on knowing all the technical aspects of flying: the procedures, aircraft performance and weather forecasts, amongst other things. He was a good compliment to Bob, who tended to favour his more practical approach to flying based on experience.

Apart from Lida and the to-be-determined second pilot to fly with Gordon, the full flight team was at the meeting—Bob, Gordon, Michael, Louise and Linda. My fiancée would fulfil a personal support role for the last half of the flight.

Opening the meeting, I shared my story and the reason for doing the flight. I told them of my experiences over the years: the negativity I'd encountered when I wanted to return to study or get a job; my ability to overcome seemingly impossible physical obstacles like learning to transfer out of my wheelchair into bed or achieving my dream to fly. I shared with them my eventual realisation that what limits us much of the time is our perception of what we think we are capable of. All these experiences and many more dovetailed into my Why: my purpose for doing the flight.

It was a turning point for the project and for the team.

'What's your Why, Bob?' I asked.

Looking up from the teacup he was fidgeting with, Bob sat back in his chair, raised a finger and said, 'I've known Gordon for years, and nothin' stops him. Like you said, it's important for people to see what you blokes can do, change some attitudes. I s'pose that's why I'm doin' it. And it's a good excuse to go for a fly, isn't it?'

Each person opened up, sharing their stories and what the flight meant to them. Gordon had his own experiences of life using a wheelchair, with all the physical and attitudinal challenges that he had to confront. The flight was a personal challenge—an adventure to take on.

Michael's mum worked in the disability area, exposing him to the normality of disability. He believed that all people should be treated fairly and with respect. 'I really like the idea of flying around Australia, changing attitudes,' he said.

For Louise, being involved in something that helped to make the community more inclusive was in line with her social values.

Linda initially agreed to be involved as I needed another person for personal support. But more than anything, she wanted to support me and help the project succeed. She believed in our purpose as she had witnessed firsthand the challenges I faced every day.

It didn't matter what each person's reason was; everyone's motivation was slightly different. What mattered was that each person had a Why, and that their Why aligned with the project.

Ultimately, it was about making a difference in our small part of the world, and each person would play a key role in making the flight a reality.

By the end of our meeting I knew the project would succeed. Each person had their purpose and believed in what we were doing.

Yes, it would be very challenging, but I somehow knew we would get through.

11

UP AND DOWN

The next eleven months was a never-ending roller coaster of ups and downs.

Easter 2012 was one of the lows. I flew Linda to Broken Hill to experience what I deemed to be one of the best parmigiana in Australia. But on our first day Linda received a call from my carer Kirsten, who was looking after Linda's dog Max. The little Maltese had been bitten by a snake and died. Linda was extremely upset and wanted to go home the next day, but then we got stranded at Swan Hill for a night with bad weather.

Our sadness compounded when I learned after we got back that my good friends Ian and Elaine Willis had died in a microlight trike crash. I could never have imagined that the entertaining night we'd spent with them, drinking Ian's home-brew Irish mint cream and sharing tall flying stories, would be the last time we'd see them.

Their deaths unsettled me; apart from the sadness of losing two generous and genuine friends, it brought home the very real danger of flying. The flight around Australia certainly had its risks. Many could be mitigated or at least reduced, but as in life, there are always curveballs you don't expect.

There was still so much to do: team meetings in Shepparton and Griffith and monthly Skype calls to review the planning and logistics; building up a following on social media; attracting media coverage; sourcing donated accommodation and transport; and gearing up to participate in promotion events at the Avalon Airshow as well as attend the Recreational Aviation Australia National Fly-in at Temora in early 2013. Also, with Linda's help, I had lined up many talks in Victoria and interstate at various Rotary clubs and corporate events to raise money for On a Wing & a Chair and get the message out.

The success of the flight did not depend on whether we circumnavigated the country. Rather, success was determined by the number of people our message reached: changing attitudes, making a difference in someone's life. But to get the message out we needed media coverage.

Louise was managing the social and traditional media. Over the coming months, it became increasingly difficult to catch up with her for planning meetings, media strategies and the myriad of other tasks that had to get done. I knew she was busy at work and with other things, but we had to get the work done or the flight wouldn't happen.

To ease her workload, we agreed that I'd find someone to help with the traditional media. Tanya, a close friend whom I'd known before my accident and who had worked on the project when she had spare time, came to the rescue. Through her network, I'd met Karen Rumley from *I.D. Yours* who'd generously developed our website, business cards and did all our graphic design work for no charge. To my relief, Tanya came through again and linked us up with Sofia Dedes, a media manager who was happy to work for us pro-bono.

Sofia was a huge blessing. With her experience and media connections, her focus and drive, she got things done. The media opportunities slowly appeared and the snowball started to gather momentum. The team was energised and excited.

Louise could now concentrate on the social media side of things, working with Matt McInnes who came on board in August 2012 as OWC's digital and social media manager.

However, in September 2012, as we headed into Louise's third year in the project, her involvement came to an end. With the project going on for much longer than originally anticipated, and given her work commitments, amongst other things, she decided it was time to move on. We both knew it was the right outcome.

Louise had been with the project from the start and she had done a lot of great work helping to shape OWC. And when I was going through my difficult time, having to delay the project twice, she was steadfast in her support, for which I was, and remain, truly grateful.

Now, with only six months to go, I wasn't sure if I'd find someone to volunteer for the role of project coordinator—another item added to my ever growing to-do list.

I had to find the right person, which wouldn't be easy given the necessary skills and availability for the flight. I wouldn't take on someone who didn't fit the role and couldn't meet the requirements. If worse came to worst, I'd do what I could myself. Taking Ernest Shackleton's lead, the advertisement for the role read:

The trip will be hard work, no pay (may have to pay part of own way), potentially dangerous, long hours, flying in small aircrafts in remote areas, no fixed completion date (flying depends on weather conditions) but an amazing life experience that you'll never forget.

I needed someone who was fully committed, able to handle pressure, an all-rounder with marketing and communications skills. But, most of all, the person had to be doing it for the right reasons and had to believe in the Why.

12

THAILAND

Amidst working full time, trying to find another project coordinator and organising the flight, Linda and I had another project on the go: our wedding in Thailand in November 2012. This pushed us from being really busy to insanely busy. As the old saying goes, *If you bite off more than you can chew, chew harder.* I was chewing like mad.

We planned to go to Thailand for three weeks, with Bangkok our first stop to sort out the paperwork so our marriage would be legal, then on to Phuket for the wedding and Chiang Mai for our honeymoon.

Apart from the valve on my full leg-bag catching on my pants when Linda transferred me from the aisle chair onto the aircraft seat, draining the contents into my shoe and soaking the carpet, the flight to Thailand was uneventful. The staff took pity and gave me a pair of socks so I could at least have a dry foot, and we got used to the smell after a few hours.

I don't like big cities, but Bangkok was an exception with the heat, colour and culture—and dodgy-looking food stalls providing cheap and delicious meals. On the third night, while strolling through the streets, Linda and I came across a stall offering samples of sweet cakes. As I finished the last mouthful, I realised my unwashed hands were probably propagating some form of toxic mutant bacteria from the grime, sewerage and spit I'd collected from pushing my wheels all afternoon.

At two a.m., as my insides churned and growled like an ice-cream machine, I thought of that innocent little sweet. 'Linda, I'm not feeling too good,' I croaked. Before she could answer, an unmistakable *thuuurp* bubbled beneath the covers, followed by an eruption on the scale of Mount Vesuvius. Hot, brown, watery, hazardous waste gushed like a broken sewer, pouring between my legs and oozing out under my sides.

It is a strange sensation having no control of your physical function while you wait for The Body to decide when it's had enough.

Linda cleaned me up as best she could, doubling our carbon footprint for the year and exhausting the room's supply with the volume of toilet paper she used.

In my misery, as I sat in the shower expelling bodily products from all three orifices for the next hour, I couldn't help but be impressed with Linda's form. She didn't flinch or gag as the acidic fumes burnt out her nasal hairs; she focused and did what had to be done. If your partner can go through an experience like that and still be willing to marry you a week later, you know you're onto a good thing. I was sure that whatever happened she would be there, regardless of how messy it got.

We had decided not to bring carers from home but to hire them in Thailand, as we wanted this to be our moment rather than having someone with us all the time. A huge mistake, as it turned out. Apart from not having a carer to help with my exploding bum episode, the language barrier made it extremely difficult to communicate my needs, even the most basic of instructions. At each location, Linda had to improvise, miming instructions with some very weird hand gestures and facial expressions to communicate what had to be done.

The morning after my horrible night, we'd planned to visit a famous temple a couple of hours' drive from Bangkok. Searching online, we were pleasantly surprised to find a travel company that offered wheelchair-accessible vans—though I was sceptical about their interpretation of 'accessible.' Throughout the morning Linda kept saying, 'We don't need to go, let's have a quiet day so you can recover.' But after a few morning chucks that turned my stomach inside out, I was feeling much better.

As the van pulled up, I was quietly confident I'd made the right decision. The driver, who spoke about as much English as I did Thai, slid the door open and pulled out the longest ramp I'd ever seen; I could only guess it was in case of a river crossing!

My confidence grew when I noticed that two seats had been removed to allow room for the wheelchair, but something was missing.

'Where are the lock-downs?' I asked the driver. (Lock-downs are clamps or straps that attach to the floor to hold the wheelchair in place while driving.)

Without a word, the side door slid closed and we started to move.

With every turn, acceleration or braking, my chair slid around the floor like an ice-hockey puck, crashing into the front and sides as I struggled to hang on and not fall out. The constant exertion and jerking was making me feel worse by the minute. Only by angling the chair against the wall and seat, with Linda jamming a foot under one wheel and her other foot on my footplate, did I become marginally more secure.

'I'm going to be sick,' I murmured, taking deep breaths to hold off the impending discharge. Just as my mouth filled with orange electrolyte fluid, Linda whipped a plastic bag under my face to catch the flow. Unfortunately, it was a dodgy supermarket bag. Linda did her best to clamp the holes with her free hand as vomit dripped from her knuckles.

Wide-eyed and a little panicked, the driver pulled to the side of the road. Linda emptied the bag outside and, being environmentally conscious, rolled it up and moved to get back in the van. 'No, no, no bag!' the driver yelled, waving his arms.

'I can't litter the place!' she exclaimed.

'Linda, turn around,' I said.

The bag joined the million others stuck to the fence, fluttering in the wind like prayer flags.

I was sure it couldn't get any worse—until I had to push through a covered market: hotter than a greenhouse and smelling of sewerage, body odour and the rotting corpses of some sort of dried fish. It almost finished me. In my gagging fit, Linda hurried me to relief in the sweet clean air of the temple.

Returning to Bangkok was no less of an ordeal; we made it to within one kilometre of the motel before another round of my weight-loss treatment struck. At least Linda had picked up some extra plastic bags.

Spotting tan-lines at a nudist beach is easier than locating a resort with wheelchair-accessible rooms in Thailand—or any other developing country for that matter. Some, such as the Hilton, claim to have wheelchair access; however, I'd have to learn to levitate up a flight of stairs to get to the room. At other resorts, even if I could've made it to the rooms, the showers had doors so narrow the average-built person would have had trouble fitting through.

We eventually found accommodation at the Laguna Resort in Phuket, set amidst tropical gardens overlooking the beach, with crystal blue water and rolling waves. With ramps and a lift, it was easy to get around. The room was great apart from a small step at the entrance which was more of a trip hazard, and a bathroom with more handrails than a ballerina's dance studio.

Our wedding was small and intimate, shared with my family

and a few friends. Linda's parents had died a few years back so her close friend Dave Miller came as her bride's man.

Every day preceding the wedding it rained; but on our wedding day the sun shone beautifully. Linda came by boat to the glass chapel which overlooked a lagoon. Gliding through the double doors accompanied by Pachelbel's Canon in D major, she looked like a princess.

Caught up in our increasingly busy lives, we hadn't had much time to stop and enjoy ourselves for a long while. We flew to Chiang Mai for our honeymoon, leaving the Dhara Dhevi Mandarin Oriental resort only once to visit a temple. The rest of the time we lay at the pool on huge beds, ordering club sandwiches and mojitos, and listening to audiobooks. It was the first time I'd done absolutely nothing in years, and it was just what I needed to recharge my batteries before the frenetic lead-up to the epic flight.

13

THE TRIAL FLIGHT

Straight after getting back from Thailand in December, we hosted our after-party for friends who didn't come to our wedding. I had another UTI and had picked up a dog of a cough which I couldn't shake. I felt tired, and even more fatigued by the thought of the trial flight in early January, which was always at the back of my mind. We'd agreed that the entire team would participate in the trial flight from 3–6 January 2013.

It was a critical step before the big flight to check how we worked together as a team. The trial flight would allow us to refine each person's role and responsibilities, to fine-tune our systems and processes and, of course, to have some fun.

When I emailed everyone after Christmas, Gordon came straight back: 'Not a problem. I'm in!' I could always count on him, as well as on Paul McCaw, Gordon's son, who would be flying as second pilot with him. Michael was initially tentative, but eventually participated.

At crunch-time, Bob couldn't get away from work and Lida had to help paint her brother's house. This was disappointing because we'd agreed to the dates and this was our only opportunity to assess our teamwork. I knew that individually each person was very capable, but I didn't know how they'd perform in a team environment.

I'd planned a moderately challenging round trip from Tooradin in Victoria, via King Island (located out to sea between Victoria and Tasmania), then on to Portland in Victoria, across to Murray Bridge in South Australia, then back to our respective home-bases through Ballarat in Victoria.

To my mind, completing our first big milestone, our first water crossing to King Island on Day 1, was what started to pull the team together.

Gordon and Paul were in their Piper Archer, a low-wing single-engine four-seater, while Michael with Adrian (a pilot from Griffith who flew in place of Bob) were in a Cessna 172, a high-wing single-engine four-seater. They had flown down from Griffith that morning and met up with Linda and me in my Jabiru. We set off from Tooradin and headed for King Island, our tongues drooling for their fine cheese. King Island was also the monkey on my back; I was nervous about my first-ever water crossing.

Flying over a great expanse of water is a psychological challenge—it requires overcoming a fear that is fairly irrational, as the plane doesn't know it is over water, and if everything is running fine there is no reason the engine should suddenly stop. But when the mainland off Cape Otway passed by beneath me, with nothing below except lots and lots of water, I had a moment of 'gulp,' as I looked back to see the shore disappearing out of gliding range. However, within a few minutes, at 7500 feet and in clear skies, a hazy shape appeared in the distance, bringing relief and moderate comfort.

Unfortunately, the cheese lady in the airport shop had just closed as the first two planes, the Archer and Cessna, arrived. By the time Linda got me out of the plane, the others had been waiting for a while. Following a quick lunch of sandwiches and Cup-A-Soup, and a photo in the warm blustery conditions, it was time to get going again.

For Linda, getting me into the plane was a slow process: get the lift out, position it, plug in the power, raise me up, lift in my bum and legs, lower and remove the chair and lift. Then, set me up in the cockpit with maps and check that my condom drainage connected to my leg-bag is free-flowing so I don't blow off my condom and piss myself. Then pack my wheelchair and everything else in the back. The others would have to wait for at least twenty minutes before starting the engines.

Heading out again over the vast ocean, my newfound confidence lifted me higher in my seat, and the flight from King Island to Warrnambool to refuel was far less daunting.

Sofia, our media manager, had lined up a story about us with the *Herald Sun*. On landing, Linda and I had to quickly email wedding and flying photos for the article while Gordon, Paul, Michael and Adrian refuelled and checked the planes.

Over dinner at a pub in Portland we chatted about the day's events—a routine that would become a regular debrief—discussing ways to improve the process, who should do what, and the really, really important question: 'Guys, Linda's done the shopping. Who's making the sangas (sandwiches) in the morning?'

'Not a problem. Paul and I will do it tomorrow,' said Gordon, sipping his glass of red.

'OK, great. Michael, how about you and Adrian do it the next day,' I suggested, and both nodded in agreement.

'It's Sofia, Dave,' said Linda, handing me the phone.

'I can't hear you, Sofia. What?'

'Our story is going to be on the front page of the *Herald Sun*!' she blurted.

The three-page story took OWC's exposure from local community to national; it was just what we needed to jump-start media interest and get our message out.

At the crack of dawn on Day 2, I awoke startled and a little confused as to why my phone was ringing. 'Hello?' said Linda, answering the persistent caller.

She turned to me. 'Dave, it's 2UE radio, they want to talk to you.'

'It's five in the morning and I've got to get up for a crap. Can they wait?'

She returned to the caller. 'David isn't available now but he will be free at seven a.m.,' she said.

All morning I was inundated with calls from radio stations wanting to chat on-air, and Channel Seven and Nine competing to be the first to nab the story. I was totally unprepared for this but Linda stepped up, calling them back, managing my schedule as we were flying most of the day, and liaising with Sofia as she would decide which TV station would get the interview. It was a little overwhelming but very exciting.

It quickly became apparent that my initial plan of having Linda as a personal support to get me in and out of the plane and set me up was a very slow process and already making her tired. After discussion with the team, I decided to change the procedure and have Michael and Paul alternate getting me in and out, while Linda would set me up in the cockpit.

'Ready, Dave?' said Paul, grabbing the back of my pants.

'Yep, let's do it!'

Paul gave a quick lift, my bottom half levitated and twisted into the plane.

'OK, he's all yours, Linda,' said Paul, moving the lift and wheelchair out of the way to start packing it in the back while Linda set me up in the cockpit.

'Dave, looks like you need a couple-hundred mil,' said Michael, showing me the engine oil dipstick from the passenger side door while Linda got me organised.

'Yep, put in two hundred mil.'

'Two hundred mil, roger that,' said Michael.

THE TRIAL FLIGHT

With Paul packing the back, Michael doing the oil check and Linda getting me organised in the cockpit, we started to gel as a team, saving ten minutes each time I got in or out, which enabled us to be ready together.

We left Portland with strong headwinds, which made our flight to Goolwa in South Australia very slow. When we landed, the temperature was in the high 30s. Although I was out of the plane in record time, I was roasting by the time Paul wheeled me into the aeroclub. While the team refuelled the planes and ate lunch, Linda arranged the phone interview with radio station 2UE, and I did my best talking about the flight. I was unprepared and it took me a few interviews, with Linda's coaching, to succinctly convey the information they wanted and get my message across—although by the following day my fifteen minutes of fame would be over.

The purpose of the trial flight was to replicate the routine we'd follow when flying around Australia, so for the remainder of the trip Linda was with Gordon and Paul in the Archer. As I sat alone in the cockpit, engine idling on the taxiway, waiting for Michael and Adrian to take off, Gordon radioed, 'The outside temperature gauge shows 52 degrees. It's a hot one!' With the sun streaming into the cockpit, I felt I was being roasted alive in a slow-cooker: way beyond my limits for thermal body regulation.

As my wheels left the dry grass runway, I knew I was in serious trouble. The massive thermals knocked and punched my little plane in all directions as I fought to get it to climb and keep flying straight, at the same time desperately trying to cool myself with my spray bottle and the small amount of air seeping through the vents. It was then I realised I'd made a very big mistake: I was overheating. My brain had slowed down considerably to the point of making mistakes: I had inadvertently turned off one of the engine's magneto switches instead of the fuel pump. (The engine has two magneto switches and with both off the engine would have stopped.) I was just hoping I wouldn't pass out. It was too late to turn around and land.

Under full power my little plane slowly climbed in the thin, hot, turbulent air. The higher I ascended, the more relief I felt as the air became cooler. After what seemed an eternity, I finally reached 8500 feet, levelled out, turned the back of the plane to the sun and sprayed myself until my body temperature returned to normal.

Over Kangaroo Island, I noticed the fuel gauge for the left-wing tank indicated almost empty, which was impossible as both were full when I left Goolwa forty-five minutes earlier. With my brain now working normally, I figured the gauge must be playing up, but I didn't want to risk it so tracked straight to Murray Bridge, our next overnight stop.

The thermals gave me a serious workout on approach, but it was a little cooler when I landed: only 46 degrees.

Parked under a tree away from the plane, spraying myself down, I noticed something unusual. 'What's that on top of my wing, Paul?' I asked.

He went over to inspect the object. 'It's your fuel cap, Dave!' he shouted, inspecting the cap attached by a safety wire cable. He placed the cap in the socket on top of the wing, pulled out the Allen key and tried tightening it in place, without success.

'Dave, looks like the O-ring got buggered by the heat when it was sitting on the tarmac in Goolwa. When it popped off, the rushing air over the opening must have siphoned out your fuel. I've heard about it but never seen it,' he said.

We waited in the oppressive heat for an hour and a half for a taxi that had got lost on the way to the airport; then, sitting in the wheelchair spot in the far back of the vehicle without air-conditioning finished me off. I had only enough energy to lie on the bed at the motel with two fans blowing on me, slowly cooling my body down, while the team, minus Linda, who stayed with me, went for a Chinese dinner.

We headed to the airfield early in the morning of Day 3 to fix my fuel cap and were fortunate to meet Mike Chapman, the chief flying instructor at Murray Bridge. For a few dollars he was happy to part with the O-ring seal from his aircraft to get us going again, which saved us a lot of search time in town.

With all planes operational, Michael and Adrian headed back to Griffith, while Gordon, Paul, Linda and I tracked to Ballarat via Mount Gambier for our overnight stop. It was an uneventful flight, but instead of the heat we had to contend with smoke from bushfires to the east so thick it was difficult to see the ground at times.

No matter who or where you are, aeroclubs always welcome you, and Ballarat was no exception. They offered us tea and coffee and arranged a taxi to get us to our accommodation.

'How are you navigating, Paul?' I asked.

'I'm using AvPlan, Dave; it's really impressive,' he said, eagerly pulling out his iPad and giving me a run-through on how it worked.

I hadn't interacted much with Paul until now, and I really liked him. He was thirty-one, fit with an average build and red-blond hair. He'd been flying for six years and was a gadgets man, mechanically minded, which was a great asset in helping to service and fix problems with my plane. I liked his easygoing nature, his capacity to analyse situations logically and consider options objectively.

With more than four hours' sleep that night both Linda and I woke feeling refreshed, and a leisurely breakfast gave the four of us a chance to reflect on the past few days before we went our separate ways home.

The trip had been a huge learning experience. It had opened everyone's eyes to some of the challenges we would face. We now knew that even simple things wouldn't always go to plan, requiring us to devise strategies to manage them—such as taxis getting lost or unexpected mechanical issues like my fuel-cap seals. Gordon realised he had to improve his fitness while I discovered I needed a better strategy for managing my temperature control, and to take an extra set of seals for my fuel caps.

The trial flight not only gave me a chance to assess each person's capabilities, it was an invaluable opportunity to trial each role, review our processes and identify what needed to be changed. This was particularly evident with the personal support role. Relying on Linda to get me in and out of the plane each time became too physically demanding for her, especially with all the other tasks that had to get done. By enlisting Michael and Paul to get me in and out, we spread the workload and made it more manageable long-term. It also made things significantly quicker.

Further, having Linda do my care was difficult for both of us. It wasn't her responsibility in our regular lives, so having her do it on the flight wasn't right for our relationship. Neither of us wanted her for the role in the first place, but without anyone else to fill the position at the time, she'd agreed to do it for me.

However, on the second day, when we were inundated with phone calls from the media, were busy updating the blog and Facebook, and she was still performing the personal support role with only a few hours' sleep, Linda really showed me what she was capable of. It then became obvious who should perform the role of project coordinator.

14

RAMP UP

The project coordinator role was a tough one and the more I thought about it, the more it seemed like a full-time job. Apart from coordinating various aspects of the flight, I needed someone who would be heavily involved in the pre-flight work from January onwards.

A few people had been interested in the role, but they were far from the right fit; attracting the ideal person had proved a significant challenge. Linda had the necessary skills, could double as a carer if needed, and I knew she was fully committed and had my interests, and those of the project, at heart. She had proved her dependability when it got tough, and most of all she believed in the Why.

With Linda officially in the role from early January, it took a lot of pressure off me. Putting her own business aspirations on hold, she dedicated herself to working full time on the project, just in time for the ramp-up.

I now had to find someone for the personal support position, but at least I had some breathing room as the role was for the second half of the flight.

From advertisements at carer agencies and in Explorers Connect and Seek, I had only one taker by February, a 21-year-old named Josh Foote. I met up with him at a café for coffee. My first impressions of this six foot three tall lanky guy dressed in a tight shirt and black jeans were not overly favourable; he didn't look like someone who could rough it. But with his height and strength, he wouldn't have a problem throwing me around.

'So, how do you feel about flying in a very small plane over remote parts of this country?' I asked bluntly.

'I've flown in a small plane and enjoyed it. And as far as I know, I don't get air-sick. Flying in remote areas wouldn't be a problem; in fact, I'd look forward to it,' he said.

'Yep, great. You know, there is some risk in flying and if we had engine problems out in the middle of nowhere, without any landing spots, we could possibly crash and potentially get injured or die. How do you feel about the risk?'

After a moment's pause, Josh said dryly, 'I don't have a desire to die, but if I am selected for the flight, I accept the risks that go with it. Of course, I trust that the pilots know what they are doing.'

'I'm glad to hear that,' I said. 'Another thing, if we can't get accommodation or get delayed somewhere, we might have to rough it. How would you go sleeping under a wing?'

'I've done a lot of hiking and camping overnight taking all our gear and food, so I think I'll be OK. Would we need to take a tent? I have one if we do.'

'Nah, just sleeping bags, we don't have the weight for tents.' I paused before asking the big question, 'So, Josh, why do you want to come on this flight?'

Considering his words carefully and rubbing his chin like a wise old man, Josh said, 'Well, apart from it being a once in a lifetime experience seeing parts of Australia that I doubt I'd get to see any other way, I hope to have a positive effect on people's lives, which is why I'm studying nursing and midwifery. I think the On a Wing &

a Chair flight's purpose is really important, and I'd love to be part of the team.'

Apart from that initial physical impression, I liked Josh from the first meeting. He was upfront, came across as relaxed and willing to take responsibility, but most of all his values were in line with the Why. He was experienced in the type of personal care I needed and he didn't get air-sick when I took him up for a flight on a hot bumpy day in February, which sealed the deal.

There was a daunting amount of planning still to be done, as well as the events we were to participate in, over the next two months. One of our priorities was to raise $20,000 for OWC. With Linda's help, I lined up numerous talks at Rotary clubs, interstate events and at work to try to get some extra donations. Also, we sold hats with the OWC logo to whomever would buy one and placed donation tins in local cafés. Following a talk at Telstra, the company provided the team with three mobile phones, two internet dongles and a satellite phone with unlimited credit for our use during the trip—saving us a lot of money.

In addition to working full time and doing the OWC administration, I was managing two separate teams. Linda and I were having regular Skype meetings with the flight team who were based in Griffith NSW, with Lida and Josh coming around to join us; as well as regular media meetings with Linda, Arlee, Matt and Sofia. Sofia was a 'gun': chasing up airline sponsorship, lining up radio interviews, and the biggest win of all—landing a story with *Weekend Today* on Channel Nine in early February. Airlie Walsh, the reporter, did an amazing story which gave OWC an enormous amount of coverage, resulting in lots of traffic to our website, much of which translated into Facebook followers.

Avalon Airshow from 1–3 March 2013 was our biggest event, with Linda working long hours developing the team's profiles for the website; organising our sponsored uniforms donated by Matt

Browne from Rosbert International emblazoned with the OWC logo; sourcing caps to sell; having posters printed of the route and of my aircraft adaptations; putting together information packs; hiring equipment; coordinating with Bob, Gordon and Michael for when they would be coming down to help with the display, including organising their accommodation; and building the following on Facebook, which was critical to the project's success, along with the media managed by Sofia.

I had again come down with a UTI, the seemingly constant companion of nasty bugs, common to many with spinal cord injury (SCI), and at the same time I was managing only four hours' sleep a night; I was shattered from the onset.

Michael drove down from Griffith a few days earlier and flew with me into Avalon in the Jabiru for the display. The weather was pretty crappy, but it was a memorable experience landing on the three-kilometre runway that was usually off limits to recreational pilots. Our display was away from the main area which was disappointing, but my parents, Brian and Roberta, officially our Base Support team for the project, turned it around. They stood in the sun for a whole day selling 35 caps, collecting donations and giving out business cards to anyone who passed by—verging on harassment. The flight team chatted to anyone willing to listen, Sofia did some spruiking, and Arlee and Matt dropped in for a few hours on Friday evening. From three days' work, we made $930 towards OWC—a little disappointing given the time and effort we'd put in.

Our last flying event before the big flight was the Recreational Aviation Australia National Fly-in held in Temora, NSW, on 30 March 2013. Josh and I flew up in my Jabiru, giving us an opportunity to get to know each other, as well as bring him up to speed with my care. Gordon and his wife Bronwynne put us up for two days at their house in Griffith, offering red wine and his very tasty beef and veggie pie, with Bob and Michael flying us to

Temora each day.

With my plane on display, we spent two days telling people about the flight to generate more interest, although I was surprised by how many people already knew about it. Word was getting around. With donations and hat sales we raised another $427, taking us a little closer to the target of $20,000. When I got back to Tooradin, I discovered I'd won an award of Most Innovative Design for my adaptations.

Base Support was still working in the background to finalise accommodation and transport. So far most had been sorted with donated rooms at motels, in people's houses or in accommodation owned or run by community organisations.

As the days ticked by, the tasks that needed to be done got pushed into smaller and smaller timeframes. Eventually I got to the point where if a task wasn't imperative and wouldn't stop the flight, it was crossed off the list.

15

ONE WEEK TO GO

My colleagues at Melbourne Water supported my goal in many ways. The social club raised a few hundred dollars for OWC and in the lead-up my managers allowed me to take off the occasional morning or afternoon to do a talk. Further, recognising that the end date of the flight was uncertain, they allowed me to take off whatever time was necessary to successfully complete the flight, thereby removing the pressure of having to be back on a specific date. I was very fortunate to have such supportive people on my side, who appreciated what I was trying to accomplish and were willing to make my life a little more manageable so I could achieve my goal.

Nevertheless, the final week before D-Day on 29 April 2013 could only be described as insane.

I finished work one week before the flight to give myself time to finalise my flight planning, get myself and the team organised and work out how Linda and I would do the social media, blogging, filming, backing up of media, and the multitude of other tasks we had to accomplish every day during the flight.

Each night over dinner Linda and I reviewed what we had to do to coordinate our precious time during the few days ahead. Flicking through my to-do-list, I said, 'Tomorrow I've gotta go to Moorabbin airport to get our new headsets and some oil for the plane. Are you picking up the camera sound equipment?'

Taking a moment to swallow her food, Linda said, 'I can order it but I don't know when I can pick it up. I'm meeting Peter tomorrow to run me through the filming for your video blogs. Can your parents pick it up?'

'Maybe, I'll ask. I've still gotta get my wheelchair fixed, buy stuff for my survival kit and sort out the 'sat' phones. I have to get down to my plane at some stage to work out where to put the GoPros and program the radios. Which reminds me: I need to check with Geoff if he has finished the spray system and serviced the plane.'

'The Facebook countdown to the flight is working well,' Linda said. 'We're getting a lot of interest and a good following. I think Bob is enjoying it too; he's getting a few likes from people he knows.'

'Ha-ha, thought he'd like that! Oh yeah, forgot to mention the donor didn't come through with the camera so we'll need to buy another GoPro for the plane. Can you pick one up?'

'I've still got to test out the Telstra WiFi dongles for uploading photos and the blogs, also sort out the information for Sofia, and still do my tax. I just don't know when I will find the time,' Linda said.

'OK, that's fine. I'll see if Mum or Dad can pick one up.'

The list of things to do never ceased; as we ticked one thing off, another went in its place and the pressure wasn't about to let up.

Running on little sleep, trying to get as much done as we could each day but still having so much left, I was nearing exhaustion and Linda wasn't far behind. A good mate Craig Fraser put on a benefit gig with his band, The Legends of GOFPOS and included the bands Signal X, Neil Wise and The Night Before Tomorrow, who donated merchandise sales to OWC, raising $1100. It was a great night with family, friends and even some ex-girlfriends turned up; but I was so tired, I struggled to keep my eyes open and stay coherent.

I feared I'd devoted so much time to promoting and raising donations for OWC over the last three months that I hadn't properly prepared myself. In particular, I still needed to finalise the finer details of the flight planning by listing all the information on a spreadsheet to make it easier for me to manage while flying. Also, I had hoped to get in some flying hours or even fitness training, but to no avail. My life was characterised by ever-increasing stress levels; all I wanted to do was get in my plane and fly away, leaving everybody and everything behind.

But six days before D-Day came the real kicker, turning my barely manageable stress into a state of overwhelming loss of control. For the past year I had been trying to get an exemption from CASA to allow me to fly through controlled airspace (airspace that is controlled by air-traffic control), as my Recreational Aviation Certificate didn't allow it. Specifically, I needed the exemption for safety reasons so I could fly into Cambridge airport in Hobart. Otherwise, there were only two less-than-ideal alternatives, one of which was Sandfly, an airstrip on the south side of Mount Wellington. Even with perfect conditions, it was hard to land at, with an approach descending at the same angle as the mountain slope, some 50 feet above the trees. The other option was Jericho, north of Hobart at a higher elevation inland; but again, I was told this could be difficult as it was susceptible to cloud and fog.

The weather in southern Tasmania is quite fickle, sometimes changing within hours. With limited options, I could be left with nowhere to land, which didn't fill me with confidence. The two support planes—Bob and Michael in the Piper Lance and Gordon and Paul in the smaller four-seater Piper Archer—had private pilots' licences (PPL) and could fly through controlled airspace. For this section of the flight, I was the weakest link.

It had been a long and drawn-out process going back and forth with CASA, answering one request after another. I had to provide detailed information on the flight, including where I was going to land. I explained that I only needed it for Tasmania. Their lawyer requested that I acknowledge the risks of flying with my quadriplegia, undertake a medical assessment and a flying assessment with a CASA representative.

'How many hours have you done in the Jabiru?' asked the representative.

'Around five hundred,' I said.

He looked at me with a smile and said, 'I think you'll be right.' He watched me take off, land, then signed me off.

Six days before D-Day came what I had been waiting for but virtually given up on: CASA's exemption. For a brief moment I was almost as excited as a vegan with a falafel—until I realised I'd never have time to get the required controlled airspace endorsements for classes C & D airspace given my existing mountain of commitments.

'Fuck!' I shouted at my computer screen as I read the document.

'What's wrong, David?' Linda called from the lounge.

'You wouldn't believe it; the CASA exemption came through!'

'That's good, right?'

'It would have been had I got it earlier, but now I'm stuffed. I don't know how I can get the controlled airspace endorsements done before we leave,' I said, completely deflated.

I was so frustrated that it had come so late; it would have been better had I never received it, as now it just added extra pressure. I felt like the world was conspiring against me, throwing everything it had at me, just to see when I would break.

For half of the next day I frantically rang all the flying schools to find a suitable instructor with the right qualifications—but no luck. After calling CASA and describing my problem, to my surprise I received an email from them saying Dick Gower, an instructor with the right qualifications at Coldstream airfield, could help me.

The next day, 24 April, I flew to Coldstream with my dad who gave me a hand getting in and out of the plane. I felt bad: Dad had cancelled a doctor's appointment for a check-up on his prostate cancer recovery in order to help me out, as no one else was available. My parents always go out of their way for us kids.

Dick walked up to my plane. 'There's a front coming through so we'll need to make this quick. Do you have maps?'

'Yeah, here they are, I printed them off,' I said, pulling them from my knee-board.

'Are you familiar with Class C airspace procedures?'

'I've read up on it.'

Running his finger along the route on the map, Dick said, 'OK then, we'll fly from here, past Doncaster Shopping Town where we will need to make a call to Essendon and then follow their instructions in.'

'OK, got it,' I said as he jumped into my plane and I fired up the engine.

The flight became a case of mental overload: I had to head southwest from Coldstream to Doncaster through unfamiliar territory, made more difficult by having to identify foreign landmarks for positioning; I had to remember unfamiliar instructions from the controller and repeat them back without stuffing up; then I had to put it all together and land at Essendon, an unfamiliar airport, receive more unfamiliar instructions, and taxi to the holding bay, before more unfamiliar instructions and take-off. Although it was only a forty-minute run in and back, I was shattered and felt terribly disheartened on my return.

The next day I was to fly into Moorabbin airport, and I was close to breaking point. If I didn't get the endorsement tomorrow, there would not be time for another go before D-Day on Monday.

At seven a.m., as I checked the weather forecast on my computer, my heart sank. It was windy at 15 knots gusting to 25 knots and getting worse. I called Dick and said, 'Given my attempt yesterday, do you think I could get it today?'

A brief pause. 'It would be a miracle,' he said.

I knew it, too.

'It usually takes a couple of weeks to become proficient to fly in and out,' he said.

I hated to quit but it was a massive weight off my shoulders; I felt so bloody relieved. The reality was, even if I did the training for the next four days, I still might not complete the endorsement. It was simply not possible in the time available. Once I got to Tasmania, I would decide what to do given my options.

Brian and Roberta were helping out, picking up camera and sound equipment and providing emotional support for Linda, who was doing an amazing job but also nearing her limit. It was not so much the physical effort but the constant mental strain—dealing with people who didn't appreciate the urgency of delivering what they'd promised, media demands for information and interviews, social media deadlines … the list went on and on.

I'd had the grand delusion that we would rest up in the final week, but it had just got busier and busier to the point where we couldn't even think about what had to be done, we just did it—hoping it would all be enough on D-Day.

The pilots—Bob, Michael, Paul, Gordon and his wife Bronwynne (who would later fly back)—flew down from Griffith on the Saturday. With 30-knot winds and a few attempts they managed to get both planes on the ground at Tooradin airport: a damned good effort considering the conditions. This gave us a few days to do final tweaks on equipment and plans, and also time to attend the On a Wing & a Chair dinner that night.

The Saturday-night dinner was the first time the whole team had come together; previously we'd been working in our smaller groups.

The flight team was at one end of the long table, I was in the middle, and the executive team and ground support on the other end.

The flight team, in particular the pilots, had an air of excitement and confidence about them, leaning back in their seats (apart from Gordon, who'd fall backwards in his wheelchair). They reminded me of excited WWII pilots eager to take to the air. Arlee, Nick, Sofia and Matt had briefly met the flight team at Avalon, so the dinner was a little awkward initially, like a group of strangers coming together at a party. However, after a few drinks everyone settled, introducing themselves and getting to know each other.

As I sat looking at the team, eating, laughing and chatting across the table, I couldn't help but think back to when I'd first shared my idea with Steve Ruffels seven years earlier. What a roller-coaster ride I'd been on since then. Through my most challenging moments when I'd wanted to throw it in, I had finally reached the point of facing my ultimate challenge and hopefully making the flight around Australia a reality.

Ching, ching, ching, Linda tapped the side of a glass to get everyone's attention. 'OK, I want to say a few quick words,' I yelled. 'I just want to thank you all for being here tonight. If it wasn't for you and the many others who've been involved with On a Wing & a Chair, we wouldn't be here today.

'There have been a few ups and downs over the years and it's taken a bit longer to get here than I first thought back in 2010, but all that is now in the past. The weather is looking good for Monday, so we'll finally start the *On a Wing & a Chair Around Australia Flight!*'

The cheers went up.

I talked about other things, but it was important to recognise that reaching this point had depended on the efforts of so many people who'd helped along the way and consequently owned part of this moment. For each team member, and for some who'd come and gone, it had been tumultuous at times. I hoped that in the end they would look back with a sense of achievement, knowing they'd played a part, whether big or small, in making it happen.

The boys from Griffith had been frantic getting themselves organised over the last week and didn't feel as well prepared as they would have liked to be, which made me feel better knowing that Linda and I weren't alone.

Sofia gave us a rundown of the media, and for the first time I started to feel excited: it was about to happen.

'Make sure you don't lose these supplies on your trip to Darwin,' I said to Josh in the hotel carpark as Linda handed him a large green sports bag containing half my medical supplies, which I would need for the second half of the trip.

'No worries, Dave. I hope you don't have any drugs in there?' he said, grinning.

'The only drug is Senokot. If someone wants to pop those, they'll get a nasty surprise. I'd be more worried about airport security thinking you're doing some weird kinky shit with all the latex gloves, lubricant and condoms in there,' I joked.

He didn't look too excited at the prospect.

I really enjoyed the night, in part because it was the first time in ages we could switch down a gear for a few hours. But I also felt that with only one day to go, everything that had happened was now over, and I could forget about it. Getting in the air and starting the trip was a new beginning.

16

ONE DAY TO GO

On Sunday Bob, Gordon, Paul, Michael and I spent the day at the airfield packing, repacking and tinkering with the planes.

'Shit Bob, you're going to get all that in there?' I asked, looking at the huge pile of gear.

'We've taken out a row of seats, saving some weight. Should be able to get it in.'

'You're not taking the disposable barbeques, are you?' I asked.

'Well, we might need them. If we get stuck. What do you think, Michael?' Bob asked.

As Michael meticulously weighed each item, writing down the number to calculate the aggregate weight and balance for the plane, he said, 'We're almost at maximum weight. We'll have to lose a few things.'

Bob picked up the barbeques and slid them under a seat in the back of the Lance. He really wanted them.

I could only take limited weight in my plane, so much of my gear had to be transported in the Lance with Linda and her gear.

I was hoping Geoff, my aircraft mechanic, would be at the airfield adjusting the throttle on my plane, which was magically moving on its own accord. I wanted to make sure it was set to go for tomorrow and called him.

'Geoff, I'm at the airfield. Have you adjusted the throttle?'

'I did it yesterday.'

'OK, so it's all fine then?'

'It should be,' he said.

I really hate the word 'should' when my life depended on a machine's reliability.

'What do you mean "should"?'

'It was too windy to start the plane outside of the hangar yesterday, but I think it will be fine. It was only a problem with the cable, so there's not much to it,' he replied, leaving me still somewhat uneasy.

'OK then,' I said, putting my trust in him. 'What about the spray system. You haven't connected it in?'

Following my overheating episode on the trial flight in January, I'd asked Geoff to develop a water-spray system in the cabin that I could activate while flying to cool myself down instead of relying on a pump-up spray bottle that was difficult to use.

'I couldn't connect it into your air system because I need a T-connector. I'll get it tomorrow.'

'I'm leaving tomorrow, Geoff!' I said.

'I know, sorry. I'll send you the part en-route and you can get one of your team to connect it. It's very simple. You won't need it until you get up north anyway,' he explained.

I had briefly tested the spray system during the week with low air pressure, which seemed to work OK. I'd hoped to have it all completed a week earlier so I could try it out properly under full pressure and sort out any problems. From my experience, something usually goes wrong with anything new and untested. Now I'd have to wait until I was up north.

I spent most of the day with Sue, my carer, working out where to put the GoPro camera mounts to get the best view, a task made a little complicated because she wasn't very mechanically minded.

'Turn the camera to your left. No, your other left!' I'd say. She was better at helping me program my radios with the frequencies of the airfields I'd be passing—I'd read out the numbers and she would dial them into the radios. I spent a lot of time reorganising the inside of the cockpit to get it as comfortable as possible as I needed all my maps, flight information, drinks, food, electronic equipment, the Personal Locator Beacon (PLB) and survival kit easily accessible during flight.

Gordon and Paul reorganised their gear for the third time in the Archer, fuelled up and did final checks to make sure the plane was ready for the water crossing the next day.

Sofia finalised media arrangements with Channel Seven and Matt was planning to transfer the website to a server with more capacity for the potential influx of high traffic. This added to Linda's already high stress levels because she was worried that if anything went wrong in the transfer, all the work she'd done building up the social media presence might be affected. Also, with the Spider Tracks tracking unit donated by Chris Dixon from Thomson Aviation, which would show the position of my plane on a map, the website had to be operational on Day 1 so our followers could see where I was in real time.

By late afternoon we'd had enough fiddling and headed home fluttering with anticipation and excitement. We were out of time, had done as much as we could, and anything else on the to-do-list was crossed off. The flight was now or never.

Paul, Gordon and Bronwynne got a taxi to a hotel near the airfield and I dropped off Bob and Michael at Brian and Roberta's place.

'Your mum dropped off two GoPros for you,' Linda said, obvious frustration in her voice.

'How are you going?' I asked.

'I still have so much to do and I haven't even packed yet.' She was looking very tired.

I could barely wheel through the lounge room with our gear spread all over the floor. Linda was still working out how to use the cameras, sorting out equipment, labelling a dozen chargers and deciding what clothes to pack.

At 11 p.m. I checked the weather on the Bureau of Meteorology (BoM), which was thankfully still looking good, checked my flight planning and finally worked out how to operate the GoPros with my Samsung Galaxy tablet that I would also use for navigation. I was shattered, and went to bed for a short sleep until my carer arrived at four a.m. Linda was up until two a.m., packing and paying bills so our electricity and gas wouldn't be cut off while we were away.

17

D-DAY

Monday 29th April, Linda and I arrived at seven a.m.; a few of the local pilots at Tooradin airfield were milling around waiting for the team. Gordon and Paul were already checking over their plane, and my parents with Bob and Michael soon arrived, thankfully with take-away coffees to charge up Linda and me. With Lida and Josh arriving not long after, the Magnificent Seven, my amazing support team, were now together, raring to go and looking the part dressed in our black polos, fleecy windcheaters, caps and name tags, all emblazoned with the OWC logo.

We couldn't have planned a more perfect morning. The air was still with high scattered clouds against a bright-blue backdrop. I felt my body re-energising with the warmth of the sun—well, that and the coffee.

I hadn't expected so many friends and even strangers to come down and support our departure. With Channel Seven wanting to chat about the flight, take photos, film how the plane worked and interview Linda and me, it was becoming very busy and I started to feel a little overwhelmed by the attention.

Between chats, I slowly got my plane checks done. 'Your oil looks good, Dave,' said Michael, showing me the dipstick as I wheeled around the plane, indicating to Paul where to position the

GoPros—two on the wing and one inside the cockpit. I was hoping to put together a short film of the flight when we got back, if it all went to plan.

Our nine a.m. departure was pushing out to ten a.m. and I started to feel an urgency to get going. It was only a short leg for the first day from Tooradin to Flinders Island to top up with fuel and lunch, then on to Wynyard, Tasmania, for our overnight stop. But if we were delayed with unexpected weather or mechanical issues we could easily run out of daylight, and I didn't like the idea of flying into an unfamiliar airfield in darkness.

As I wheeled around to each person, shaking hands or giving closer friends a hug and kiss, everyone was quiet. It felt really weird, as if I were leaving the shore for an unknown land and may not come back.

'See you in Tassie, Mum,' I said as she hugged me. I could tell she was worried but trying not to show it.

'Fly safely, David.'

'Yes, Mum!'

'See you tomorrow, David,' said Brian, shaking my hand and patting me on the shoulder in a half man-hug.

Paul and Michael loaded me into the plane with my wheelchair in the back and Lida set me up in the cockpit.

With my life-jacket on (a requirement for the water crossing over the Bass Strait), the survival kit in a plastic container in the passenger seat (not that I'd be able to use much of it if I went down, apart from the satellite phone and Personal Locator Beacon attached to me), the Camelback with water, muesli bars, maps and flight-detail sheets with all my radio frequencies and distances for when to change them, I was set to go.

Velcroed to my knee-board was the Samsung Galaxy tablet with all the aeronautical charts as moving maps, provided by my friend John Kidon to use for navigation. He also gave me a backup tablet and a Walkman power pack to ensure I didn't get lost by running out of power. In addition, I had a GPS on my dashboard with the route programmed in. There was no way I'd get lost—and if all else failed, as long as I kept the land on my left, I'd be all right.

'Clear prop!' I yelled as the six cylinders slowly cranked over and burst into life with a throaty growl. I pushed the choke off and pulled back on the throttle, but it remained at 1150 rpm, revving too high.

I thought through the possible causes but was pretty sure I knew what had happened. When Geoff had fixed the problem with the throttle on Saturday, because he couldn't run the engine he was unaware that it was revving high; it should have been idling at 900 rpm.

I shut down the engine to check what was going on and Michael came over. We concluded it was only a simple adjustment issue, and I decided it would be best to sort it in Wynyard when we had more time. It didn't affect the performance of the aircraft at all, I was just annoyed that the plane wasn't in perfect form as I had tried to make sure everything was right before leaving. But if this was to be my biggest problem, I'd be happy.

With a quicker than usual taxi to Runway 22, the support aircraft followed. Gordon, Paul and Lida in Sierra Delta Whiskey (SDW), the Piper Archer—a four-seater, low-wing, single-engine with a cruise speed of 120 knots—were behind me. They were followed by Bob, Michael and Linda in Whiskey Mike Quebec (WMQ), the Piper Lance, or Sir Lancelot as Bob named it. It was a big six-seater, low-wing, single-engine aircraft with retractable undercarriage and a quick cruise speed of 160 knots.

My plane, Jabiru 5558, was the slowest at 115 knots cruise. The plan was for me to take off first with the Archer catching up and flying at a safe distance. If something happened, at least we could identify each other's position and relay it to Melbourne Centre (en-route air-traffic control) in an emergency. The Lance would take off last, fly ahead, land at the airfield and start getting fuel, media, transport and anything else organised before I arrived.

'Tooradin traffic, Jabiru 5558 rolling on Runway 22 for immediate departure, Tooradin,' I called over the radio. As I puffed on the mouth tube, the engine revved to a roar. The pressure of the seat on my back increased as the plane quickly gathered speed, hurling us down the runway like a sprinting racehorse. Feeling the wheels skipping, I gently pulled back on the control column, the ground instantly fell away and my windscreen turned blue.

Bright sunshine cut across my body as I climbed to a thousand feet, turned left to join the circuit and went in for a low-level pass over the runway, the support aircrafts following. As I roared past, my family and friends stood clumped together in a small group waving. Pulling up to gain height, turning left, and with the coast on the horizon—so began the *On a Wing & a Chair Around Australia Flight*.

'Good luck Dave, safe flight!' said a familiar voice over the radio.

'Thanks Ian, see you when I get back,' I said, exultant to be on my way at last.

I felt a mixture of disbelief, relief and excitement: I was actually doing it. I was finally on my way, seven years after sharing my dream with Steve. I also felt a little apprehensive at the thought of the massive task ahead. 'I'm flying around Australia,' easily rolls off the tongue, but as the miles slowly counted down on my GPS, the endless coastline reaching into the distance, it began to sink in just how ambitious this flight was. But right then, I had to push that thought out of my mind; I had to focus on my immediate goal—getting to Wynyard, Tasmania.

We had two VHF radios in our planes; I had one set to our chat channel of 123.4 MHz and local CTAFs (Common Traffic Advisory Frequency) for local airfields en-route. The second radio was programmed to Melbourne Centre that covers the southern half

Surfing at Smiths Beach, Victoria, in 1987. Friends and I would regularly head down to the coast on weekends, surf all day, then replenish our energy on dim-sims, hot chips and Coke on the drive home.
Photo: Rebecca Burt

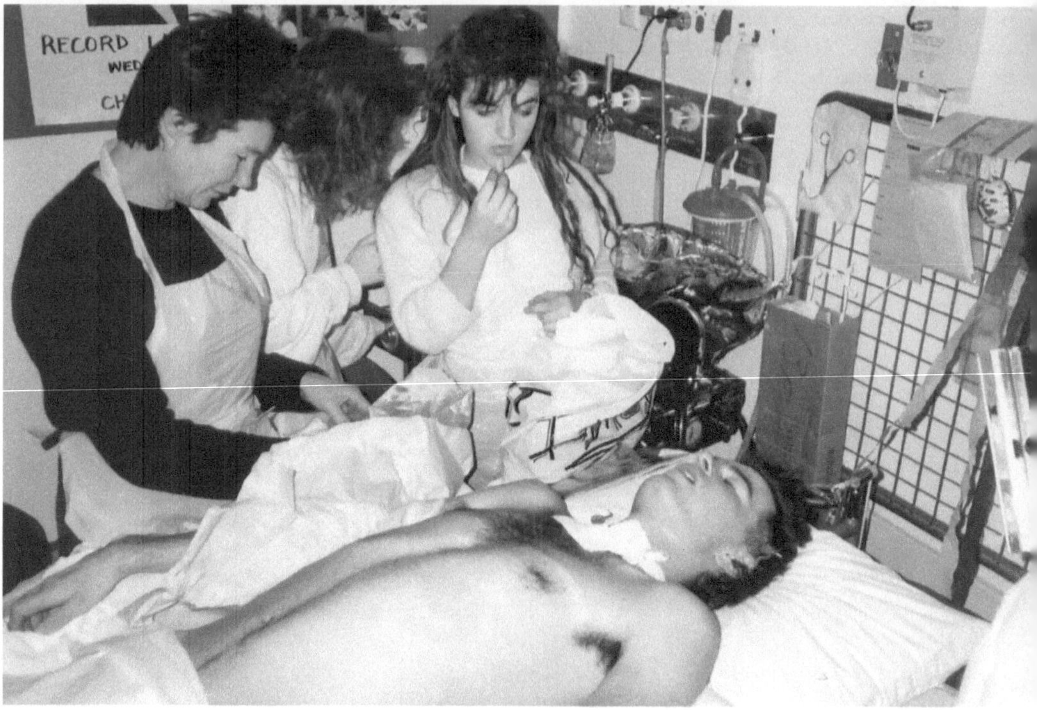

I spent my first two months lying in bed with head tongs screwed into the side of my head, pulling my neck straight, to allow my broken 5th vertebrae to heal.

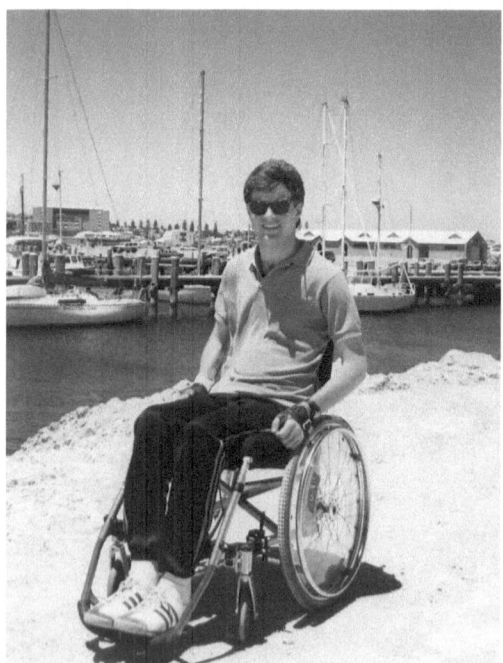

Challenging as it was, it was great to be out in the community, getting back into life after nine months in hospital.

The hook, attached to my bed, which holds the wheelchair in position, enabling me to transfer independently. It was such a simple idea, and one that changed my life.

Top: First solo flight at Porepunkah Airfield, Victoria, February 2006.

Left: Ready to take off in my adapted Airborne Edge X 582 microlight trike. The cockpit had my new base-bar adaptation with push buttons for the throttle control. My left hand is on the ground steering lever, and the go-cart seat with harness provided good lateral support. The magneto (kill) switches are on the right side out of view.

Steve Ruffels and I celebrating with champagne. My boyhood dream of flying had become a reality, as I completed my first solo flight on 14th February, 2006. *Photo: Lisa Ruffels*

Landing at Hay, NSW, on the 2007 Navex flying trip. A gust of wind caught my wing, pushing me into a two-foot-high bank on the side of the runway and rolling the trike.

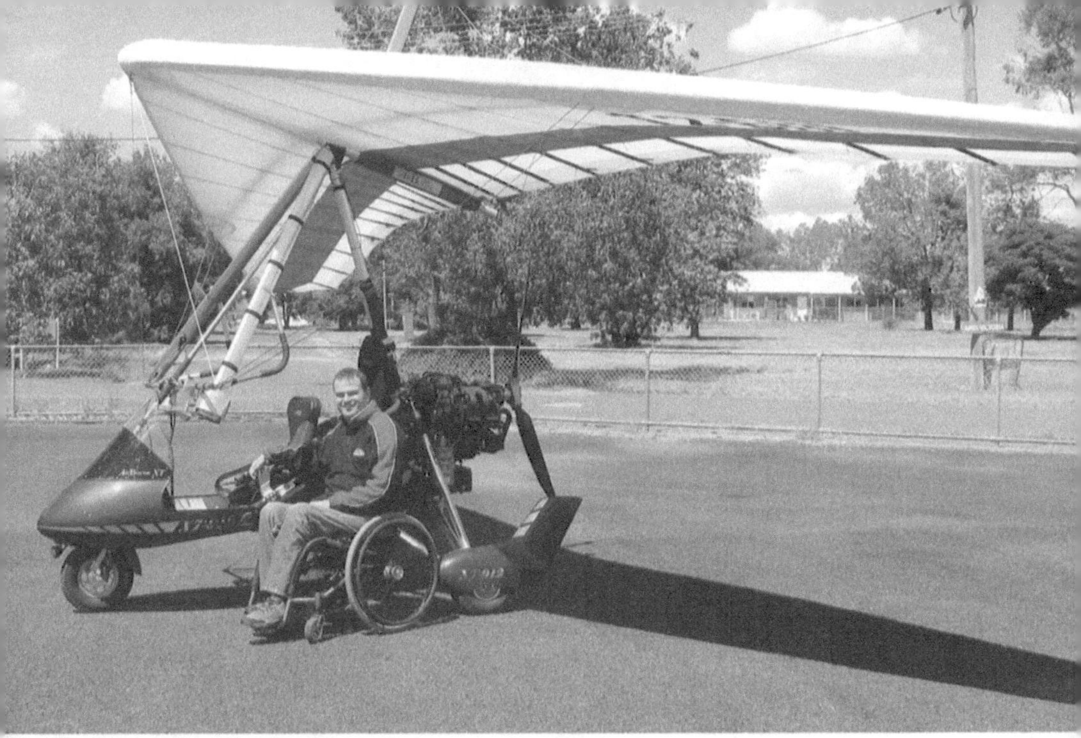

Upgraded to an Airborne XT-912 trike in 2007 after my eventful first cross-country flight. Developing the sip/puff system to steer the front nose wheel for taxiing was a game changer!

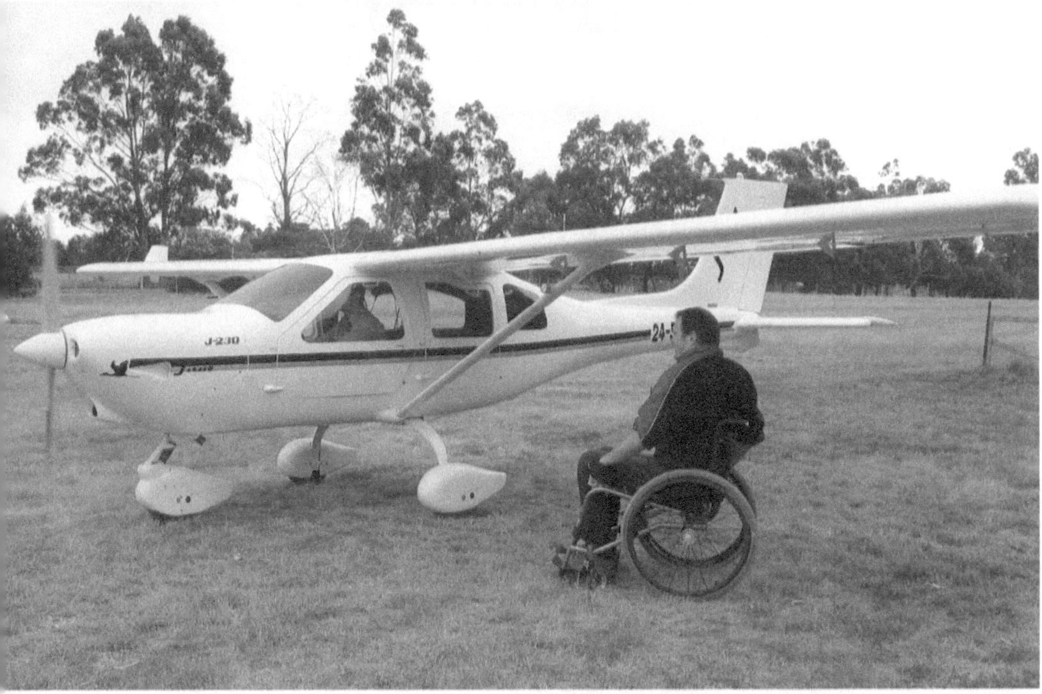

The day my new Jabiru J230D arrived in December, 2008. I couldn't wait to fly it, but would have to wait until I developed the adaptations to enable me to pilot it with quadriplegia.

Inside the cockpit of the new Jabiru J230D fitted out with my custom adaptations.
1. Sip/puff tube is used to control the speed of the engine.
2. Control column, with wrist support, locks my hand in place so I can control the pitch/roll of the aircraft.
3. Rudder lever (with wrist support) is used both to operate the rudder during flight and steer the front nose wheel when taxiing. Incorporated in the top are red and green push buttons to operate the flaps and a black push button to change the programmed radio frequencies.
4. Toggle switch to operate the elevator trim adjustment.
5. Toggle switch to operate brake.
6. Small levers attached to instrument knobs to enable easier adjustment

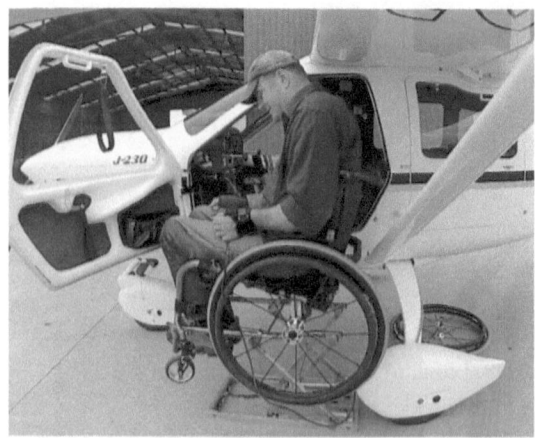

A compact scissor lift, positioned under my wheelchair, raises me up to the height of the door sill. I then require assistance transferring into the pilot's seat and positioning. The lift folds down flat and fits neatly into the rear of the aircraft.

Left: Despite the Bangkok incident, Linda, my beautiful princess, still married me, November 2012.

Below: The Magnificent 7 on D-Day, 29 April 2013, ready to start the On a Wing & a Chair Around Australia Flight.
(Back L–R) Lida, Michael, Paul, Bob, Linda, Josh (Front L–R) Gordon, me.
Photo: Linda Sands

The Piper Lance PA-32R-300, the big six-seater support plane with retractable undercarriage and a cruise speed of 160 knots. Piloted by Bob and Michael with Linda, our project coordinator, as passenger. *Photo: Linda Sands*

The Piper Archer II, our smaller four-seater support plane with a cruise speed of 120 knots. Piloted by Gordon and Paul, carrying my personal support, Lida, for the first half of the flight, and Josh for the second half. *Photo: Linda Sands*

First leg of the epic flight, heading out over the seemingly endless expanse of water of the Bass Strait towards Flinders Island.

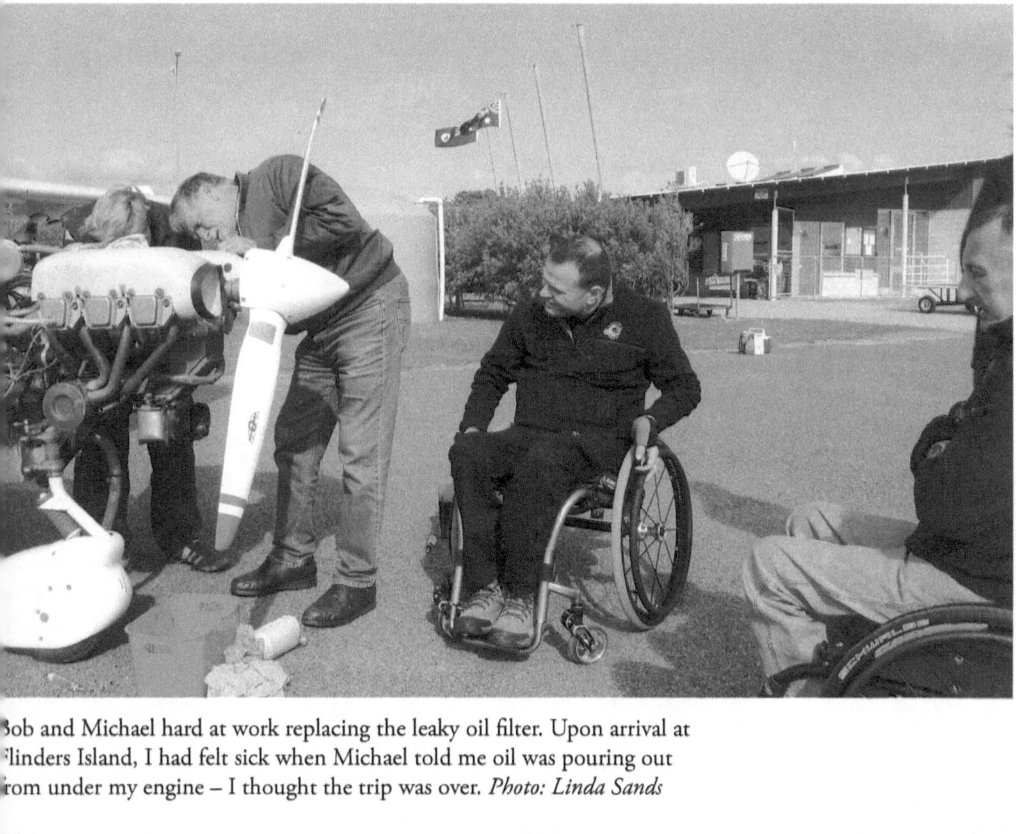

Bob and Michael hard at work replacing the leaky oil filter. Upon arrival at Flinders Island, I had felt sick when Michael told me oil was pouring out from under my engine – I thought the trip was over. *Photo: Linda Sands*

Refuelling the aircraft with jerry cans at Strahan in the chilling wind and rain. *Photo: Linda Sands*

Settled in my warm cocoon above the ocean we crossed our first milestone, the most southerly point of Australia, South East Cape, Tasmania. *Photo: Linda Sands*

Flying along Victor 1, the VFR route past Sydney Heads with the iconic Sydney Opera House and Sydney Harbour Bridge in the distance.
Photo: Linda Sands

The members of East Gippsland Aero Club looked after the team so generously with a warm fire, smorgasbord of food and accommodation.
Photo: Linda Sands

Passing our second milestone, the most easterly point of Australia, Cape Byron, NSW. *Photo: Linda Sands*

I'd been looking forward to flying along the beach of the Gold Coast, QLD, another highlight ticked off.

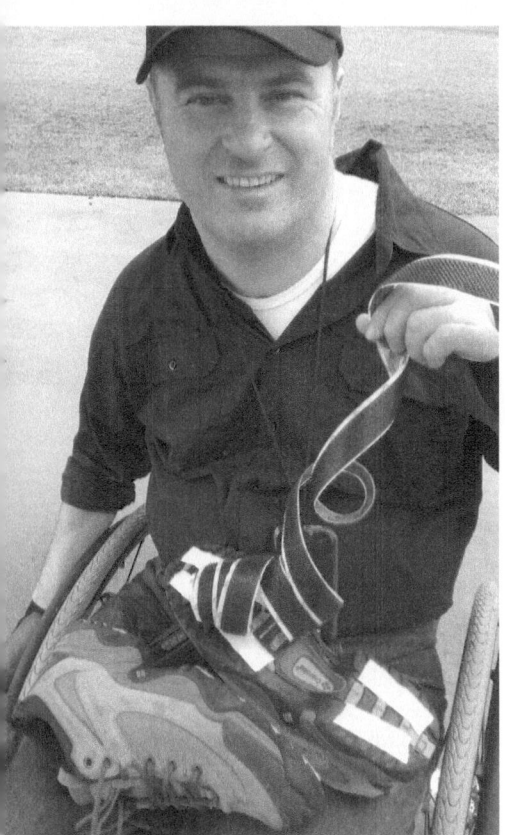

Top: Linda found a brief moment to take a quick sleep amongst all the gear in the back of the Lance during the hectic flight up the east coast.
Photo: Bob Frauenfelder

Left: Following my battering with turbulence coming into Shute Harbour, I got some industrial Velcro to secure my feet to the foot plate in my plane.
Photo: Linda Sands

Running into deteriorating weather near Hinchinbrook Island, separated from both support planes and with lowering cloud and rain ahead, I turned around and headed to the safety of Ingham, Qld.

After being separated due to bad weather, the Lance with Bob, Michael and Linda got stuck on Dunk Island, with the remainder of the team landing at Ingham. Here Michael and Bob are tying the plane down for their overnight stay. *Photo: Linda Sands*

With the team reunited at Ingham, low cloud and rain prevented us from progressing further north. We had daily planning meetings to work out our options for getting out. *Photo: Linda Sands*

Finally out of Ingham, we were again held up with a flat tyre on my Jabiru as soon as I landed at Cooktown, Qld. Without a jack, the team improvised by manually lifting the wing and supporting it with the refuelling ladder topped with Linda's yoga mat to raise the right tyre off the ground so we could fix the puncture. *Photo: Gordon McCaw*

Third milestone down, crossing the most northerly point of Australia, Cape York, Qld. *Photo: Linda Sands*

Top: Patchwork of scars on the earth from bauxite mining around Weipa, Qld. *Photo: Bob Frauenfelder*

Below: With a hot day ahead, Paul tried to connect my new spray system so I could cool myself down, but to no avail—it wouldn't hold air pressure. We'd have another go in Darwin. *Photo: Linda Sands*

Trevor 'Snoddy' Snodgrass from the SES was ready with an Esky full of ice-cold soft drinks and beer to wash down the dust when we arrived at Weipa. *Photo: Linda Sands*

of Australia (Brisbane Centre covering the northern half), enabling me to hear if there were other aircraft near. In an emergency, they could assist by notifying Search and Rescue or other aircraft.

Approaching Wilsons Promontory, I heard Bob and Gordon giving their respective positions, relaying back and forth. I was a fair way behind, but in the rush and hustle at Tooradin, I didn't get myself set up right and felt disorganised trying to navigate, change frequencies, give calls of my location and height as I passed airfields and tried to operate three GoPro cameras. I hate being flustered when I fly.

In the end I switched on all three cameras, forgot about them and concentrated on the important bit: flying. I'd work out the rest later.

Ahead the clouds were getting denser and the further I progressed the lower they got, feeding my nerves as I approached South East Point, the tip of Wilsons Promontory, our drop-off point into the abyss of Bass Strait.

I had hoped for a clear day to get up to 7500 feet, providing more time to glide in case of an engine out—assuming I was close enough to land; or if no land, more time to think how I might die. In fact, height was more of a psychological security blanket; in reality, it was a false form of reassurance. Today, it wasn't to be. Reaching a disappointing 2500 feet, the thick layered cumulus cloud with the occasional patch of blue breaking through, it felt a lot lower than if I was over land.

I called Melbourne Centre to notify them of my crossing and reporting schedule (SKED), making a radio call every ten minutes confirming Operations Normal, location and track. Missing a SKED report would activate Search and Rescue (SAR) action.

As South East Point drifted past, my stomach tightened like the strings on a tennis racket. Below me and into infinity was a dark, cold grey ocean bubbling away with small whitecaps. I climbed as high as I could to 2500 feet, lined up the nose of my plane with Hogan Island and headed for it, following the line of islands (more like rocks) to Flinders Island.

My senses were in overdrive. A little nagging voice of doubt in the back of my mind said softly, *What was that, was it a miss, a cough? Is the engine OK, maybe there's a problem with the fuel, you have enough oil, don't you?* Every few minutes I scanned the instruments, making sure everything looked normal to shut down the annoying voice.

Giving my first SKED to Melbourne Centre, a friendly guy received my call, logged my position and gave me a time to call him back in ten minutes. I felt a little more at ease knowing there was someone watching over me.

Isolated cloud-bursts of rain in the distance resembled massive pipes sucking up water from the ocean. I couldn't fly through them as the rain would effectively sand-blast my wooden propeller to a stick; my direct track to Hogan Island became a wavy line as I weaved around the rain showers.

The Archer, a white dot in the distance, was also zipping around the showers. I gave them a call for a chat and to see how they were doing. 'We have you in sight, Dave,' Paul said, making me feel a little less alone over this endless expanse of water.

I started to settle in, relax and feel more organised after the mad rush, and had another go at operating the GoPros on the Galaxy tablet. Without an autopilot, I had to fly hands on all the time. I could only play around with the tablet for a few seconds before having to look up, otherwise I'd find the aircraft in a slow banking turn even though I thought it was going straight. That's why flying in cloud is so dangerous; without a reference point you don't know whether you're up, down or sideways as the force on your body confuses your balance.

Passing Hogan Island, I completed the regular scan on my

instruments, noticing the oil pressure dropping a little but still in the green. This was of no real concern as it had always fluctuated, but at the halfway mark across Bass Strait it dropped into the yellow—now it had my attention. The oil and cylinder head temperatures were reading normal in the green, the fan was still turning so I figured it might be the sender for the oil gauge playing up, which had happened in the past. There was nothing I could do anyway except keep going and hope it wouldn't drop any further.

As the outline of Flinders Island became clearer in the distance, the small knot in my stomach loosened; it would be just a short time until I was back over land. The cloud started to get higher and break up with more patches of blue, allowing me to gain height as I crossed the coast, ready for my descent into Flinders Island airport. Tuning to the Flinders Island CTAF, I picked up the Lance 10 NM out giving their inbound call; I still had another 20 NM to run with the Archer in front of me.

Feeling much more relaxed and confident about achieving my first challenge, I enjoyed taking in the picturesque scenery of Flinders Island with the patchwork of natural bush and green farmland against the varying shades of blue along the coastline.

As I joined circuit, I suddenly got a whiff of a burning smell. I couldn't see anything behind me and there was no smoke from under the dash, confusing me a little as to where it was coming from. Not taking any chances, I did a very quick circuit and was on the ground in record time.

As soon as I took off my headset, I heard a hissing sound. For a moment I couldn't work out where it was coming from. 'Ah shit!' I yelled once I realised my next problem. When Geoff had tapped into the pressurised pneumatic brake system air line to connect the new spray system, the connection hadn't sealed properly and was leaking air. This explained the burning smell: the compressor had become hot from running more often than normal.

As Lida started to extract me from the plane, Michael came over looking concerned. 'Dave, do you realise you have oil pouring out from under your engine?' he asked, dropping to his knees for a closer look.

My heart sank. 'What? What do you mean?'

'You have oil dripping onto the nose-wheel cover and the ground.'

Images of a cracked block or sump filled my mind, oil spurting everywhere.

I can't fucking believe this. We had just started, and now it was over before it even began! was all I could think of. I felt sick.

Michael knew the Jabiru well, and with Bob's help quickly pulled off the cowling to get to the engine. I held my breath, hoping it was something simple. 'Looks like the oil filter's leaking, Dave,' said Bob, wiping the oil with his finger and showing me. It explained my drop in oil pressure over Bass Strait.

A wave of relief washed over me like a fresh breeze. I was so happy it was an easy fix, as I had spare filters in the plane; but then my thoughts turned to disbelief. I couldn't believe what had happened. I could deal with the fast idle and air leak, but to have the oil filter leak left me quite annoyed. I didn't know whether it hadn't been installed properly, whether it had worked loose or if the gasket was faulty. Whichever way, it didn't matter; if it had leaked a little more and I had run out of oil over the crossing, the engine would have seized and I'd be dead. It's the little things that catch you out and bring disaster. And I thought I'd had it all covered.

With the planes refuelled and Bob and Michael finishing off with the oil leak, we sat in the warmth of the terminal building to eat the sandwiches Mum had made along with the dinner-plate-sized Anzac biscuits, washing it all down with Cup-A-Soups, which soon became a daily staple of the flight.

'I'll take the Jab for a run down the strip to check the leak,

Dave,' offered Michael, munching on his ham and cheese sandwich.

'Yeah, that'd be great, mate. See if you can tighten the air leak while you're at it?' I asked.

'Roger that,' he said and headed out.

The oil leak was fixed, but the air leak needed smaller tools to tighten the connector and would have to wait until Wynyard. To stop the compressor from overheating, I decided to turn it off while flying, then back on before landing. It wasn't a big issue, providing I didn't forget to turn it on.

Linda's role as project coordinator was to liaise and coordinate with the various people at each stopover to confirm our arrangements as well as keep people in the loop with our estimated time of arrival. Over lunch, Linda contacted Michael Dykstra, the president of the Wynyard Aeroclub, to check our arrangements for accommodation, transport and the media, as the local paper wanted a story.

'Dave, good news; I told Michael about your plane problems and he'll get someone to look at it when you land,' she said.

'A LAME?' I asked.

'Yeah, I think that's what he said; there's one at the airfield.'

'Ah great, good work, honey,' I said, feeling much happier having a Licensed Aircraft Maintenance Engineer (LAME) take a look and sort out the problems.

The oil filter issue really brought home to me the danger of this flight and how something so simple could very easily kill me or my team members. With three things going wrong on the first day, I felt a little less confident and more apprehensive about the flight. It began to sink in that there was no guarantee I would make it around Tasmania, let alone the whole country.

It was after two p.m. by the time we left for our next leg, which was only 1.5 hours flying time. Although it was getting late, we still had plenty of time to get there but, with the day's events so far, I didn't want to risk racing daylight.

Heading south down Finders Island, I then turned right to follow the northern coast of Tasmania, passing little towns surrounding the calm sea inlets. The oil pressure was back up in the green and, whether it was psychological or not, the plane seemed to be running beautifully. The cloud had cleared to blue skies and the air was silky smooth with the sun shining in through my windscreen, sinking lower to the west.

'Jabiru 5558, Whiskey Mike Quebec, you there, Dave?' asked Bob over the radio.

'Go ahead, Bob,' I replied.

'Linda is asking, have you forgotten something?'

I had to think for a moment, then looking at the dash, I realised. Aw shit. 'I forgot the Spider Tracks, didn't I?'

'Roger that.'

The one thing I had to remember without fail was to plug the Spider Tracks tracking unit into the power outlet in my plane. The Spider Tracks showed my location, height, direction and speed on a map of Australia linked to the OWC website, so followers could track my aircraft in real time. In the rush to get going I had forgotten to ask Lida to plug it in.

In the back of the Lance, Linda would update Facebook when we took off and indicate our ETA at our next destination. Linda had posted that we had left Flinders Island, but on the website the Spider Tracks showed I was still there. One of our followers quickly picked this up and Facebooked us. We found out later that Dad had also been watching the Spider Tracks and was starting to panic, thinking we were stuck. It was nice to know we had at least two followers.

Touching down at Wynyard, the air was still: a beautiful autumn afternoon as the sun started to set. Completing the first leg, I felt I had really accomplished something, despite the few problems that I hoped were now behind me.

Members of the Wynyard Aeroclub were at the door of the

hanger waiting for us to arrive. As I opened the door of the plane, the cold air hit me like a slap in the face. We pushed my plane into the hanger so I could get out and meet Dale Triffett, the LAME from Island Air Maintenance. Dale gave my engine a good once-over, fixing the engine idle speed and air leak, and we decided to lock-wire the oil filter to ensure it couldn't come loose. I felt much happier when he gave it the OK.

My legs were like ice blocks and I managed to get pole position in front of the heater in the aeroclub to warm up. The club had organised a barbeque dinner for us, which really hit the spot; I was ravenous. It was great to relax for a moment and chat with the members, but Linda and I had a lot more to do before we could even think about going to bed.

While Bob, Michael, Paul, Gordon and Lida chatted over a few drinks and celebrated the completion of the momentous first day, Michael Dykstra drove Linda and me to our motel accommodation, generously donated by the aeroclub.

Once we got there, Linda had to charge up all the batteries in stages, check and answer emails, copy photos from cameras and GoPros to three backup hard drives (one went in each plane in case one crashed), sort through the photos to put in the blog and adjust them, liaise with Sofia for media the next day and send information if required, liaise with base support about accommodation and transport for the next day, assist me with the blog (I would dictate and she would type), then lastly, update Facebook.

While she did most of that, I reviewed my flight plans for the next day, checked the weather and caught up on emails. Oh, and there was the video blog which I didn't get to on the first night, as I ran out of time.

By eleven p.m. I was exhausted and had to go to bed, but Lida was still at the aeroclub with the rest of the team having a drink. I called her on the team phone and Mike Dykstra shuttled her back to our motel. As personal support, her main role was to do my personal care: get me into bed and get me up in the morning as well as fix me up in the plane.

I lay in bed dictating the day's events to Linda as she typed the blog. But when she hit the Save button, she cried, 'Oh no, it's gone!'

'What's gone?'

'The blog, it crashed! I've lost everything.'

I dictated it again, Linda tried to save it but again it crashed. 'I don't fucking believe this!' she screamed and burst into tears of frustration and exhaustion; but she refused to quit. This was our first blog of the trip. It had to go up without fail; people were waiting for it. Through tears and snot dribbling onto the keyboard, the third time lucky, Linda finally managed to post it.

We had been up since four a.m., had done 3.8 hours flying, it was now past midnight and we had to get up at five a.m.

18

FIRST MILESTONE: SOUTH EAST CAPE

God, I'm tired, was my first thought as I was jolted into consciousness by Lida knocking on the door at five a.m. I had to think for a moment where I was.

As the previous day's events drifted into memory, I became conscious of where we were heading that day, the awareness increasing my uneasiness.

Of all the flying legs on the trip, Day 2 was the one I was most concerned about. It wasn't that we were heading down the notoriously challenging windswept west coast of Tasmania that receives the brunt of the Roaring Forties winds. Many pilots I had spoken to reported it was very windy, very changeable, and there was no place to put down in an emergency. If you're going down the west coast you need a good day, they'd cautioned. This had lodged in my mind, adding to my uncertainty.

However, my main worry was: where would I land when I reached Hobart? Without the controlled airspace exemption, theoretically I wasn't meant to fly into Cambridge airport, at least by myself. Cambridge was a small airfield next to Hobart international airport with its commercial jets flying in and out, but to get there I would have to fly through controlled airspace.

If the conditions were good, I planned to fly over Sandfly, see what it looked like and possibly give it a go. But at this point I was anticipating going to Jericho, which was around 70 kilometres north of Hobart, inland.

This morning's five a.m. start was considered a sleep-in as I didn't need to have a poo (I do it every second day), which adds at least another hour to my morning routine, requiring a four a.m. start. Then it was out the door and transported by a couple of aeroclub members to the airfield by seven a.m. for breakfast. Lida had to be up before me and go to bed after me, getting limited sleep at night; but at least she could rest up and sleep in the back of the plane during the day.

With the day's challenges on my mind, I could only stomach a slice of cold toast with jam and a coffee.

I ran a briefing each morning to discuss the plan for the day: the route with alternate airfields, midpoint stops to refuel and have lunch, a review of the weather and any concerns held by team members.

'It's a big day today,' I began. 'With a bit of luck, we're going to tick off our first milestone and cross South East Cape. How are we feeling?'

'Good,' Gordon said.

'Looking forward to getting going,' Paul added, everyone else nodding.

'How's the weather looking, Michael? Can you give us a run-through?' I asked, knowing he loved the detail and was across it.

He brought up the forecast on his phone. 'Looks like we'll have a moderate northwesterly with a few showers. Should be OK. Cloud base is broken around three thousand. Weather at Strahan is a few scattered showers and winds around 12 knots from the northwest.'

We would have preferred a higher cloud base for safety, especially down the southwest where the coastline is rugged with no beaches, but I was very happy it wasn't too windy, especially at Strahan. With a north-south runway, it would be a crosswind of around 10 knots, within the limits of my aircraft and my ability—nothing I couldn't handle.

'Fair enough. Are we happy to fly, guys?' I asked.

'Yep, all good,' said Bob, to accompanying nods.

Each pilot had different skills, experience and comfort levels in taking on risk. Flying can be dangerous, especially if the pilot is operating beyond his or her ability. As a team, we had to operate within each person's level, which varied depending on the conditions. Before embarking on the flight, we agreed that each pilot had to agree to fly, otherwise we wouldn't go.

'OK, at Strahan we'll check the weather for Hobart and decide where I'm going to land. If it's no good, we'll wait. We're all good with that?' I wasn't going to take off unless I knew I could land safely down south.

With no objections, we headed for the planes.

I'd hoped to get in the air by nine a.m., but no one was organised: planes weren't packed and Bob was on the phone trying to sort out a few issues with his shed-building business back in Griffith. It was only our second day and I knew it would take time to get used to working with each other, as had occurred on the trial flight back in January. Lida and Bob hadn't been with us then, so the team was different now. We had to readjust our systems and processes to suit.

My lesson for that morning was to provide more detailed direction so each person knew what we were doing and what was required of them.

Landing down south was still playing on my mind, but as I was about to get into my plane my week was made. I got a phone call from Stan Tilley, the manager of Sandfly airport near Hobart, whom I'd spoken to the day before. Aware of my concerns, and keen to take care of a brethren pilot, he'd contacted the top guy in the control tower at Hobart international, getting approval for me to fly into

Cambridge airport. I was so happy, I called up the tower to confirm the procedure and thanked them for going out of their way to make my life easier and safer. I was allowed to fly 'in company' (follow) one of our support planes as all the pilots had controlled airspace endorsements. They would do the radio calls and all I had to do was follow one of them in. My biggest worry and risk instantaneously vaporised. I now felt revitalised and looked forward to tackling the notorious west coast.

We finally managed to get in the air at 10.30 a.m. (once we got Bob off the phone), this time making sure the Spider Tracks was plugged in, and headed west along the coast. Dodging the scattered rain showers wasn't a problem, but we only managed 2500 feet, at times dropping to 1500 feet with low cloud.

My goal was to fly over the water as much as possible in order to say I'd truly circumnavigated the coastline. I wasn't going to cut corners or go inland unless I absolutely had to. Initially I felt a little uneasy going too far offshore, tending to hug the coast tightly; but the more comfortable I felt in my warm cocoon, the more my confidence grew. I flew straight across the smaller bays instead of going around them, taking less time to cover the same distance, but I was still within gliding range to the beach if the fan stopped.

The string of curved bays along the coast ahead reminded me of bites in a sandwich, the frothing ocean rolling onto the yellow beaches, sand dunes stretching inland until they met the dense low-lying bush. I couldn't imagine humans had ever set foot on this pristine environment.

Shit! The oil pressure gauge suddenly dropped to zero: it was déjà vu. As I scanned the instruments—*fuck!*—the oil temperature was maxed out into the red. *I've really got a problem now*, I thought.

Without thinking, I checked my map for the closest airfield. Smithton was 20 NM back with nothing else around. My engine was still running and the cylinder head temperature was normal; I figured I had some time, but not much before it seized. Scanning the coast ahead, there were plenty of wide beaches so I felt confident I could get the plane down in one piece.

Suddenly the oil pressure returned to normal and the oil temperature dropped to 90 degrees, also in the green. *What the…? Was I seeing things?* The aircraft hit a bump. Again, one gauge dropped and the other climbed. Seconds later, they were both back to normal. I hit another bump and it happened again. This time they didn't return to normal, so I did what Fonzie (from *Happy Days*) would do in a crisis: I gave the dash a thump and the gauges went back to normal. To my relief, this time it wasn't a lack of oil pressure, but a problem with the instruments. 'Sierra Delta Whiskey, Jabiru 5558, you copy?'

'Copy, Dave,' radioed Paul.

'My instruments are playing up. Ever had your oil pressure drop and the oil temp max out then go back to normal?'

'Sounds like a loose earth wire,' said Paul.

'That happened to me a few years back. Definitely an earth,' commented Gordon.

'I'll take a look at it at Strahan, Dave,' Paul suggested.

'Cheers. See you on the ground.'

I was hyper-conscious of the risks, as was the whole team, when planning this flight. I had put together a detailed risk assessment, and during our team-planning sessions we reviewed each issue, making sure we had everything covered and were comfortable with our management of each one. For all team members, the risks of weather, fatigue and mechanical problems could be managed to a point. It was the unexpected things that bit and could potentially end in disaster—like my oil-filter leak. However, being prepared allowed us to deal with the unexpected a bit more easily.

Most of the coastline around Australia is extremely remote with little opportunity for a safe landing. As a team we had discussed this extensively. If there wasn't an adequate clearing or beach for a forced landing, Bob, Michael, Gordon and Paul would put down in water, as they and their passengers could get out of the plane relatively easily. As a last resort, I preferred to attempt the coastal bush rather than water. My biggest problem flying solo, in a forced landing situation, was the difficulty of exiting the aircraft by myself. Even if I successfully ditched into the sea with the aircraft remaining upright and staying afloat with the buoyancy of the wings, it would not help me as the cockpit is below the wings and would fill with water. If I did manage to get out, down south I would be stuffed anyway, hypothermic within minutes—while up north I'd be a floating hors d'oeuvre for the crocodiles and sharks. Having this scenario constantly in the back of my mind was one of the psychological challenges I had to manage.

The wind was getting up at Strahan and I was nearing the maximum crosswind of 14 knots for my plane. Using full rudder, on approach I was buffeted around like a leaf in the wind.

Cracking open the door of my plane was like sitting naked in the snow beneath a hurricane fan: it was *unbelievably* cold.

The terminal building, an old asbestos-lined box resembling Mawson's Hut in the Antarctic, had nothing inside except a power outlet that I hoped worked. Plugging in the fan heater Mum had bought me before we left, it came to life with a gentle purr. The warmth on my face was like slipping into a hot bath.

'You're soft, Jacka!' Bob said, giving me shit about bringing the heater.

'At least I'm not a quadsicle, Bob!'

Strahan airport didn't have fuel, so prior to the flight Bob had arranged for Geoff Ayton to drop some off. Geoff was obviously part Inuit, dressed in Stubby shorts and a thin jumper. In the wind and rain, he helped Michael siphon fuel from the jerry cans into the aircraft.

FIRST MILESTONE: SOUTH EAST CAPE

The forecast looked better down south, but the weather at Strahan was deteriorating. The showers from the west were coming in more frequently and we knew that if we didn't get out soon, we would most likely be stuck there. Through the fogged-up window of the hut we stared, willing the heavens for a break. As I slurped my last mouthful of soup, the sun broke through the cloud, blasting warm rays into the room, and a blue sky miraculously appeared in the background.

The reprieve wouldn't last long, so we had to move quickly. Before I was even out of the hut, Gordon was in the Archer preparing to go.

We took off towards the very remote southwest coast to our first milestone, South East Cape. In the rush, which isn't a good way to start a flight, the control panel for my Bose noise-cancelling headset got stuck at the side of my seat out of reach so I couldn't turn it on, making it a very noisy few hours to Hobart.

The long beaches gave way to remote bush-covered mountains, the Southern Ocean licking the cold grey rock faces. Low cloud kept me at 1500 feet and a few showers sprinkled the windscreen as I veered quickly around them, the northwesterly tailwind giving me a blistering 140 knots ground speed on the GPS.

Towards Port Davey the cloud lifted and the rain started to clear; gaining height gave me psychological comfort. Rounding the southwest coast, I had to track about 4 NM offshore to get out of the rotor coming off the mountains. In too close, it became scarily bumpy.

In the back of my mind I knew that if the engine stopped I was dead as there was nowhere to land. This part of Tassie is classified as a Designated Remote Area, meaning it is extremely remote, with little to no population. If anything happened, we were definitely screwed. It was unlikely help would come for some time—assuming there were any survivors—so we had to carry survival equipment in each plane. Apart from the satellite phone, the most important piece of equipment was the PLB. Activating this device would give Search and Rescue a location within 50 metres. I figured that if I was going down and if I had time, I would activate it before I hit, as it was unlikely I'd be in any condition to do it after.

Cruising above the churning ocean, with all instruments reading normal, the little voice in my head had stopped nagging and I felt relaxed and comfortable. Out my left window the rugged coastline was so majestic, its isolation filling me with peace. In that moment I wasn't worried about what could happen; I was fully present, living the experience.

Climbing as high as I could to 2700 feet, I rounded South East Cape, the most southerly point of Australia. 'Well done, everyone!' I congratulated, radioing both aircraft. I felt very proud of the team; it was a huge achievement to get there.

'Dave, Linda needs a photo of the Jab passing the Cape,' radioed Michael, Linda obviously giving him instructions from the back seat of the Lance.

'Where do you want me?' I radioed.

'Just keep flying straight.'

With open ocean ahead, I was getting more nervous the further I went from the coast.

'Hurry up, Michael, we're halfway to the Antarctic!'

'Almost done, Dave … OK, Linda got it. You can head back.'

Frustratingly, I tried to take photos with the GoPro on the wing but it decided to stop working at that moment. At least Linda got a good shot.

I felt elated; we had done the job and now we were heading to Cambridge for our final stop. Tracking towards the northeast I lost my tailwind so was back to 115 knots, but the air was smooth with a clearing sky, allowing us to climb to a more comfortable 3500 feet. Crossing Bruny Island brought us back to civilisation, houses on the

FIRST MILESTONE: SOUTH EAST CAPE

sides of the hills appearing more frequently. It was beautiful.

With a few radio calls the Archer found me and took the lead to fly into Cambridge airport. I tuned into the tower frequency so I could hear Paul chatting to air-traffic control for directions, making it easier to follow them in. Hobart airspace was deserted with no air traffic; a couple of turns with the Archer in the lead and we were lined up on final, gently touching down at 4.30 p.m.

Brian and Roberta had flown down on a commercial flight and were waiting for us to arrive. If I'd had to land at Sandfly or Jericho they had planned to pick me up in a hire car, but as it turned out they had a relaxing day and were very glad we had made it without incident.

Flying time: 4 hours.

With the best night's sleep I'd had in a long time, I felt like a million bucks, thanks to the Paraquad Association of Tasmania picking up the team from the airport and putting us up in their awesome wheelchair-accessible Glenn Moore apartments. I was particularly impressed with the hoist system that could lift and transport a person from the bedroom to the bath or toilet, like a carcass moving through an abattoir.

I had initially planned a lay day at each major city for additional media and school talks; however, as it became impossible to guarantee our arrival day or time, I had to scrap the idea. Nevertheless, having the extra day turned out to be a blessing early on.

Although we had only been going for two days, the events of the past few weeks had taken their toll and Linda and I needed this rest day. It wasn't a day off, but it gave us some breathing space to sleep in and catch up on things.

In the morning, the team attended the launch of Wheelies Van Rentals, a great initiative enabling wheelchair users to get around and see Tassie in an accessible vehicle. We also met with the Minister for Human Services, Cassy O'Connor, who told the audience that I was flying around Australia in a private jet. 'Didn't realise you traded in the Jab!' quipped Paul.

'I wish!' I replied.

Before Bob, Michael and Paul were to head off to the airport to work on the planes, we had to sort out meals. 'What do you want to do for dinner tonight?' I asked.

'I can make a beef stew,' offered Gordon, who enjoyed cooking and was particularly good at it.

'Oh, I can cook a risotto and help Gordon,' added Lida, eager to make one of her specialties.

'Sure. We all good with that?' Everyone nodded.

'Let us know what to get and we'll do the shopping,' Roberta offered.

'OK, last thing: who's making lunches tomorrow morning?' I asked. 'Bob, do you and Michael want to do it?'

He didn't look up as he was scrolling through text messages on his phone, still trying to sort out a few problems with his business.

'Gordon and I can make them,' Lida said.

'Lida, you won't have time. You'll be busy getting me up and packing.' Lida was eager to get in and help with everything, but I needed her to focus on helping me. My priority at this point was to get the team working as one efficient unit as quickly as possible, and to achieve this each person had to stick to their role.

'Paul and I will do it,' offered Gordon, arms folded with one leg up on his other knee.

The pilots set off for the airport to refuel and check the planes in the rain and bitter cold; there was even snow on Mount Wellington. While there, they managed to get into Hobart's control tower and chat about our route out the next day. Lida did the team's washing and took some time out while I stayed indoors to keep warm with

Linda; it was bloody freezing outside. The two of us had a relatively slow day, responding to Facebook comments and emails. Linda sent photos and information to newspapers Sofia had organised, and got in touch with the people who'd help with accommodation and transport at our next stop. I even managed to squeeze in three radio interviews for South Australia and Queensland. Our endeavour, and the purpose of the flight, was gathering momentum around the country. With the accumulating messages of support on social media and via email, it was evident we were making an impact, whether it was challenging a person's assumptions of what a person with a disability could do or inspiring someone to explore their potential and set new goals. Either way, it appeared we were making a difference. It was tremendously encouraging to know that whatever trials we would face, it was worth it.

Having my parents meet us in Hobart turned out to be a godsend. Not just for their help with buying groceries or a transport service for the pilots, but for their emotional support and encouragement.

Dinner that night was a mini-celebration for the whole team, including my parents, our Base Support. It had been a tough few days with the weather and other challenging flying conditions, but we had completed our first big milestone. Gordon and Lida put on a fantastic meal, and with a few beers and wines our stories got a little inflated—which didn't ease Mum's tendency to worry!

19

SICK AS A DOG

The cold front from the previous day had passed, leaving a sunny but bitterly cold morning. My hands felt like semi-frozen John West Fish Fingers as I vigorously shrugged my shoulders up and down, trying to keep warm in the cockpit as Lida set me up.

'Safe flight, David,' Mum whispered as she hugged and kissed me.

'Of course. I just want to get out of here to Bairnsdale. I'm bloody freezing,' I uttered through chattering teeth.

Dad shook my hand and patted me on the shoulder. 'Have a good flight, Dave. We'll be in touch tonight,' he said as he closed the door.

We were getting better at organising ourselves; with an early start we made it to the airfield at eight a.m. and were in the air by nine a.m.—on time!

Air traffic was light; we had to wait for only one passenger jet to clear our path before departing. It was the same procedure to get out as getting in to Cambridge. Following the controller's directions, we tracked east to the coast, climbing over the mountains.

Heading towards Flinders Island, the morning was magical as the glorious sun poured through my windscreen, energising my cold body like a recharging battery. I melted into the seat. Mist hung low in the valleys, while scattered cotton-ball clouds dotted the blue sky in the distance with air so smooth I could take my hands off the controls and play with the GoPros. The contrast between the windy, rugged west coast and the tranquil east was like swapping hessian undies for silk.

'When did you get here, Gerard?' inquired Gordon, as a person in a wheelchair rolled over with his mate Mark at the Flinders Island airport. Gordon and I knew them from the Disabled Pilots Association fly-ins we attended each year.

'We flew in yesterday. Thought we'd spend the night in a motel to meet up with you guys,' Gerard replied.

'Ah, good to see ya. How did you go with all the weather yesterday?' I asked.

'We got out OK, but had to dodge the front and rain to get over here,' Mark said.

'Man, good work!'

As we were chatting, two guys—who reminded me of Penn and Teller (a big loud bloke with his short sidekick)—approached. 'You the guy flyin' round Austrayya?' asked Penn.

'Yeah, trying to,' I said.

'We heard about you in Perth,' Teller added.

'Really? Over there?'

'You're famous!' Teller said with a smile.

While the team refuelled the aircraft, I chatted with them, 'kicking the tyres' so to speak, talked flying and showed them my adaptations, which impressed them. 'You don't want to sneeze, ay!' jested Penn when I explained how I operate the throttle by sucking and blowing on a tube.

'Na, ha-ha, that's right,' I replied, despite having heard the same comment for the millionth time—it had lost its originality.

Over an early lunch we discussed how to get through East Sale Military Restricted Airspace on the coast, which we had to navigate before Bairnsdale when we got back in Victoria. 'What do you want to do about East Sale, Dave?' Michael asked.

'Maybe we could fly through it like Hobart,' suggested Paul.

'That'd be a lot easier,' Gordon added.

'Yeah, that'd be good. I'd prefer not to fly out to sea if I can avoid it,' I said. During the week, the base is active, becoming controlled airspace. To fly through the VFR (Visual Flight Rules—able to navigate by visual reference to the ground or water and clear of cloud) route along the coast, you need clearance.

Michael called up East Sale Tower for a chat, then reported, 'Good news, Dave: they agreed to let you through in company.'

'Awesome, Michael, good work!' This was turning out to be fairly easy.

With the team briefing out of the way, Bob and Michael checked my engine which showed no sign of oil leaks. With my mind at rest, we set off for the last water crossing: back over Bass Strait to the mainland.

I wasn't nervous this time. Flying down the west coast had built my confidence and I felt more comfortable over water. I wasn't complacent, but the little voice in my head remained quiet.

Following the line of small islands at 3500 feet, as high as I could go with the cloud, I traced back to the tip of Wilsons Promontory. As I flew, I did some mental calculations to estimate how close I needed to be to a rocky island to reach it if the engine quit—it worked out to be around 5 NM, or five minutes in the air in ideal conditions. It sounds a bit fatalistic, but if the fan stopped, I wanted to know instantly whether to try for land or try my best at ditching in the sea.

'Made it!' I declared out loud, taking a deep breath and expelling it slowly, fully relaxing my body as I crossed over to the mainland.

We had reached Tassie and back without getting delayed; luck had definitely been on our side. I'd figured that if we were to be delayed anywhere, it would be Tasmania. Fortunately, the weather gods had been very kind to us.

With clearance from East Sale Military, I followed the Archer up the VFR route at 1500 feet. Suddenly I felt an almighty whack hit the plane, scaring the crap out of me.

'Shit, that was exciting. I just flew through your wake turbulence!' I exclaimed, radioing the Archer.

'Well, you'd better not fly behind us,' Gordon replied, laughing. I tracked well to the side after that.

'Welcome to Bairnsdale, Dave. Congratulations to you and your team on making it around Tasmania,' welcomed John Chester, president of the East Gippsland Aeroclub.

Although I had the warm sun shining on me and the heater going in the plane, I felt cold. When I got out of the plane I started to shiver and felt quite unwell. I hoped I was only feeling lingering effects from the morning chill. Usually it took me hours to warm up; also, I was possibly a little dehydrated as I found it hard to drink in the cold. I just hoped I wasn't coming down with something.

'I'll take you over. They have a heater,' Lida offered.

'OK, let's go,' I said, shivering as she pushed me to the club room, parking me in front of a roaring wood heater. I needed warmth like I needed air, and holding on to the handle of my wheelchair backrest, I leant my upper half forward, almost falling on top of the heater, absorbing as much of the wonderful heat as I could through my face—one of the few places on my body that I can feel warmth. The club members who could cope with the tropical temperature sat at the bar sweating and red-faced; I'm sure beer sales went up that day.

The OWC team were VIPs for that night's dinner. Many of the club members brought plates of their gourmet specialties—lasagnas, curries, roasts. It was a delectable smorgasbord and we stuffed ourselves full. Gerard, Mark and their mate Terry, who had followed us to Bairnsdale, tracked the smell of food and dropped in for a feed.

After dinner I felt worse, with no energy, and forcing myself to talk to the folk was a real effort. I just wanted to go to bed and wake up in a year. I did manage to get through my presentation, which must have been OK as the members were very generous when the bucket was passed around, donating a few hundred dollars to OWC.

It was a long day of flying. The pilots stayed at John Chester's house while Linda, Lida and I stayed in a motel with two rooms donated by the club. By eleven p.m. I had passed out.

Flying time: 4.4 hours.

Even with a four a.m. start the next morning I felt much better than the previous night. I felt OK to fly, but I still didn't feel quite right. I wasn't yet sure if the dreaded urinary tract infection was brewing, or whether getting cold and dehydrated had knocked me around more than I thought.

The morning was crisp with frost in the shadows of the trees. I sat in the sun absorbing its gentle warmth while Paul set up my GoPro cameras in different positions, experimenting to see what angles worked best, while the rest of the team packed the support planes.

Bairnsdale was my backyard and I was feeling restless to get further north; it would then feel like we were making progress. Also, the thought of heading north to warmer weather was drawing me like Charlie Sheen to cocaine.

At 9.30 a.m. we tracked out over Lakes Entrance towards the coast with Martin Higgins and his daughter Chloe escorting me in their RV, a cool-looking low-wing aerobatic aircraft. Although only nine years old, Chloe was already a talented pilot and had set a goal to get her private pilot's license at the earliest possible age of seventeen. A very young voice came over the radio with their position and I looked out my left window to see a red and white RV off my wing. I gave a wave to the bizarre but inspiring sight of little Chloe, barely able to see over the dash. Approaching Lakes Entrance, the RV banked away to head back to the airfield as Chloe was late for school.

I sat back in my 'office' and pointed the nose along the coast, grateful for the easy flying conditions, not having to deal with water crossings or changeable weather; it suited me just fine.

Merimbula, our first stop, felt a little more tropical—well, in my mind at least. The Frogs Hollow Aeroclub put on an array of tasty Subway sandwiches to feed the hungry team. And not being in a huge rush for a change, we enjoyed a leisurely lunch with time to chat.

'Ryan can't make it, Dave. He had to get to Melbourne at the last minute to sort out a problem with sponsorship of his plane,' Neil informed me.

'That's a shame, I was looking forward to meeting him.'

Ryan Campbell was a nineteen-year-old pilot who was attempting to set a new record as the youngest person to fly solo around the world. Later that year he achieved his goal, an amazing accomplishment for anyone, let alone someone so young.

While the team chatted to the members, Bob was in his element making new friends. I did a phone interview for a Sydney newspaper.

'Yes, I have quadriplegia,' I explained.

'But how do you fly a plane without arms that work?' the journalist queried.

'I can move my arms, but I can't move my fingers.'

'So, you are a paraplegic then?'

'No, I have quadriplegia. There are different levels of quadriplegia; some people have arm movement and some don't,' I informed her, getting somewhat frustrated.

The reporter couldn't understand what quadriplegia was or how I could possibly fly a plane, even after I explained it a few times. The next day the paper read: 'Paraplegic pilot.'

Linda was really pissed and called her. 'The article is wrong. Dave has quadriplegia, not paraplegia. That's why it's so amazing that he is flying around Australia.' The newspaper changed the online article immediately.

The day was working out nicely: Nowra Military Base was inactive, which allowed us to fly coastal instead of diverting inland, maintaining our track north with a nice tailwind to Wollongong in southern NSW. Paul had previously lived in Wollongong so was familiar with the airfield; his only advice: 'Watch out for the hills!'

Upon our arrival, the plan was for the Illawarra Flyers to put on a barbeque for the team and I'd give a talk. I was unaware that Lyndal, a friend of mine, had driven down from Sydney with her kids that afternoon and was driving around the airfield looking for me. After a few calls to give her directions, we eventually caught up.

'I didn't know you were coming!' I exclaimed.

'I told you we'd come down when you arrived.'

'But you said that over a year ago!'

'Yeah well, I know. But I said I would!'

I really appreciated her and her family making the effort to drive down. It was so nice to see her as it had been a few years. However, as the team members were guests, I felt obliged to spend time with the club members, which made me feel guilty and a little awkward as I couldn't spend much time with her.

Many people didn't understand how much planning had gone into the flight and how serious and strenuous it was. Some comments were along the lines of: 'You must be having a great holiday!' For Linda and me it was a nonstop job. And it was hard work for the rest of the team—certainly not a holiday.

Everything had been planned ahead, whether it was meeting

with groups, media interviews, arrangements for transport and accommodation and so on, which made it difficult when people just rocked up to chat as I invariably had other commitments to attend to.

Little issues like this came up, but we learnt from them. Going forward, we decided that Linda would post on Facebook the times when the team and I would be available at an airfield, which was usually about an hour after landing. This gave an opportunity to those who wanted to meet and chat with us. It made things a lot easier for us and, more importantly, it meant we didn't disappoint those who took the time to drop by and see us.

Although it was a relatively easy day flying, I was shattered and felt considerably 'ordinary.' After a sausage and my presentation, we caught taxis to our accommodation. The only thing on my mind was to pass out in bed.

Flying time: 3.5 hours.

As I gained consciousness the next morning on Day 6, I knew I was very sick. The overnight bag I'd peed into was full of what looked like yellow ginger beer. What I'd long suspected had reared its ugly head: a nasty UTI. I was relieved it was a rest day as I wouldn't have wanted to fly the way I was feeling.

I had anticipated this scenario, so before leaving I had stocked up on antibiotics, which I started taking immediately to avoid escalation and a potential hospital stay which would have ended the flight.

Following a relaxing breakfast with Linda and Lida, Linda and I caught up on the usual admin while the rest of the team went to the Illawarra regional airport and took up the opportunity for a private tour of the Historical Aircraft Restoration Society Museum (HARS). Bob seemed particularly excited and was a little more talkative than usual when he got back; a highlight for him was sitting in an F111 and speaking to the last pilot who'd flown the aircraft.

We were staying at the Terralong Terrace Apartments and were given discounted rates for our two nights in Kiama, a small town south of Wollongong. Paul and Michael spent the first night visiting friends and going to parties while Gordon met up with Bronwynne at their accommodation. It was good for everyone to change the routine and have some space before the long haul to Darwin, where we planned a four-day midpoint rest break.

I had purposefully arranged shorter legs for the first week as I knew it would take time to get our systems working and settle into a routine. From Day 7 onwards, the flying times would increase from 3.5–4.5 hours to up to 5–6 hours per day. It doesn't sound like much time in the air, but added to everything else the team had to do, it became a very, very long day.

A typical day for me started at 4 a.m. as it took me around three hours to get up and dressed, have breakfast, pack and be out the door by 7 a.m. Then the drive to the airfield, preparing the planes, a team briefing and in the air by 9 a.m. I would then fly the first leg of around two to three hours, land, refuel, have lunch, another team briefing, get back in the plane and be in the air by one p.m. On finishing the second leg of another two to three hours, I would land and refuel, then do media interviews or meet supporters at the airfield. At the same time, the team would put the planes to bed while Linda organised transport to our previously arranged accommodation. We would then drive to our accommodation by six p.m., unpack and have dinner. Afterwards, while the rest of the team caught up on personal tasks or flight planning, they usually had time to relax, have a few drinks, play pool or take in some sightseeing (on the shorter flying days). Linda and I would go back to our room to charge the batteries, download photos, sort and adjust them for the blog, write the blog, update Facebook, catch up on emails, check arrangements for the next day—media, accommodation, transport—answer comments on social media, do a video blog if I remembered, and finally roll into bed around eleven p.m. That is, if it all went well; midnight if it didn't. There was always so much to do; flying was the easiest part.

It was Day 7, flying from Wollongong, NSW, to Caboolture, Queensland. We arrived at the airfield at six a.m.: a new record. Gordon Griffin had let us park our planes in his hangar for the two nights, which saved us time as we didn't have to untie planes and pack up covers.

Today's flying would be one of the hardest—not so much because it was long but because it would be mentally draining. We had to pass many airfields en-route and weave around lots of controlled airspace; and we planned to cross our second milestone: Cape Byron. We had to be on the ball to make sure we flew at the correct altitudes and along the designated routes.

I wasn't feeling great, but the bug was manageable and I felt good enough to fly. The antibiotics would take a couple of days to kick in, so in the meantime I was in survival mode, doing only what was absolutely necessary to get through the day. With this added burden, I had to rely more on Linda to help manage the team, as I needed to conserve my limited energy to concentrate on flying.

On the previous day Linda had bought plastic name tags as Bob had lost a bag in a taxi on the first night in Wollongong. As Linda attached a tag to each bag before the pilots loaded them into the aircraft, Lida grabbed her plastic bag out of the pile and removed the name tag.

'All the bags need a name tag, Lida,' said Linda.

'No, not this one, I'm taking it on the plane.'

I could hear the discussion from the cockpit. 'Lida, we agreed to have a tag on each bag, so it stays on,' I barked; I didn't have the energy to debate it.

After making a short video that Linda would upload to Facebook once we were flying, we got underway by 7.30 a.m. As we taxied out, the airport was starting to come alive as the Illawarra airshow was due to start at nine a.m. We'd been invited to attend but with such a huge flight ahead of us, we'd turned them down so as to make an early start.

It was another beautiful day—sunny with blue skies and a forecast for a nice southeasterly tailwind to push us up to Caboolture—which slightly reduced our mental burden.

The Great Dividing Range to my left was quite a sight, standing like an impenetrable wall to the vast interior. As we approached Sydney, I had to descend to 500 feet to get below the controlled airspace where the jets fly, and into Victor 1, the VFR route to the north. There is a set procedure, with each plane required to call at every reporting point to inform air-traffic of our intentions, which was easy.

Entering the route south of Sydney at Jibbon Point, I turned on my landing light to make it easier to be seen and gave my call to other air-traffic: 'Victor 1 Traffic, Jabiru 5558 is at Jibbon Point tracking northbound 500 feet. Victor 1.' Apart from the Lance and Archer behind me there was no other chatter. I'd expected it to be busier but at eight a.m., most sensible people were still in bed.

I had wanted to fly this route ever since hearing about it a few years earlier, and now I was doing it. It was a little unnerving flying so low out over the water; if the engine quit, I doubted I'd have much time to get more than a Mayday out, so I put it out of my mind and pulled the strap on my lifejacket a little tighter.

It took a lot of concentration to maintain height, keep a lookout for other traffic and weave the aircraft around the coastline; then, in the distance from behind the sheer cliffs protecting the bay, the most famous icons in Australia came into view, standing boldly against the inner-city landscape. It was a remarkable experience seeing the majestic arches of the Sydney Harbour Bridge stretched across the bay while the glow of the morning sun reflected off the white shell of the Opera House. I wondered if the architect, Jørn Utzon, had been thinking of the teeth of the Great White shark when he designed it.

The palm trees at Port Macquarie put a smile on my face, bringing a more tropical feel and some warmth in the air. The small town had expanded massively since the last time I was there in 1987 when I was eighteen and on a road-trip with Pete and Mick. It was where my passion for surfing had begun.

The Hastings District Flying Club was a friendly bunch and welcomed us to their clubrooms for a cuppa and biscuits. At each stop I was greeted with the customary, 'Can we see your modifications?' —which I was more than happy to show.

When I say I'm a quadriplegic pilot many people just nod blankly because they can't get their head around how I fly. After explaining what does and doesn't work in my body, then running them through the adaptations, the penny usually drops and they become suitably impressed, asking lots of questions and taking photos.

As we'd decided not to make lunch this day, we were punished with tasteless stale sandwiches from the airport café. Satisfactorily disappointed, we had a quick team briefing to confirm our photo shoot of me crossing Cape Byron, the most easterly point of Australia, and our intentions regarding controlled airspace. I planned to bypass the airspace by going inland; however, the other pilots would decide en-route.

With a tailwind picking up, I still had three hours in the seat, which is close to my sitting limit in the plane. Most people's limit is determined by their bladder capacity but for me it is my bum tolerance. Although I sit on a Roho, an air-cushion designed to relieve the pressure on my bum which minimises the chance of pressure sores, I still become uncomfortable after three hours or so and start sweating. This is my body's way of telling me there is a part of me that is in pain, although I can't feel it. The sweating is a result of autonomic dysreflexia, common to people with spinal cord injury. When it occurs, our blood pressure can rise very high, accompanied by an increase in heart rate, sweating, headaches and, if it gets really serious, it can be fatal. Through experience and deduction, I can work out what the cause is, which is usually my bum, and that I need to get off it. If I were to get a pressure sore from sitting too long, it would mean the end of the flight and months in bed waiting for it to heal. I'd never had one and I certainly didn't want to get one now.

Between 2500–3500 feet became my cruising altitudes, limited mainly by the cloud-base level. Approaching Coffs Harbour, the Lance went through controlled airspace while the Archer and I tracked inland. The cloud-base was lower than expected, with only a few hundred feet of clearance above the highest mountain peaks, which kept us on our toes choosing our path ahead.

'Second one down. Congrats, everyone!' I radioed as I circled the Cape Byron lighthouse. Trying to coordinate a photo wasn't as easy as it sounds. I had to fly continuous circles around the lighthouse while the Lance, being much faster, sped around the outside and above, attempting to line up with me to get a shot. I must have flown around six times to get the photo, and by the end I was starting to feel a bit dizzy. Ticking off the second milestone was an achievement; we all felt a sense of accomplishment to be halfway through the list—although there was still a very long way to go.

There were a few parts of Australia I had really wanted to see, and flying along the Gold Coast was at the top of the list. Passing the mishmash of apartment buildings stretching along the coast, with the modern monoliths and Q1 (the world's seventh-tallest residential building) casting long shadows over the beach when the afternoon sun found a hole through the clouds, it was a spectacular sight.

The demands of my concentration in the cockpit were wearing me down, as was a sore bum and accompanying sweats; I couldn't wait to get on the ground at Caboolture.

The last stretch was simple: follow the coast of North Stradbroke and Moreton Islands to Caboolture. Switching on my landing light for safety, I kept to the east side of the island, as was the standard incoming procedure, to avoid a head-on with another aircraft coming down the west side. Out the corner of my eye I glimpsed a white object pass down my left-hand side; it wasn't at all close, but with a closing speed of 440 km/hr, I didn't see it coming.

Was that another aircraft? I wondered if I was seeing things.

A voice came over the radio: 'Is that you, Jabiru 5558?'

'Yes, who's this?'

'It's me, Dave!' I then realised who it was: Dave Coulston from Caboolture. He had been following me on Spider Tracks in real time in his aircraft with a mate and came up to meet and fly in with me—very cool!

I must have been really tired because I couldn't make out the Caboolture airfield from my approach. Usually, airfields are relatively easy to spot, but this one blended into the surrounding landscape. It was only when I saw Gordon and Paul in the Archer, and drew a mental line to where they were heading, that I sighted it.

Just as I got out of the plane, half a dozen people came up for a chat. 'I'll be back in a sec,' I said, trying not to be rude as Lida rushed me off to a patch of grass to empty my swelling 'calf muscle' (leg-bag) before I pissed myself. It's a little hard trying to explain these things.

'Dave, this is Chris Sharp and members of the Rotary Club of

Caboolture,' Linda introduced me. They had been patiently awaiting our arrival.

'Chris, we really appreciate what the Rotary club is doing for us,' I said, feeling that my words didn't come close to expressing my gratitude. They had been extremely generous in arranging a four-bedroom house, two brand-new cars from a dealer and, the best bit, a fridge full of home-cooked meals.

'When your parents contacted us last year, we were glad to help you on your mission. What you are doing is really inspiring. Can we get a photo for our newsletter?'

'Of course, it's the least I can do.'

There were so many people waiting to see the team when we landed—local flyers, Facebook followers and Josh's parents, who no doubt wanted to check out who their son was flying with.

By the time we'd washed and refuelled the planes and chatted to our supporters, it was almost dark. As I wheeled to the cars I asked Linda, 'Is the team ready yet?'

'They still need to tie the planes down.'

I looked over; they were still standing around.

I wheeled over. 'Guys, what are you doing? We should be ready to go!'

Chris and another Rotary member were waiting to drive us to the house, and I felt a little embarrassed that we were keeping them waiting. We needed to get better at this!

It had been a very long day, for even with good tailwinds we spent 4.7 hours flying. It was one of the hardest so far, but also very rewarding, ticking off our second milestone. I felt very satisfied, but absolutely knackered.

The team relaxed and had a few well-earned beers. We had to take a vote on which prepared meal we would eat—the lasagna won. 'Not bad,' said Gordon, a generous compliment considering he was a pasta connoisseur.

I was so thankful that tomorrow was another lay day. My UTI was wearing me down and I was struggling more than ever: I had to rest. But I wasn't the only one; Linda was getting little sleep, constantly exhausted, and I was worried she would burn out. The rest of the team seemed to be going OK, but they were also getting tired. I was conscious that the longer we went, the more fatigued we would get, and the greater the challenge it would be to work as a team.

Flying time: 4.7 hours.

Everyone slept in. I was tired from being up most of the night with a headache, but on the plus side the symptoms of the UTI were a little better with the antibiotics starting to do their thing.

The four-bedroom house felt like a home away from home and everyone settled in—maybe a little too much, as they were hanging washing over the couches and doors. Paul and Michael went up the street for supplies and Gordon cooked a huge bacon, sausage, tomato and egg breakfast for the team, a welcome change from the regular muesli each morning.

After the late breakfast, the pilots and Lida went out to the airfield for the day. Bob flew the Lance to Gympie to visit friends while Gordon and Paul investigated the Archer's higher-than-usual oil usage, which thankfully turned out to be a simple fix: a loose hose-clamp on the oil-line. Paul and Michael's mechanical talents were huge assets, saving me the trouble of flying to Bundaberg for my plane's 25-hour oil change as they could do it themselves.

I found a quiet spot and finally had a chance to write in my journal—which I hadn't had time for since the first day. Apart from creating a record of each day's events, I enjoyed writing it as it gave me time to reflect on my experiences.

In the afternoon I was able to steal a short snooze, but as I lay on the bed in a semi-conscious state while Linda uploaded photos onto the hard drives, I heard a sudden *pop!*

'Oh no … it's stopped working!' Linda said frantically.

I immediately snapped awake. 'What's stopped working?' I asked as a horrible electrical burning smell filled the air.

'The hard drive. It has all our photos!' she exclaimed.

This was the only hard drive that held all the media, as we hadn't had time to update the other two. If this was cooked, we had lost all our videos and photos from the past seven days.

'Try another power adapter; it may be that,' I suggested.

With shaking hands Linda plugged in another power adapter. For an anxious moment there was nothing, then a gentle whirring came from the small black box.

'It works: lucky!' I said, both of us exhaling with immense relief.

That night Paul helped copy the media to the other drives so at least we had backups.

20

THE AIRLIE BEACH INCIDENT

'Chris, a local helicopter instructor, reckons we shouldn't worry too much about the weather,' I said to the team. 'The showers are fairly scattered; we can come inland a bit and go around them. If the weather gets crappy we can divert and go somewhere else. So, what are your views?' I asked.

Michael began, 'Bob's driving today. If it looks like crappy weather just come back. It's not worth losing a plane; I don't care if we don't have a bed tonight.'

'Na, na, of course not. We're not going to push through just to get to a destination,' I said. 'If it's not looking good, depending on where we are, we either turn around or go to an alternative, wait it out or stay the night if we have to.' I wanted to make sure we were all on the same page.

'Yeah, OK,' Michael agreed.

'I chatted to my uncle and aunty,' I said, 'they'll be at the mouth of the Noosa River waiting for us. I'll go inland around controlled airspace then go coastal. What about you guys?'

'We plan to get clearance through Sunshine Coast airspace,' Gordon said, with Paul nodding in agreement.

Bob kicked a tuft of grass clumped on the edge of the concrete in the ensuing silence.

'Anyway … wanna get moving?' I ventured.

'Yep, let's rock 'n' roll,' Paul chimed in.

The weather was perfect when we left Caboolture and headed north, skirting inland around the Sunshine Coast controlled airspace, close to the cone-shaped Glass House Mountains, named by Captain Cook as he sailed past in 1770. To him they resembled English glasshouses but in fact are remnants of volcanic activity millions of years ago. The Archer and Lance got clearance and went through the controlled airspace.

Over the mouth of the Noosa River I noticed a couple of people waving below but I couldn't make out who they were. I hoped it was Hayden and Joan as they'd been following us via Spider Tracks and were looking forward to catching a glimpse. I circled twice, then blasted north.

From where I was sitting at 2500 feet, with a nice tailwind of 15 knots giving me a ground speed of 130 knots, the weather ahead looked perfect, with some scattered high cloud. A highlight of this leg was seeing Rainbow Beach from the air. As I passed over, the various shades of yellow, red and orange that streaked through the steep banks burst out from the green bushland; it made the effort of getting there all the sweeter.

Approaching Gladstone, the scenery changed from gentle bush and beaches to industrial coal ports tinged with grey, made worse by dirty brown mudflats.

As I was about to turn onto final approach, a Rex (Regional Express Airline) gave an inbound call, a signal to get on the ground quickly to avoid a big passenger aircraft up my bum. These guys do a straight-in approach, taking minutes to get on the ground, and I didn't want to be in their way. The commercials are on a tight timeframe so it's good manners not to hold them up, if possible. If it was going to be tight for me to get on the ground before them, I'd let them in first.

Having parked the planes we were met by security personnel at the airport who were very serious, checking that we had our ASIC cards (Aviation Security Identification Cards) required for unescorted access in a security-controlled airport.

The airport manager was very interested in the flight: Michael gave him the OWC spiel of why we were doing it and where we'd been, and he kindly waived our landing fees and offered the boardroom to eat our lunch.

I was continually thinking of ways to make our processes more efficient, in particular to devise a plan to avoid delays, as recently experienced in Caboolture where the team was waiting for directions to put the planes to bed. It wasn't their fault, but it was evident we needed better coordination. Although the team had been given detailed information packs for each day's schedule, Linda and I thought it would be helpful if, at each midpoint stop, she gave a detailed rundown at the team briefing on what was to happen when we landed at the end of the day—who we'd be meeting, what I'd be doing, what the team needed to do, time of the pickup, where we were staying and in what rooms, and anything else that was important. This would hopefully ensure we were coordinated and working more efficiently.

In my mind I had a postcard image of the Whitsundays from ads I'd seen on TV: a gentle sea breeze caressing the hair of a bikini-clad Barbie as she strolled hand-in-hand with a bronzed, muscled Ken along a perfectly white beach under a cloudless blue sky, palm trees reaching over to touch the turquoise sea. But the further north we pushed, the more my paradise image receded. Instead, we had low-hanging cloud, sporadic showers and strong winds that whipped the sea into a bubbling grey soup. We had run into the forecast weather.

Ross Millard, a local flyer from the Townsville area, had emailed me earlier in the flight to offer his assistance if we needed it. He also mentioned that Shute Harbour at Airlie Beach was a challenge to get into when windy and could be a little turbulent on final. This played in the back of my mind as I dialed in the radio frequency for the Aerodrome Weather Information Service (AWIS) for Hamilton Island.

Paul came over the radio. 'Dave, have you got Hamilton weather?'

'Affirm, not the best: 28 knots on the ground at 100 degrees,' I replied.

'Yeah, it should be OK as the strip is sheltered,' he remarked.

'Roger that, let's see how we go.'

The strip was at 140 degrees which wasn't the best as the crosswind would be around 18 knots, beyond my aircraft's capability. However, it was situated between two mountains that sheltered the worst of it. If it was no good, we'd head to our alternative, Proserpine.

I wasn't too concerned but remembered Ross Millard's words: I had to be on my toes. I had planned to cut across over the mountains, but with low cloud I couldn't get through and had to go along the valley. Passing Proserpine, I could see the valley I had to follow to get to Shute Harbour. The Lance was long gone and the Archer was ahead of me as I entered the valley, only managing around 2000 feet with the thick dark cloud base blocking the sun.

'It's a bit bumpy ahead, Dave,' Paul radioed.

'Roger that,' I said, preparing myself to get a little knocked around.

Nearing Pioneer Bay, the intensity of the turbulence suddenly ramped up. The wind passing over the top of the mountains on my right was generating severe rotor: churned air on the leeward side where I was passing. Flying my trike in thermals during summer at Benalla had been good experience for tough conditions, so I felt well equipped for a few bumps as my fibreglass bubble rode the invisible waves—lifted up on one, then slipping down the side of another like an out-of-control boogieboarder until the next grabbed me, jerking at the wings.

With each whack the aircraft jolted hard and my comfort level began to rapidly drop. It was far bumpier than I'd anticipated so I reduced the throttle to slow the engine, thereby dropping the aircraft air speed to avoid overstressing the wings. The control column seemed to have a will of its own, trying to push my hand left and right. 'I'm in command, follow my orders,' I muttered as I forced my hand where I wanted it to go.

Without time to process what was happening, I felt my bum lift off the seat, my head thump on the roof as the aircraft suddenly dropped, and then I crashed down, falling to the right. My initial reaction was *fuck!* as I desperately hung on to the rudder-lever with my left hand, struggling to hold myself up. Instinctively, I sipped on the throttle tube to slow the aircraft further. As I was about to reach to adjust the trim control to pull up the nose of the plane—*whack*—the plane dropped again, finishing me off. It was a moment of *oh shit!* as my hand came out of the rudder-lever hand-support, I lost my balance and flopped onto my survival kit in the passenger seat.

As I tried to grab hold of anything to raise my twisted body, I looked up and, to my horror, the windscreen was filling with the grey sea as the plane banked over and nosed down.

It seemed like an eternity—although it was only a few seconds—before my survival instincts kicked in. I heaved myself off the survival kit, grabbed the underside of the armrest on the door with my left arm to hold myself up, while I pulled the control column back and to centre, bringing the aircraft level again.

Whack!—another hit. I fell over again but this time I quickly pushed off the survival kit, grabbed the top of the door to steady myself and powered the engine back up to get the plane level.

A wave of panic suddenly came over me; my mouth went dry, the heat of the adrenalin rushed through my body while my racing heart pounded against my chest. Then, as quickly as it came, it dissipated into serene calm as a thought momentarily flickered in my mind: *Why don't you get someone to help you?* It seemed a reasonable request.

But I was promptly plunged back to reality with another hit, which reminded me that I was flying solo. 'Fuck!' I shouted.

It was at that moment that I realised what being solo was all about: there was nothing anyone could do. It was up to me whether or not I survived, whether I lived or died.

All I knew was that I had to get out of the washing machine, so I headed straight over the bay to find clear air.

But I had a problem. My bum had slid back and to the left in the seat, making me very unbalanced as I have no trunk body function. The only way to stay upright without falling over was to hang on to the rudder-lever with my left hand. But the biggest issue was my knees. My feet had come off the footplates, causing my body to twist with my knees falling to the right, which jammed the control column. I couldn't turn left and this was a very serious problem. In my current position, I wasn't even sure if I could land the plane in good conditions, let alone a crosswind.

I orbited over the bay in clear air to give myself a chance to gather my thoughts and figure out how to untwist my body. By pushing on my knees and leaning to twist my body to the left, I managed to inch my bum a little to the right, which in turn held my knees to the left, but not by much.

Michael came over the radio. 'Dave, where are you? You should be on the ground by now.'

'I have a small problem; I fell over and I'm trying to straighten myself up. Stand by,' I said.

My delay in getting down didn't raise Linda's concerns, as I had taken a bit of time to land on other occasions, and she thought this was just one of those.

When I'd come through the valley earlier, I couldn't see the airfield as it had been behind a mountain. Out over the bay it had become apparent what my path in would be, and I was feeling nervous. The approach I had to take was between two mountains with a slight left turn to line up. My concern was that with a crosswind coming from the left, without enough left turn capability I could end up getting blown into the hill on the right.

'Gordon, what were the conditions when you came through?' I radioed.

'A little turbulence on final but it wasn't too bad,' he reported.

Yeah, but what the Archer experienced doesn't translate into what it will be like for me in an aircraft half the weight. After what I'd just been through, I was expecting the worst.

My plan was to fly in close to the left mountain, and if there was a strong crosswind, I hoped to have enough time to get through before it blew me into the hill on the right. If it was too bad and I couldn't get in, I would abort and fly to Proserpine.

As I continued to orbit over the bay, with some more body-twisting and knee-pushing, I managed to get my bum over a little more and move my knees to the left, which gave me about a third left-turning authority. I knew it wouldn't get any better, so I had to give it a go.

I felt calm and in control of the situation, ready to make an attempt. I had a plan and knew what I needed to do to get back on the ground.

On final approach, tensed up in anticipation, I hung on to the rudder-lever for balance with my left hand while I steered with the right. I knew if I let go of the rudder-lever I would fall over, with little chance of recovery from such a low altitude.

Approaching the gap between the hills, my wings bounced left and right, shaking through the turbulence as I waited for the big hit and crosswind. Banking left a little, the runway ahead got bigger in my windscreen. *I'm almost through, I'm going to make it,* I thought, surprised it had been so easy.

With only one stage of flaps set to maintain my airspeed, which gave me better control with higher airflow over the wings and rudder, I was coming in fast. Being so focused on turbulence and my route in, I had forgotten to set the aircraft up properly and adjust the trim control back to lift the nose of the plane and make it easier to land.

Unexpectedly, the approaching end of the runway appeared low as the runway extended slightly uphill, which made me a little high on approach; but as far as I was concerned, I was getting on the ground one way or another.

I didn't judge my touchdown well, bouncing twice; then a gust of wind lifted me a third time. I pulled the engine power off, held the control column back to let the airspeed drop and finally settled down nicely with a slight bump. It wasn't the most elegant of landings, but I had made it, and I didn't care. I had never been more pleased to be on the ground.

Feeling like I had won the lottery after cheating death, as Linda opened the door of my plane, I blurted, 'I'm never coming to this fuckin' place ever again!' I hadn't noticed the journalist from the local paper scribbling down my reaction. Thankfully she didn't print it.

Diary entry:
Not enjoying this, can't wait for it to be over. This is a massive challenge.
Flying time: 5 hours.

21

THIS IS NO PARADISE

The beautiful Airlie Beach Hotel donated free accommodation and the Whitsunday Aeroclub organised a dinner for us that night.

'Heard you had a bit of fun coming in?' said one of the members.

'Yeah, you could say that; I could've done without it,' I responded as I self-medicated with a few wines to settle down.

The rest of the team were in their element, enjoying the night with a few well-deserved drinks and chatting to the locals and pilots about the trip.

Linda was again up till midnight backing up the media while I slept like a baby until Lida's four a.m. wake-up knock. My early start also meant Linda had to get up: we didn't have much privacy in the mornings, which added to the challenge of travel. To make use of the time, Linda checked emails and Facebook and started packing.

By Day 10, my routine was well and truly worked out and Lida was very efficient in the personal support role. While I was on the toilet or having breakfast, she would pack and organise as much as possible so as to minimise the time needed to get going.

Packed and awaiting the arrival of the wheelchair-accessible van donated by Compass Whitsundays, one by one each team member strolled through the door for an unannounced meeting—actually, it felt more like a mutiny. I could sense there was some tension, an uneasiness in their demeanour. They weren't fully packed and I could see they weren't intending to go anywhere at this point.

'Have you looked at the weather?' asked Michael.

'Yeah, it's not the best. What do you guys think?'

Outside the trees jerked and swayed in the wind, the clouds hung low around the tops of the hills and rain splashed in the puddles.

'The forecast is for low cloud and showers up the coast,' Michael said.

It wasn't looking good, and after yesterday's experience I was feeling anxious with the very thought of taking off, let alone dealing with the weather.

'So, what are our options?' I asked.

'We could wait a bit to see if it clears,' suggested Gordon.

'The weather isn't looking too good for the next four days,' stated Paul.

'If we get out, we could see how far we can get up the coast. If it's no good we could come back or go to an alternate,' Gordon added.

'Yeah, there are a few airfields up the coast,' Bob chimed in.

'It could be clear to the north or it might be like this for days. We really don't know,' Gordon said.

We canvassed our options, opinions flying around the room like ping-pong balls.

I had my views but I wanted everyone to have their say before a decision was made. All of us had to agree to fly.

'We could go to the airfield and ask some of the local pilots what they think. If they reckon the weather will be flyable, we could decide then,' suggested Paul.

'That's an option. If anyone knows the area it will be those guys. What do you think, Michael?' I asked.

'Yeah, we could try that,' Michael agreed with a nod.

'Bob, Linda, Lida. You happy?' I asked.

Bob casually nodded.

'Whatever you pilots think,' Lida said.

'I'm happy to go if you think it's OK,' Linda said.

Everyone packed quickly and we were ready just as the van arrived to take us to the airport—but without lunches made.

Michael and Paul found some local pilots to interrogate who said that once we were past Bowen the weather should clear up. Based on their local knowledge we decided to give it a go.

The real test of mental strength is not the act of getting through a tough situation—like the one I was thrown into yesterday. Rather, it's when, having fallen off your bike, confidence shattered, you push through your fears and get back on.

Although the rain had stopped and it wasn't anywhere near as windy as the previous day, I was shitting myself with the thought of taking off; my confidence was bruised and I was afraid of being in the same situation again. To be honest, a part of me was secretly disappointed that the local pilots had said we'd be fine to go because I would rather have avoided flying that day. But I knew it wouldn't be any easier the following day if I delayed it; I had to get back in the air.

'The bloke up there has something for your feet,' Bob said, pointing to the hangar.

An unshaven bloke dressed in a blue work shirt and shorts with work boots came out from behind a plane as I rolled into the hangar. 'You got a problem with your feet?' he asked.

'Yeah, hit a few bumps and my feet came off my footplate flying in yesterday.'

'Give this a go,' he said, holding up a metre of super-industrial Velcro. 'It'll stick like shit to a blanket.'

Paul fitted the Velcro to the soles of my shoes and to the footplate which seemed to hold quite well. He also added a piece of Velcro to my seat belt so it wouldn't loosen again, making sure it held me nice and tight in turbulence. I rolled up a towel and placed it behind my lower back so my bum wouldn't slide back again, causing me to lose my balance. At least this time if it got rough, I should be OK.

Three guys with some serious cash pushed out their Robinson R44 helicopters from the garage of one of the exclusive double-storey houses lining the runway, took off and headed up to the Northern Territory on a boys' holiday. If they were flying, I figured, we should also be able to get out.

After a team photo in front of the Whitsunday airport sign, and once Lida had set me up in the plane, Linda came over. 'Be careful, David Jacka. You're very precious to me.'

'You know me, honeybunch: any tougher I'd rust!' I said with a half laugh, feeling very nervous as Linda gave me a kiss and closed the door of the plane.

Taxiing out to the runway, my nerves settled and I focused on the job at hand, not giving my mind the opportunity to dream up nightmarish scenarios of how my life might end.

A moderate wind faced me head-on as I climbed out with only a few small bumps jolting the aircraft, the few functional parts of my body unconsciously tensing each time. I flew out wider over the ocean, making sure I was far from any unsuspecting rotor coming off the nearby mountains. Climbing to 1500 feet, I was sandwiched between the low scattered clumps of cloud and the higher thick grey blanket. But the local pilots were on the money: passing Bowen to the north, the low cloud cleared on the coast while the high cloud got higher. I felt relieved and settled into the seat; the day wasn't turning out too bad after all. Cooktown, here we come!

However, the weather gods decided to toy with us once more for fun. Approaching Hinchinbrook Island, the clear skies changed as a furry blanket of cloud was suddenly laid over the sky, forcing me to drop from 3500 to 2000 feet as I followed the channel between the mountains on the mainland and Hinchinbrook Island, the peaks of both hidden by thick cloud.

Visibility quickly deteriorated, the grey mist blending with the water, making it difficult to distinguish the horizon. I focused on following the thin line of beige beach that stood out from green rainforest and the water.

I radioed the Archer but got no word, which was a little odd as I thought they were ahead of me. So I called up the Lance on the chat channel. 'Michael, do you know where the Archer is?'

'No, Dave,' he answered, confusing me further.

The Lance was 30 NM ahead of me with only 6 NM to run to Innisfail, our midpoint stop, before they decided to turn around after hitting a wall of rain.

With the Lance ahead of me and no idea about the Archer, I had to work out my options. I was now down to 1000 feet and the weather was closing in, with diminishing visibility.

Cardwell airfield, an isolated grass strip, was to my left, so I decided to orbit the area so I could land quickly should the visibility worsen while I waited to hear to where the Lance was heading.

'Michael, what are your plans?' I radioed.

'We're going to land at Tully.'

Checking my maps, I saw that it was still 20 NM away.

'Correction, we'll go to Dunk Island, Dave.'

Either of those options were 20 NM ahead, and I wasn't confident I could get through; I was not willing to risk it and was on my own again.

What worried me was that if I landed at Cardwell, or any other place on my own, I couldn't get out of the plane. And if I couldn't take off again and meet up with one of the support planes, I'd have to spend the night in the plane by myself, which wasn't exactly thrilling me. Even if I did find someone to get me out and help me to accommodation, I wouldn't be able to get into bed or do my care. I would basically be a helpless turtle on its back.

In 2010, I flew up to see the Paroo River in NSW during flood, accompanied with a few other planes. On the way home, I had engine trouble and had to spend the night at Tor Downs, a cattle station south of Broken Hill. The station owner and his family were very welcoming, providing a place to sleep, and fed me and Brian, my passenger, who was also a pilot. Brian's engine had failed so he landed his plane on the same property three days earlier; I was ferrying him home.

I was lucky then as Brian could help me, but without someone to assist me at Cardwell, I would be stuck. This scenario looped in my mind as I circled; I wasn't sure how it would play out.

Before Hinchinbrook Island, I remembered passing the small town of Ingham. The weather had been clear there and the airfield was right next to the town, so I figured I might find someone to help me there if I was desperate.

Backtracking through the channel, wispy scraps of cloud hung like spiderwebs down to 1000 feet, with hills on each side. It was like flying through a grey, murky tunnel. Bursting into the bright light at the end, I gained height and tracked to Ingham where, to my huge relief, was a beautiful sight—the Archer with Gordon, Paul and Lida.

Safely on the ground, it was now a waiting game. We refuelled the planes while we waited for the Lance, then we could work out what to do. I got some spare oil from a LAME at the airfield. 'Do you think we could get through to Cooktown today?' I asked as the guy washed grease off his hands and wiped them on his overalls.

'The cloud will get worse the later it gets,' he said. 'Nah, doubt it.'

His friendly wife chimed in, 'A local bloke flew through cloud like that a few years back. He hit one of those hills.' This pretty much wrote off my idea of getting out today.

During the Birdsville flying trip in 2011, I learnt a very important lesson—don't put all your food in one basket. One of the four planes on the trip crashed on take-off while I and another aircraft continued to the Burke and Wills Dig Tree. No one was hurt, apart from pride, but unfortunately the plane that crashed was carrying most of the ingredients for our lunch, so we had to wait until the third aircraft turned up with the food from the crashed aircraft. On flying trips since, I made sure all aircraft carried lunches and any other necessary supplies or equipment in case we were separated.

Well, it had happened again and I was somewhat annoyed, because it should have been avoided. Lida did the shopping and the pilots were responsible for making the lunches each day but, because they thought we might not be leaving Airlie Beach that day, they hadn't done it. We had some meat and salad while the Lance had the bread and a few other things. At least we had our Cup-A-Soup.

As we drank our soup a young girl turned up. 'I'm a reporter for the local, heard you're a bit stuck,' she said.

'Waiting for the weather,' Gordon answered.

Damn, news travels fast in these towns, I thought. She took a few photos and wrote a short story about us which broke the monotony.

At three o'clock I called Base Support to let them know we wouldn't make Cooktown and needed accommodation for the night. I still wasn't sure whether Bob, Michael and Linda would make it.

As we waited in Ingham, the weather deteriorated further at Dunk Island and Bob, Michael and Linda were forced to stay the night. You might think, *How wonderful to be stranded in beautiful Dunk Island*—which might have been the case before cyclone Yasi hit two years earlier and damaged many of the buildings.

When the Lance and team landed it soon became apparent that the airfield was a construction site, being rebuilt as luxury accommodation. The grumpy project manager came down to tell them they couldn't land at the airstrip because the owner would be annoyed. Well, that was too bad because they were already on the ground and couldn't take off again with the crappy weather, even if they wanted to.

Weighing up their options, it was looking likely they'd be sleeping under a lean-to at the airstrip, but fortunately the multimillionaire owner, Peter Bond, arrived in his private jet and offered them a couple of spare rooms to sleep in and plenty of food in the mess.

Base Support researched accommodation options and got us into the best motel in town near the airport—with discounted rates.

Bob, Michael and Linda dialed in for our team briefing to discuss our options.

'How are you going?' I asked.

'Good. Had a feed, met the owner,' Bob replied.

'The forecast says the weather could be OK early in the morning,' I said.

'With the mountains here, it isn't the same as on the mainland. We'll have to wait and see how it looks tomorrow,' Michael said.

'No worries. Our priority right now is to get you three back here and we'll work out what to do next,' I said.

Fortunately, the Tropixx Motel had a really good restaurant and Gordon, Paul and Lida made the most of it. I ate a little of my grilled barramundi but I wasn't hungry and went back to my room. My mind was filled with worry and I now hated the flight. I regretted the entire idea it was all too hard and it just wasn't any fun.

Everything had caught up with me—lack of sleep had worn me down, making me more stressed; the UTI had weakened me further; and now I was worried about my wife. I knew Bob and Michael could look after themselves; for them this deviation was an exciting part of the adventure. But for Linda and me, this flight was a job and it was my responsibility to make it a success. I felt ever-present pressure—not so much from my own expectations of myself, but because I felt responsible for so many people. The team had put their lives on hold, we were in the media spotlight and many people were following our journey. My worst fear was letting all these people down if we failed.

Also, this delay made Base Support's job so much harder; now they had to reschedule all our future accommodation and associated transport. I wondered how much of the donated accommodation would be lost. The deal I'd offered the team was that all costs including food, accommodation and ground transport would be covered—which was the least I could do given the time they were putting in. But with only about $12,000 up my sleeve, this wouldn't go very far if I had to cover four motel rooms each night. The completion of the flight was at risk.

I called Linda to see how she was doing and to write the blog and Facebook updates. She was really upset about being stuck on Dunk. 'I never want to do anything like this again,' she growled, almost in tears. I knew she didn't mean it; she was tired, stressed and upset, and it made it so much harder for me.

After dictating the blog, I got off the phone and my tears came; I couldn't stop them. What set me off was not just the stress, the worry, the tiredness, the UTI, the effort of flying, the doubt about whether our mission was worth it, or Linda's emotions. Rather, I think now it was the aftershock of the previous day's experience into Shute Harbour. I hadn't had time to process the near-death ordeal as I'd had to focus on the next day, and the days further ahead. This day's events just pushed me over the edge—they were the proverbial straw that broke the camel's back.

Linda and I are very passionate and focused, giving our all to whatever we do. But when we give our all, and keep giving our all, we eventually hit a wall and our emotions crumble. But once we've pushed the reset button, we are ready to throw ourselves into it again.

Ten minutes later I felt much better. I opened the maps on my computer, brought up the weather forecast to assess our options and

tried to work out how to get us out of Ingham.
Diary entry:
Today really sucks!
Flying time: 3 hours.

The wind howled and the rain drummed on the roof all night, which made it hard to sleep. My thoughts kept going to Linda, Bob and Michael, not knowing whether they would get out of Dunk Island safely and meet up with us at Ingham in the morning.

I got up at four a.m. just in case the weather miraculously cleared and looked flyable. It took me so long to get up and dressed, I had to be ready each morning even though we might not be able to leave. The weather could change quickly and I always held a glimmer of hope—I suppose it was my optimistic nature—that we could get lucky. If they could make it back, I kept thinking, we could potentially get up to Cooktown that day.

Paul spoke to Michael at 4.30 a.m. to discuss the weather and the probability of them getting out. Shortly after, he relayed the message to me, saying they would see if it was possible at first light. It became a waiting game.

At 8.37 a.m., Linda sent me a text to let me know that a window had opened up in the weather and they would attempt to fly out. It was the last I heard from her.

At around 9.30 a.m., Paul got a call from Michael to say they were two minutes from Ingham. 'They're coming!' Lida yelled. We were so relieved, our spirits rose. A minute later, the Lance's deep throaty roar sounded in the distance, then it appeared with its familiar white and green markings, flying directly over our motel. My smile stretched from ear to ear.

The team was reunited, to our great joy and relief, but it was evident we wouldn't get off the ground that day because the weather had closed in. It would be another glorious night in Ingham.

It was important to hold our team debrief each day so we could chat and reflect on the day's events and learn what we could from the experience. Apart from needing to communicate better on the radio to ensure we stayed together and landed at the same location, a basic rule had been broken—lunches had to be made and carried in each plane.

I felt it was important to talk about what had happened because the flight had gone relatively smoothly until now, and I wasn't sure how people were feeling. I didn't want anyone to feel apprehensive about sharing their thoughts or emotions; it was far better to know where each person stood so that if there was a problem, we could address it. My concern was that by bottling it up, a team member might end up pulling out.

To open up the conversation I said, 'To be honest, I'm feeling tired and a little mentally drained. My UTI has knocked me around a bit. Depending on how we go with delays, I was thinking about planning another lay day so we can have some time to rest up, if needed. How are you all going?'

I hoped this would encourage the team to open up; there was no point in being stoic. Sharing our feelings, what we find difficult, isn't a sign of weakness; it's a strength. Once we understand our internal workings, both physical and mental, we can then address and manage the situation, whether it leads to changing strategy or asking others for help. We were a team, and we relied on each other to perform our roles, so as a team we had to support each other in whatever way necessary to complete the flight and make it home safely.

Lida, Bob and Paul were going well and enjoying the motel.

Linda spoke up. 'I'm fine, but I think we need to make sure we stick together and land at the same place.'

'Yep, good point,' I commented, everyone else nodding.

'How are you going, Gordon?'

'Fine, not a problem!'

Michael sat quietly and then raised his concerns about leaving Shute Harbour in the first place. He suggested we need to be more vigilant with the weather so we didn't take unnecessary risks.

No one disagreed—it was a fair call. I was glad Michael opened up and shared with the team what was on his mind. As the youngest member, I think it bolstered his confidence to speak up, and his perspective was useful and grounding.

We'd had a good run with the weather down south, and it was inevitable we'd be delayed at some stage, but I'd hoped it would have happened later in the flight. I hadn't expected the east coast weather to be so challenging at this time of year.

We were two days behind schedule, and we still didn't know when we'd get out of Ingham or whether we'd be delayed further up the coast. The situation was out of our hands; it was like rolling a dice. We couldn't provide Base Support with a fixed date, which was frustrating for them. All they could do was inform our accommodation places of our delay, and once we knew our schedule, check if they could still take us.

Due to our largish group, with two wheelchair users, we couldn't simply roll up somewhere and find a suitable place to stay, especially in the small remote towns. It had to be planned ahead, and to secure the accommodation we'd had no choice but to commit to specific dates.

I'd anticipated delays at some stage and had factored in delay days to give us some flexibility. I never would have leaned on the team to fly if it was dangerous, but there was an unspoken level of pressure on all of us to keep going.

The weather to the west looked promising when I rolled out of the motel room, but by the time we got packed up and down to the airfield at 9.30 a.m., the blue sky had been replaced with a blanket of grey.

The BoM's animated satellite images showed a small area of cloud to the north at Tully, running from Dunk Island to Innisfail, circling around in sweeps from the sea to the coast every day. This was our roadblock or, more precisely, our air block: a small area of low cloud with showers that we couldn't get through. And there was a good reason why the weather was behaving this way. Tully is the wettest town in Australia with an average rainfall of 4000 mm. In 2003, a giant golden gumboot was erected as the town's monument. I could now see why!

To the north there was rain and to the west the cloud that was meant to be above the mountains was obscuring the peaks. We were in for another night in lovely Ingham.

Although we had been held up for a third frustrating day, one positive was it allowed us to rest. I was feeling much better, my UTI was under control and the team seemed more relaxed and eager to push ahead.

Back at my room with maps laid out on the bed, we discussed our options, weighing up the risks of each one. We understood the dangers and would not fly if it wasn't safe. I felt—as did the rest of the team, I think—that if we didn't have a go soon, when would we? The weather wasn't improving and the forecast was the same for every day, deteriorating mid-morning. If we didn't try, we might be stuck in Ingham indefinitely.

The goal for our flight was to follow the coast as much as possible; however, I definitely considered going inland if the weather demanded it. After much discussion we finally reached a consensus: tomorrow we would try going north along the coast if it was flyable. If not, we would head south to the lower mountains, then west inland to Georgetown, and finally north to Cooktown. Although this route was double the distance, we had to try and get past the weather barrier.

With the afternoon free we went our separate ways to explore Ingham, quickly discovering there wasn't much to do. I'd assumed it might be the home of Ingham chickens, but not so. The main industry is sugar cane, as with most towns in the area, and the biggest attraction is the Italian festival in May. Though it was May, we'd either missed it or it was a pretty low-key event as the town—one main street, a few pubs and the essential shops—was very quiet. However, the local council had initiated an impressive redevelopment of the wetlands near our motel, with a modern and sustainable building that had excellent wheelchair access. It looked somewhat out of place compared to the rest of the town.

I needed to improve my foot attachment mechanism as the Velcro had come off my shoes, so with a little improvisation I bought bungee straps to wrap around my feet and the footplate to lock them together. I was confident it would do the trick.

22

GOTTA GET OUTTA THIS PLACE

At 7.30 a.m., the weather forecast looked significantly better than it had for the past three days with sufficient visibility for VFR. We felt that today was the day, if it was going to be any day. The west looked reasonable but with low cloud, isolated showers and high terrain, we were uneasy about the risk of getting boxed in. To the immediate north, the murky clouds hung low but, beyond that, the weather was good. Even though going coastal to the north meant a few more showers, at least there was nothing nasty to run into—like mountains.

As with all the other days, the weather started to deteriorate later in the morning so once we'd made the decision, we had to go. It felt good to be moving again as I settled into my cocoon; I even felt optimistic that we wouldn't be turning around.

The Lance took off first, while I followed with the Archer behind and headed up the coast, climbing to 1500 feet below the thick blanket of cloud. Approaching the passage between Hinchinbrook Island and the mainland, it felt like déjà vu as the cloud ahead got lower, closing in like a net. I had never realised the impact of Hinchinbrook or Dunk Islands on the local weather conditions; they create their own micro-climates, the mountains adding to the shitty weather we were experiencing.

With the Lance a few miles ahead, Michael radioed the conditions, and with Paul behind me in the Archer tapping into the BoM's weather radar, we had a pretty good idea of what was ahead. This knowledge made flying far easier, more predictable and safer, and it boosted our confidence about making it through.

Passing Cardwell, the farthest I'd reached three days ago, I was again down to 1000 feet with the lowering cloud. The showers became more frequent and I had to drop to 500 feet as I followed the beach line. I went out to sea to avoid the smaller showers, although identifying the horizon was difficult as the patchy drizzle and murky grey cloud blended precisely with the colour of the ocean. Some showers were too wide to skirt and I had to fly through them, which wasn't a problem as they were fairly light and I could keep a visual on the thin beach line ahead.

Dunk Island, to my right, had clouds sitting on top like Dr Evil's lair; as I passed it, I tried to steal a glimpse of where Bob, Michael and Linda had stayed for the night.

Secure in my cocoon, the sun's glow through the cloud gradually brightened as the weather began to clear over the water. As I passed Innisfail, Queensland, I was able to climb to a more respectable height and became more optimistic about reaching Cooktown in far north Queensland that day.

Feeling settled and relaxed, I turned my attention to testing the audio from my headset intercom and radio through the GoPro camera set up inside the cockpit. Before leaving Tooradin, no one could tell me how to get the audio from my headset to go through the GoPro. It turned out to be very simple if you knew what to do. Linda had contacted Michael Coates from XCOM Avionics, who sent us a GoPro aviation headset cable adaptor. Following a quick modification to the GoPro cover, I was in business; I even attempted some short videos for our Facebook followers.

Cairns was the last area of controlled airspace to navigate up the east coast and we decided to take the ocean route, which was less of a hassle as we didn't need ATC approval; furthermore, the weather looked pretty ordinary over Cairns. Leaping off Fitzroy Island, the VFR approach point, I called Cairns tower. 'Cairns approach, Jabiru 5558.'

'Jabiru 5558, Cairns approach.'

'I'm rounding Cape Grafton tracking to Double Island not above 1000 feet, then north, Jabiru 5558.'

'Cairns approach copy.'

As I was tracking eight miles out to sea below controlled airspace, I wanted to make sure they knew where to look if I ditched.

Flying towards Double Island reminded me of the previous year when Linda and I were on holiday at Palm Cove. One afternoon as we were enjoying a few wines on the beach, I looked across to Double Island and wondered, *What would it be like to fly past?* As the island grew larger in my windscreen, I now knew. I felt so lucky to be where I was. Listening to the voices of my support team over the radio, I felt very grateful that they and the many others involved had made this dream a reality. It was also a moment of satisfaction as another small goal was ticked off, Cairns being the last area of controlled airspace until we reached Darwin, in the Northern Territory.

The cloud fell away and it turned into a wonderful sunny day. The wind had picked up, giving me a nice 23-knot tailwind with a ground speed of 138 knots. Each time I rounded a bay with a hill or a mountain coming in behind me, the turbulence from the rotor unnerved me a little.

Ever since Shute Harbour, my comfort level with bumps had diminished significantly. I had never been concerned about a little turbulence, but now, even a small bump made me tense. I knew it was in my head, but I was afraid of hitting turbulence and being unable to reposition myself.

After Port Douglas, civilisation disappeared—as did the dodgy weather. We were now flying in clear skies with nothing to block our way to Cooktown.

'Looks like we're not getting to Weipa today,' I said as Paul inspected the flat tyre on my plane after a windy and bumpy landing at Cooktown airport. Changing a car tyre is easy when you have a jack, but as our planes didn't carry one, it made it a little harder. It became a matter of improvisation. Following a ten-minute discussion on how to lift one side of the plane, Michael explained, 'You need to lift it and support it about a third of the way in from the wing-tip.'

'Are you sure?' I queried.

'Yeah, I remember seeing someone from Jabiru do it.'

'OK, let's give it a go then,' I said nervously.

Bob found the refuelling ladder and with Linda's rubber yoga mat placed on top to protect the underside surface of the wing, in synchronised teamwork Linda, Paul, Michael and Lida lifted the right wing to raise the right wheel off the ground while Bob positioned the ladder where Michael directed. I watched on, tensed and ready to scream 'STOP!' if anything unusual happened—like the tip of the wing breaking off. Gordon was in his element, snapping photos in anticipation of capturing one of those *Oh shit!* moments that attract numerous likes on Facebook.

What should have only taken an hour or two was looking like a day's work as the tube stubbornly thwarted every effort to pry it from the tyre.

We had planned to be in Cooktown three days earlier to attend a dinner hosted by the Endeavour Lions Club, which we obviously never made due to the weather. Jill Williams, the club member who'd coordinated the dinner, transport and accommodation, met us when we arrived. Jill was a real-estate agent, around seventy years young, dressed smartly in a red shirt with gold badges, blue pants and sandals. Despite our delay, she was very happy to see us.

'Welcome to Cooktown,' she said, hugging me and the rest of the team and posing for a photo. People in these remote communities understand that things don't always go to plan and there's not much you can do about it, especially when you're dealing with Mother Nature. 'You get there when you get there,' is their philosophy.

Fortunately, Jill had seconded Tony Likiss, director of engineering services of Cooktown shire council, to help with transport and, luckily for us, he drove Bob to the tyre repair shop to replace the tube minutes before it closed, which avoided a delayed departure the following day.

With the tyre fixed and back on my Jab, the planes had to be tied down securely, given the strong wind. Meanwhile, Linda organised transport for the team and our gear to the motel.

Tony was very proud of his town, giving us a royal tour on the way to our accommodation, showing us the main attraction—the lookout that had recently been improved by the council. You can't miss seeing the plaque where Captain Cook ran the *Endeavor* aground in 1770, hence the name of the Endeavour River on which the town is situated; and the name Cooktown, which gives its colonial history away.

With most of the afternoon free, I enjoyed a nice snooze, feeling much more rested than I had been for some time. Linda caught up on emails and organised the next few stops; Lida found a supermarket with Gordon to buy lunch supplies; meanwhile the boys went to a pub displaying a sign that read: *Beer—helping ugly people have sex since 1862*—which, I was informed, was a likely necessity for some of the blokes at the bar.

Although we had missed our dinner with the Lions Club, Jill joined us at the Cooktown bowls club for a meal. The barramundi was fantastic.

Flying time: 2.1 hours.

23

THIRD DOWN, ONE TO GO

There was an air of excitement amongst the team as we packed into the cars and headed for the airport at seven a.m. to get an early start; it would be a long day. Having recovered from my UTI, I felt great and the team was going well. Everyone seemed to have a little more energy, spurred on by the anticipation of completing our third milestone—rounding Cape York in Queensland and reaching Weipa.

Most mornings, Linda filmed some of the activity as we got ready at the planes, including my usual short spiel describing our plans for the day. Once we were in the air, she would upload the footage onto Facebook.

If Bob wasn't on the phone, flying or chatting to a stranger, he was jotting poems in his notebook.

'Give us a poem, Bob,' Linda asked, rarely having to persuade our resident bush poet.

'I might have one for ya,' he said, clearing his throat.

'Round the Cape we go today,
On a Wing and a Chair, up, up and away,
Tyres are mended, planes OK,
So round Cape York we fly today.'

'Those clouds are moving really fast,' Linda remarked, looking at the grey sky.

'It blows 30 knots continuously in Cooktown,' Tony Likiss advised, which explained the windy conditions.

As the dark clouds and a band of rain passed over—the high wing of my plane keeping us dry—Paul secured me by adding an extra piece of Velcro to my seat belt and tied the bungee straps I had bought in Ingham around my feet, just in case it got bumpy. I felt confident that another occurrence of Airlie Beach magnitude wouldn't shake me loose.

'So, does this change the Dave installation procedure?' Linda asked as she filmed the process.

'Yeah, it does. The guys will need to be recertified,' I said.

'We should add an "air worthiness directive" on the Dave installation,' Paul quipped as he fiddled at my feet.

The low dark-grey clouds that had brought the rain scooted to the west. The north was looking reasonably clear with broken cloud, but of course there was a lot of wind and intermittent showers.

Although the wind-sock was horizontal, the wind direction was almost down the runway, so getting away wasn't an issue. I headed off first, now the standard procedure, with the Archer and the Lance in my wake.

Passing Cape Flattery at 1500 feet and dodging isolated showers, I came across the world's biggest silica mine oozing from beneath the green vegetation like cream out of a chocolate eclair.

We reached Lockhart River in under two hours, an obliging tailwind pushing me to 147 knots, and had an early lunch. Lockhart River airport, known as Iron Range airport, was a military airbase built in 1942 by the US 46th Engineers and was used for bombing and communications during the threat of invasion in WWII. There is a lot of Aboriginal and aviation history there, including plaques dedicated to the Aboriginal and Torres Strait Islander service personnel and residents for their contributions during WWII, and for the servicemen and civilians killed in aircraft crashes, as well as information signs describing the extensiveness of the base, with cinemas, bakeries and a hospital. It was a small secret town, as far as you could get from anywhere. Beyond Lockhart River, there are few tracks or signs of civilisation until Weipa.

We had over three hours flying to round Cape York and then down to Weipa; in fact, from Lockhart River we could have flown west, cutting across the Cape, and arrived at Weipa in under an hour as it was only 82 NM away. Although we joked about it, we were never tempted to take the short cut: we had our third and most northern milestone to achieve—Cape York.

Along most of the east coast, including today, it had been demanding flying with the wind, the showers and the cloudy conditions. By the end of the day I was exhausted, having to manually 'fly' the plane as it was knocked around so easily due to its lightness. Continuously correcting the control column and pushing or pulling the rudder-lever to keep the aircraft flying straight, with the added challenges of changing radio frequencies, plotting the best path around rain showers and keeping a lookout for potential emergency landing spots, was a relentless exercise. The unremitting mental and physical demands were very tiring over a long period, especially for a flight of our length and duration—it was now over 7,000 kilometres and 14 days since departure.

Approaching the Cape, the Lance was waiting high up for me to pass under and do a few orbits for a photo op. The cloud had cleared but it was very windy and turbulent; I wasn't comfortable going any lower that 1000 feet for the shot. Banking left, I rounded Cape York, the most northerly point of Australia, thereby completing our third milestone. I felt triumphant as a smile spread across my face.

'Well done guys, third milestone done!' I radioed.

On my third orbit, I radioed Bob. 'Have you got the shot yet?'

I'd had enough of the turbulence knocking me around like a pinball, giving the bungees and seat belt a good workout.

'Once more round should do it, Dave,' he said as Linda snapped away in the back of the Lance, eventually taking the 'money' shot.

What kept surprising me was the ever-changing landscape and vegetation, especially rounding Cape York. Compared to the east coast with its thick green bush and seemingly constant rain and cloud, within minutes the vegetation had become sparse and dry. The wind dropped off and the cloud started to clear and get higher. Before long I was at 2500 feet and, although I had a 10-knot headwind, it was smooth air all the way to Weipa. It was brilliant to finish the day with some easy and comfortable flying, giving me time to relax and enjoy the view for a change.

On approach to Weipa, the green bush was pocketed with a patchwork of red scars from the open-cut mines and roads dividing the landscape.

'You made it! Great to have you in Weipa team,' said Trevor Snodgrass—'Snoddy' as he's known—who was waiting at the airport with an esky full of beer and soft drinks to wash down the dust. Dressed in his orange State Emergency Services overalls, Snoddy was in his sixties, very fit, tanned and willing to do whatever he could to help. He'd come to Weipa for work in the mines many years ago and ended up staying. It seemed to be a common theme amongst people I spoke to: they fell in love with the lifestyle and never left. An outsider might look at the town and think, *Who in hell would live here, so far away from the cities?* But I think the sense of the community draws and holds people; in the outback you depend on your neighbours for survival.

With so many workers for the mines and the refugee detention centre at the RAAF base close by, there was a severe lack of accommodation—as is the case in many country towns where mining has taken over. Our delay meant we had lost some of our precious wheelchair-accessible accommodation at the caravan park, but were lucky enough to get discounted rooms at Albatros Bay Resort for the four pilots. Peter from the Anchorage caravan park, a quirky but kind man wearing an '80s Hawaiian shirt, shorts, thongs and leathered skin, provided Linda, Lida and me with a two-room cottage that gave the women a workout lifting me up the three steps. Nevertheless, it was free and we had beds.

After dropping off the pilots, we headed to our accommodation to unload our luggage. I stayed in the 4WD, mainly because to get in or out I needed two of the guys to lift me. Normal cars weren't much good in remote areas, the roads being mainly dirt and gravel which becomes muddy and inaccessible in the wet season.

Getting me in and out of the 4WD was a small ordeal. To enter the vehicle, I'd park myself at the side of the front passenger door and place my feet on the floor so my legs were horizontal. Paul would then grab the back of my jeans and lift while Michael leaned across from the driver's side and pulled my knees up so my legs would bend, allowing my bum to raise to the height of the seat. Paul would then swing my bum onto the front passenger seat, invariably slamming my forehead onto the dash. But I would finally be in. Getting out was much the same process—in reverse.

It was Bauxite Bills for dinner, maintaining the theme of what the town mined, with Snoddy and his wife, Pam, joining us.

'Snoddy, what's that fence for?' I asked, pointing to what looked like plastic construction mesh composed of wire strands and green shade-cloth, with big star pickets driven into the ground to hold it up.

'It's to stop the crocs coming up from the river,' he replied.

'Oh, they must be big crocs?'

'Yep, you don't want to go near the water. We lose a few that way. Down at the pier, they wait near the ships. If you went in there, you wouldn't get out,' Snoddy added matter-of-factly.

It had been a long, tough day with 5.4 hours' flying time. Before bed I did my periodic podcast, with *Plane Crazy Down Under*, while Lida sat outside drinking coffee, stealing some time to herself.

Our arrangement wasn't ideal with Lida having to come in each morning to get me up and put me to bed at night. Over an extended period, the lack of privacy was becoming somewhat overwhelming for Linda, but also for Lida as she'd never had another person, let alone my wife, in such close confines when she did my care. On previous flying trips, she'd worked only with me and she did everything—at which she excelled. But with Linda in the room, the dynamics were challenging.

This situation was new for all of us. Linda, who is an introvert and needs her space—or 'cave,' as she calls it—had only been in my life for a year and a half and was still getting used to having carers around. Given that I'd had twenty-four years to get used to it and could tolerate limited privacy, it was much less of an issue for me.

It had been a hard two weeks. In my mind the lack of personal space, the uncertainty during our unscripted days and the stress and fatigue of flying in challenging conditions added to the strain. To ameliorate the situation, Linda would find a room or a space somewhere to do a little work or go for a walk while Lida got me up in the morning and into bed at night.

We would be in Darwin in a few days, where the team could recharge and Lida would swap with Josh, which would change the dynamics of the team.

Flying time: 5.4 hours.

24

BURKETOWN SCHOOLKIDS

Snoddy dropped us off at the airport, and with typical outback hospitality, Pam made the team sandwiches for lunch. We transferred our supplies from Snoddy's well-cooled esky to the planes' lunch bags, hoping the food would stay cool and not turn rancid in the heat.

Snoddy assured me it would be a hot day so I decided to install my new, sophisticated pneumatic spray system. Geoff had sent the spare part I needed to Cooktown and I was excited to see how it worked. I hoped it would make keeping cool much easier than hand-pumping my spray bottle as I flew.

'It's very easy to connect,' Geoff had assured me before we left. Following his instructions, Paul, our gadgets man, connected the air-tubes and switched on the compressor.

Burrrrrr, rattle, rattle, brrrrrrr, hisssssss.

'That doesn't sound too good, Paul,' I said.

'You're right about that,' he said as he fiddled a little more, but couldn't stop the leak.

'I don't have the right tools to tighten it, Dave. We'll have to wait till Darwin.' So the spray system went back in the boot and I had to resort to my pump spray bottle again.

Our routine was now embedded—each person knew what to

do, we were a finely tuned machine and in the air by nine a.m. To have beautiful weather with perfect flying conditions was such a contrast to the last few weeks. I felt relaxed and looked forward to the day ahead.

Our initial planned refuel stop was Kowanyama, but that morning Base Support informed us that Kowanyama no longer had fuel. Prior to the flight, I'd contacted all our planned refueling airfields to confirm availability. But in these isolated areas, if a truck can't get through due to rain, or if demand is too great, fuel can dry up and the only choice is to wait until another supply comes in.

We headed for an alternate airfield, Normanton, further south, but with over three hours flying on my bum, it was going to be very sore by the end.

Peering out of my perch I marvelled at the landscape; it was some of the most spectacular scenery I had ever seen, unique to the Australian outback. From my bird's-eye vantage point, the rivers resembled lone trees in a barren landscape: thick trunks snaking into the distance, estuaries shooting off to the sides like branches, with smaller creeks like twigs, all outlined by dark-green mangroves.

I caught sight of what looked like large logs floating at the mouth of a river so I dropped down for a closer look. It seemed strange that the logs were aligned with the flow of the river, fanning out rather than randomly drifting. As I drew closer, I realised what they were: 'Shit, they're not logs, they're crocs!' I said aloud—and very big ones at that. I immediately climbed to a more sensible altitude.

In the months leading up to the flight, Linda had contacted hundreds of schools to let them know about our quest. As we made our way up the east coast, a teacher at Burketown State School contacted Linda to say the kids were eagerly following the team around Australia. The kids were very keen to visit when we arrived but as an exercise, they had to first write a letter to the principal, persuading him to allow them to come to the airfield and meet the team.

The letters were so kind and honest, making us laugh, in particular one that finished with: '... *this motivates people to get off their lazy backsides and try things they have never done before. Dave may be disabled, but that doesn't stop him from achieving his goals. In conclusion I think most people love to meet him and if you say no I won't like you, but if you let us go I won't hate you. Please Mr Campbell, can we visit Mr Jacka.*'

Needless to say, the principal was sufficiently persuaded and permission was granted.

After a leisurely lunch at Normanton enjoying Pam's tasty sandwiches—they had not turned rancid in the heat—we refuelled and headed to Burketown, known for its rare meteorological phenomenon called Morning Glory: a cloud mass resembling a rolling wave across the sky. I could barely see the town as I approached—it was like a pimple in a flat, expansive brown landscape—but the airfield stood out like a burlesque dancer at the G20 Summit with its 1372-metre-long bitumen strip.

Not long after touching down the kids arrived in their school uniforms, and most with bare feet. The kids from this community are Aboriginal, and the school has about thirty students, of which eleven came to meet us, ranging from grades four to seven.

In the shade of a tin-roofed awning that sheltered us from the scorching sun, the kids surrounded me and presented a wonderful gift: a poster the class had made with drawings of Linda and me, my plane, jellyfish and wonderful personal messages, some of which read:

'*Thank you for coming to Burketown it means a lot to me and my class. You have inspired us to dream as if there are no impossibilities. From Mayarr. PS. I'm your biggest fan.*'

'*You have inspired me a lot I will never give up thanks to you. From Latreya.*'

A girl with a beaming smile came up and handed me chocolate biscuits—a tad melted from the heat. 'This is from the class, thank you for coming,' she said.

Kids have no inhibitions and were soon launching question after question.

'Do your arm thing!' one yelled.

'Yeah, do your arm thing!' they yelled in unison.

Not wanting to disappoint, I raised my right arm, then let it fall on my head. They burst out laughing, the girls squealing, then yelled, 'Do it again, do it again!' I duly repeated the exercise two more times before the teacher told them, 'That's enough!'

They had seen me on TV talking about my disability, in particular having no working tricep muscles which prevents me from holding my arm directly above my head.

'Do you play sport?' asked one boy.

'I played wheelchair rugby and went to the Paralympics.'

This set off a barrage of questions. Being Queenslanders and into their rugby, they were very excited, quizzing me about how I played and what team I barracked for. I think they were a little disappointed to learn I am from Victoria and the game I follow is Aussie Rules (AFL).

The experience was one of the most memorable of the flight. I loved their honesty, openness and acceptance, but it was their energy and potential that stood out. It made me hope that even if we had only a small effect on them and their futures, our quest would be worth it.

After showing the kids my plane and demonstrating how I flew with my adaptations, a guy from the Savannah Lodge, our accommodation for the night, picked us up in a ute that resembled a wreck from *Mad Max*. We were lucky to have the cabins as we'd lost our reservation due to our delay at Ingham, but fortunately a fishing group had cancelled at the last minute, freeing them up for us.

While Linda and I updated social media and made plans for the next day, Gordon went into town with Lida as she was struggling to find anything suitable for our lunch that wasn't canned. In the end, we resorted to prepackaged salami and a loaf of frozen white bread.

Bob and Michael went to the pub and got chatting to Trinity, a Māori New Zealander. He had a special talent: removing the top of a can with his incisor, just like a can-opener, hence his nickname, the Burketown Can Opener. Not sure what his dentist had to say, but it was an entertaining party trick.

Daniel, one of the teachers, dropped around with a few beers and Gordon and Paul stayed chatting with him. I had to get up at four a.m. the next morning and felt shattered from the flying and heat, so I didn't stay long and was in bed by seven p.m.

Flying time: 3.5 hours.

25

DAYS 16 AND 17 NHULUNBUY NT

Our cabins at the Savannah Lodge didn't have bathrooms, so at four a.m. Lida had to wheel me to the accessible bathroom about thirty metres away. It was very dark; soft lights illuminated the path of the wooden deck which was surrounded by tropical palms and bushes. Creatures scuttled away as I rolled along, massive cane toads thumping like little wallabies as they jumped and landed, while other nocturnal animals left me puzzled as to what they could be. There seemed to be so much wildlife at night but during the day they seemed nonexistent.

While the planes were being readied, I was interviewed by ABC radio in Mount Isa. We were in the air by 8.30 a.m. and looking forward to another perfect flying day.

Having flown through four states so far, the Northern Territory was our first and only territory. At 50 NM from Borroloola, our lunch and refuel stop, we headed slightly inland. The landscape transformed to green bush with hills and valleys of red rock; I half-expected to see Gina Rhinehart out there digging it up.

'Jabiru 5558, Whiskey Mike Quebec, what's your location, Dave?' radioed Michael.

'Mike, 40 miles to run to Borroow…borrool…Borurala…. Borllooo. Forty miles to our lunch spot!' I replied, getting seriously tongue-tied.

'What's your location again?' he asked. I swear Michael would ask for my location when he knew it was at a place I'd have difficulty saying—just for fun. I imagined him smirking, if not outright laughing, as I fumbled to pronounce the names.

Talk on our chat channel of 123.4 MHz interrupted us, and I heard Michael call up to see who they were. They were the voices of the three Robinson 44 helicopters that had left Airlie Beach the same day as us.

'Where have you been?' I asked.

'Went to Nhulunbuy but couldn't get accommodation so we're heading back home,' came the reply, shaky from the aircraft's excessive vibrations. 'Where are you going?' he added.

'We're flying around Australia and are on our way to Nhulunbuy. But we have accommodation with Rio Tinto.'

'How did you get that?'

'We applied for it months ago and they gave us a couple of nights in the workers' accommodation,' I said somewhat smugly.

Between Borroloola and Nhulunbuy, both in the Northern Territory, we knew there was some dodgy weather coming but weren't quite sure how significant it would be. From bright sunshine one moment to having a cloud blanket pulled over my head, I hoped the showers ahead were light as dark, murky clouds enveloped the path into the distance. Inland out of my left window, I saw heavy tropical downpours that I definitely couldn't fly through.

As we headed up the coast, my track resembling a zigzag, a local pilot, Andrew Daken, flying a Beachcraft Twin was following our flight and realised we were hitting some dodgy weather. He Facebooked Linda in the Lance, providing details on the conditions ahead and added that if we couldn't get through to Gove, he could arrange accommodation on Groote Eylandt, an island to our right with an alternate aerodrome. It was a very generous offer.

DAYS 16 AND 17 NHULUNBUY NT

I wasn't aware how many followers we had on social media, but at various times people would contact us out of the blue, letting us know they were watching out for us. It was very comforting when alone in the middle of nowhere to know that should we need help, they would assist us if they could. To me, this is the real spirit of Australia, especially in the outback—a helping hand to those in need, no matter who they are, for no benefit other than knowing they have made someone's life a little easier.

Ten miles before Gove airport (south of Nhulunbuy township) we burst into brilliant light, the 2200-metre runway glistening in the sunshine from the recent rain. I landed a little long, and with the exit point for the taxiway up the other end, I had about 1.5 kilometres to track back. It took ages, and I realised why my tyres were wearing out: I was doing far more taxiing than usual on these longer strips.

At the refuelling pump I was surprised to run into Andrew; I chatted with him about flying in the top end and thanked him for his thoughtful and generous offer. These young pilots have a tough job flying in the outback. Many have their ambitions set on the big commercial jets but need to accumulate hours and experience, so they come up to the remote areas and work for minimal pay. It's a tough job but they do it because they love to fly—it's their passion, what they live for.

The accommodation in Arnhem Village provided by Gove Operations Pacific Aluminium (Rio Tinto) were portable rooms, comprised of dongas or site sheds, each fitted out with a bed and bathroom with baby-blue wall linings. Each person had a separate room except for Linda and me, which offered some much-appreciated space and privacy.

Chris Wallace from Gove Operations went the extra mile to look after us, and to our surprise even installed a double bed for Linda and me. Our room and Gordon's had concrete ramps and wheelchair-accessible bathrooms; it was awesome.

I later asked Michael and Paul, 'What was the best part of the trip?' They both agreed: Nhulunbuy.

I was a little surprised. 'Nhulunbuy, really? Why?'

'The food!' Paul said with a grin.

The food was indeed impressive. The food hall, a massive banquet, was open eighteen or so hours a day. The bain-maries offered a dozen hot dishes of varying cuisines, along with a huge selection of cold foods, salads and half a dozen desserts. If you wanted steak, the chef would cook it for you on the spot and to your liking. We were a little heavier after our stay.

Flying time: 5 hours.

The original plan was to spend only one night in Nhulunbuy; however, as we had lost one night's accommodation in Weipa, Rio Tinto put us up for another night. It would have been nice to go straight to Darwin but our accommodation there wasn't available, and our stay had reduced from four to three days due to delays.

I had imagined the flight to be 'an adventure of a lifetime'—chatting with the many interesting people we'd meet over the course of our journey. But in reality, with all the work Linda and I had to get done each day, when we reached our accommodation, we didn't have the time or energy to do much else. Maybe my expectations had been unrealistic; nevertheless, I was a little disappointed. However, the extra day in Nhulunbuy granted a rare opportunity to visit a community, and this time I was determined to see at least one town.

Paul and Michael went their separate ways to explore and catch up on their domestic duties. I joined Gordon, Lida and Bob for a stroll into town. It didn't seem that far in the taxi the day before, but after a tiring hour of pushing down the footpath in the heat and humidity, I definitely decided to get a taxi back.

DAYS 16 AND 17 NHULUNBUY NT

Nhulunbuy is the largest town in East Arnhem Land—the area of which was leased from the traditional Aboriginal land owners by Rio Tinto for the bauxite mining site. It is a pretty standard mining town with a pub, a shopping centre, a couple of cafes and expensive takeaways.

The most surprising aspect of the town was their surf lifesaving club. I was a little puzzled as I couldn't see any surf, just flat water. Maybe a cyclone would generate big-enough waves, but I was at a loss. 'Why are the gates to the surf club locked?' I asked a middle-aged lady walking past with an arm full of shopping.

'There's a big croc hanging around along the beach there,' she responded, pointing. 'Until he goes it won't open.'

According to the locals, people swam a lot around here, but not during the stinger (box jellyfish) season.

When I spoke to another woman, a resident who worked for the mine, I asked, 'Don't you worry about the crocs?'

'Na, you just throw your dog in first.'

'So, you must go through a few dogs then,' I quipped.

'Ah … not that many,' she said.

I wasn't sure if she was joking or not. I left it at that.

26

DARWIN HERE WE COME

Today we'd be in Darwin for a three-day break, which must have spurred on the team as everyone moved at a cracking pace.

With only a short flight to Maningrida, an Aboriginal community on the coast of West Arnhem Land with an impressive art and culture centre, we'd then fly on to Emkaytee, a small airfield around 20 NM south of Darwin.

The day was so clear as I climbed out, heading west over Gove Harbour. It was an impressive sight with three massive ore ships lined up and waiting for their loads in the bay. A white line of beaches stretched endlessly into the distance and estuaries lined with mangroves wove inland through the bush.

At 4500 feet it was pleasantly cool in the cockpit, but upon landing at Maningrida the heat hit me like a furnace; I quickly had to get out of the plane and into the shade before I overheated.

'Get this into ya,' said Bob, handing me my usual Cup-A-Soup. But with the stench of something dead near the terminal building, combined with the heat, I couldn't stomach it.

Apart from Tassie, the daily temperatures had been fairly mild, so I was unprepared for the sudden heat of the top end. After refuelling and our team briefing under the shade of the wing, I got in the plane in record time. The sun streaming through the windscreen gave me flashbacks of my experience at Goolwa. *God, it'd be nice to have my spray system working*, I thought. Lida sprayed me down one last time, and with air streaming through the vents, ruffling my loose papers and maps, I felt adequately cool and headed for Emkaytee two hours away.

Sixty nautical miles out of Emkaytee, heading inland, the beaches, mudflats and mangroves transformed into thick bush and rock. The air was also getting warmer, pushing my cylinder head temperature up, a little too high for my liking at about 110 degrees Celsius, just on the red. I pulled back the revs to avoid working the engine too hard and the temperature slowly came down into the green, which made me much happier.

The sight of cleared bush with crops was a change from the natural landscapes we'd consistently seen since Cairns; in the distance the city poked up its head in defiance of the natural world.

'We've arrived in Emkaytee, woo-hoo! Thank God we're here,' I said to the camera as Linda filmed a Facebook update. I was so damned happy to have finally made it to our halfway point, as was the rest of the team.

It was a pretty basic airfield: a red gravel strip, a few hangars and fuel. 'Dave, you need to see Scott for your service,' Gordon reminded me. Gordon had booked in my Jab for its fifty-hour service with Scott Barlow, the local LAME. The Archer and the Lance also had a few issues to sort out; we wanted our planes to be in tiptop shape before we left.

I wheeled to the hangar, finding Scott in his grease-stained white-and-blue singlet, blue shorts and runners. 'So, you're flying round Austrayya?' Scott said.

'Yep, that's the idea.'

'It's a long way,' he remarked.

'Sure is. We've been going eighteen days and are only halfway.'

'Bedda make sure your plane's all good then.'

'If you can give it a fifty-hour and a good once-over that'd be great.'

'Too easy, I'll see what I can do.'

It was a relief when Mark Christee from the Top End Flying Club arrived, welcoming me to his cool air-conditioned car; I was roasting. He had arranged two vehicles to drive us to Darwin as the airfield was a forty-minute drive south. Travelling up the highway, I noticed what looked like sections of an old road running parallel.

'It's an old WWII runway,' Mark told me. 'There are lots of airfields around here built to fight the Japanese,' he went on.

Although the remnants are fading, Darwin and the top end have a lot of history that indicates the area's role in defending Australia. Looking at the faces of those young soldiers in museum photos—dirty with grease, tanned in their shorts and boots—they seemed a tough breed, able to withstand harsh conditions.

Given our delays, we were lucky to still have our accommodation at the Darwin Central Hotel, despite it being peak season and in a fantastic location in the centre of town. The manager had generously donated three rooms for the team and managed to rearrange other guests so we could still have the wheelchair-accessible rooms.

Bronwynne had flown up to meet Gordon and Paul for the three days, and Josh looked very happy to see us. He had come up north a week before our anticipated arrival to have a short holiday, but with our delays, his holiday had turned out to be a little longer—which was difficult for him as he couldn't cope with heat and hadn't been sleeping.

We had ticked off three of our four milestones; we'd endured tough weather, illness, lack of sleep and, in my case, a near-death experience. We had definitely earned this much-needed rest. It was now time to recharge for the second half of the flight.

Flying time: 3.8 hours.

Lida was leaving the next morning on a commercial flight back to Melbourne and I wanted to catch up before she left.

'You're ready to go?' I asked, noting her packed bags.

'Yes, just waiting for the taxi.'

'Thanks for coming on the trip, Lida, I really appreciate everything you've done.'

'You're welcome. I got to see things I never have before.'

'But no crocs.'

'Bloody shit, no way, thank God!' she said, laughing.

'I know it's been a tough trip but I hope it's been worthwhile?'

'Gordon asked me if I would do it again, and I said yes. I'm glad I was part of it.'

After a little more reminiscing, we hugged. As I went out the door she said, 'Good luck for the second half. I'll come to Tooradin when you finish.'

Lida had been a valuable team member who'd worked very hard, generously giving her time to make the flight possible.

The rest of the team had gone their separate ways and Linda was back at our room. I needed to get away from everything for a while, to have a bit of me time. I rolled around the centre of Darwin until I found a bar where I could sit outside, self-medicate with a few beers and completely relax, switching off from thoughts about the flight. It was glorious, and for the first time in so long I let myself just be.

A few hours later Linda called to see where I was and joined me; then Bob, Michael and Josh wandered in. We sat in the late-afternoon heat drinking beer and nibbling tapas, reminiscing about the flight. The more beers we drank, the grander and more epic our stories became. Josh may have wondered what the hell he'd signed up for as he laughed along with us.

On the second rest day, we went out for brunch. Sitting in the sun, devouring my bacon and eggs with extra oil-soaked hash browns felt so extravagant compared to the hasty early mornings we were used to.

After our meal, and feeling somewhat heavier, Linda and I wandered around town. Darwin has a lot of history: it was bombed by the Japanese in WWII, and has also withstood a few natural disasters. In the centre of town, the bent metal star from the old Star Theatre is displayed, a reminder of that fateful Christmas Eve in 1974 when Cyclone Tracey blew Darwin off the face of the earth. Although I was six years old at the time, I remember the vivid images of total devastation flickering across the screen of our black-and-white TV.

It was Bob's birthday in a few days—he had made sure we knew it—so Linda and I decided to get him a present.

'How about this?' I suggested, waving a bottle-opener made from a stuffed kangaroo scrotum.

Linda rolled her eyes and I gathered she didn't approve.

'Maybe something he can remember Darwin by,' she suggested, picking up a small stone painted with an Aboriginal design; but it looked a little sloppy.

'How about something by a local Aboriginal artist?' she said.

At a classier shop, we found a stone about three centimetres in diameter decorated with an unusual pattern. It was quite pricey, but very nice.

I asked the saleslady the name of the artist.

She gave me the name and told me he was a local. 'Been here for thirty years,' she added.

'And where was he before that?' I asked, assuming he came from a remote Aboriginal community.

'In America.'

'America? Is he an Aboriginal artist?' I continued.

'No, he is American,' she said, a little annoyed by my persistent questioning. Then the penny dropped.

'But he is a local,' she insisted.

I was a little dumfounded as I'd assumed all the art in the shop was by local Aboriginal artists, not just by any local who could paint. I think most people would have made that assumption. I was pretty annoyed because I felt misled and would never have known had I not asked.

'Maybe the kangaroo scrotum bottle-opener will do after all?' I said to Linda with a shrug.

Day 21 was our third and last day in Darwin. *I'm not doing anything today* was my waking thought. *No emails, no Facebook, no blog …* Then I pulled myself up: *OK, I'll do one Facebook post and a very quick blog so our followers know we haven't forgotten them and I'm not dead.* We had an enthusiastic social media following and if we were late with a blog post, our supporters would send us messages, even at eleven o'clock at night, asking for it. The interest was, of course, fantastic, but it put pressure on Linda and me to stay up to date. She was working relentlessly, doing an amazing job; in the end, it was this effort that would make the flight a success by getting our message out.

As well as giving us time to rest and recharge, the last two days allowed me to step back and reflect on the first half of the flight, to assess our procedures and consider where we could improve.

Travelling up the east coast had been harder than I'd anticipated given the varying weather conditions, the mechanical delays and my UTI. But each team member had stepped up to the challenges when needed, which made me proud and very grateful.

Upon reflection, what I hadn't fully appreciated was how each person, as an individual, functioned in the team environment, especially given the duration of the flight and the necessity of working in such close confines. While it's not always possible to predict people's reactions in a given situation, I felt I should have been more sensitive to the challenges posed by the limits on personal space, and in turn, the strain it put on interpersonal dynamics—as occurred with Linda and Lida towards the end of the first half of the flight.

It wasn't just living in small motel rooms, but rather the lack of privacy, and the intrusion into personal space. Without a small private sanctuary, having to retreat with all her possessions to one side of the room while Lida, in the rest of the room, did my personal care made life on the journey a very stressful experience for Linda.

I also sensed that Lida felt uncomfortable having others in her space, in particular when working with me. This was compounded by minor events that would normally be brushed aside—such as the disagreement in Wollongong when Lida didn't want to put a name tag on her bag. I was aware of the building tension, but not of the extent. I had expected some team members might get a little cranky and figured that the tiredness and stress of being continually on the go was the main cause—which at the time didn't seem a big issue and one which would likely resolve with a few rest days.

This situation wasn't helped by the onset of my UTI after leaving Bairnsdale. It left me feeling lousy and exhausted, without the mental or physical energy to fly as well as effectively manage the team. This made it more difficult for Linda to coordinate the team's routine with the community support at each stop. In turn, this led to her feeling frustrated and stressed—as occurred on our arrival in Cooktown when Lida wasn't around to help transport luggage to our accommodation.

My lesson was that as team leader, as the visionary and driving force of the project, the buck stopped with me. I had to lead all the time without exception. I had to recognise developing issues and manage them quickly. In this, I needed to be aware of personality differences within the team, coach members to fulfill their roles and responsibilities, and maintain team well-being by minimizing stress and fatigue as much as possible. I had to ensure these factors didn't undermine the team, and in turn, impede achievement of our goal.

With Josh now onboard the dynamics of the team would change; but also, as we had established effective processes over the last three weeks, I had to make sure he slotted into his role quickly.

It was necessary for Josh, Michael and Paul to coordinate with each other and assist me, so I called a meeting to discuss how we would work together. Josh was assigned to helping me with my personal care, organising me in the plane and anything else I needed. Although Michael had to help Bob with the Lance and Paul to assist Gordon, I also needed them to share Josh's load to assist me getting into the plane, prepping it and putting it to bed after the day's flight.

Talking things through with the guys, I understood better the constraints Michael and Paul were under, given the demands of their own planes and everything else they were responsible for. Although we had our systems, we retained some flexibility to adapt to the demands of each day.

Early in the afternoon of our last day in Darwin, we held our team meeting to discuss the next day's schedule: the flight to Kununurra, just over the border into Western Australia. I wanted to start afresh, putting the first half of the flight behind us, and to view the next half as a new stage in the project. It would offer different challenges but we were all feeling good, eagerly anticipating heading off. And looking at the map, it was all downhill!

Paul, my ex-boss from Melbourne Water, was living in Darwin so Linda and I caught up with him that afternoon at Monsoons, a bar around the corner from the hotel. Paul hadn't changed, except he looked far more relaxed in shorts and T-shirt than when he worked at Melbourne Water.

He watched his kids while we downed a few ice-cold Asahi beers in the hot and humid afternoon. I updated him on work and we reminisced about the good-old days. Our lives had changed quite a bit in only two years; I wondered what was around the corner for us in the next few.

I noticed Bob walking past and called out, 'You look like a derro with all those plastic bags!' But I did notice his new haircut and trimmed beard, a habit from his army days.

'Do ya reckon I can get in with me shopping?' he asked.

'While they're not looking, Bob,' I said, waving him over. He hurried in and shoved the bags under the table.

After a few more beers in the sun, and increasingly relaxed, I found myself singing 'Khe Sanh' along with the musician while Linda handed out our business cards, making sure everyone in the bar knew about the flight and could follow our onward journey. To this day, Bob talks about our time at Monsoons. It was a very memorable way to end our Darwin stay.

27

STAGE TWO: KUNUNURRA

I was glad to see Scott Barlow waiting for us in the blistering heat at Emkaytee.

'How'd you go with the Jab, Scott?' I asked.

'Yeah, all good. I changed the oil and filter and everything looks fine,' he said. Just what I wanted to hear.

'So what do I owe you?'

'Just cover the cost of the oil, Dave. Nothing for the labour,' he replied.

'Really? OK, thanks Scott, really appreciate it.'

Considering he didn't give Gordon and Bob a freebee, I was extremely grateful for his generosity.

The right tyre had been wearing more than usual so Bob and Michael checked the undercarriage and mounting bolts but saw nothing out of the ordinary. My only concern was that if the tyre wore out, I didn't have a replacement. I'd been trying to source one for the past few days, but there weren't many options in the far northwest.

With plenty of time for the short flight to Kununurra, I was eager to get my spray system working before we left. After the previous failed attempt, Paul had worked out the problem: we had connected it backwards, which explained why it wasn't holding air.

The system worked by pressing a blue button the size of a coffee-cup base with my elbow; a fine spray of water then shot out of a nozzle on a flexible hose that I could direct onto my face to cool myself down.

By 11.30 a.m. I was beginning to feel like a roasted chicken in the cockpit. Readying to taxi out, I decided another spray was in order before taking off, knowing it would be difficult to coordinate once I was on climb. I hit the blue button, there was a short delay, then *whoosh*: a high-pressure water-stream shot out of the spray reservoir, splashing the windscreen and gushing all over the electrical equipment and instruments. As the high-pressure fountain subsided and turned to a dribble, large droplets of water dripped off the windscreen and roof. I was soaked, my Galaxy tablet drowning in the pool of water in my lap.

'Shit!' I yelled, then radioed the support aircraft as they warmed up their engines. 'I have another problem, guys!'

Paul quickly came to my rescue.

The tube leading to my spray hose had blown off the top of the water reservoir from the high air pressure. On closer inspection, it was evident we'd need a very small clamp to fix it. We didn't have transport or the time to go back into Darwin, and by the time we'd likely find something suitable in another town along our route, we'd have reached the cool south.

Once again Paul disconnected it and threw it into the back where it would stay permanently, to my annoyance. Again, I resorted to the trusty pump spray bottle to keep cool.

One advantage of being well soaked was that with the outside air from the vents blowing onto me, I was at least temporally cooled as my little plane slowly climbed in the thin, hot air over the airfield. Hot air reduces the performance of the aircraft, decreasing the climb rate, and as my engine was air-cooled, it could easily overheat in those conditions. To keep the engine cool, I had to make a series of step climbs. Climb for 500 feet, level off, then climb again. This allowed more air flow over the engine during level flight as I tracked southwest to Kununurra in Western Australia.

I was excited to be in the air again; looking forward to getting on with the job and back to Tooradin. Each day's travelling was one day closer to home, and this thought kept me going as I calculated our remaining flying days. By making it to Darwin, we had psychologically broken the back of the flight; now it was just a matter of reaching our final milestone: Steep Point, WA, the most westerly point in Australia, for the downhill run home.

Back on the coast the air was cooler, reducing the likelihood my engine would overheat and giving us smoother air away from the thermals over the land.

Peering out my window, I was amazed by the dazzling aqua of the rivers and ocean as I tracked from Port Keats across the Joseph Bonaparte Gulf. Beginning our track inland from the coast, crossing the WA border, I was filled with anticipation as I'd been looking forward to seeing the Kimberley ever since I'd unfolded a map of the region and tried to imagine what it would be like. The vast and alluring red landscape of hills and canyons stretched into the distance, with trees latching on to the rocky surfaces—it was breathtaking. Then came the unexpected twist: civilisation burst out of the earth with roads, train lines, dams, crops and buildings as Kununurra gradually emerged.

The wave of heat enveloped me like molasses as I opened the door to my plane on the tarmac at Kununurra airport.

Gordon and I sat in the shade of the wing while Josh, Paul and Michael unpacked the gear. Josh looked a little warm in his black long-sleeve OWC shirt and shorts, his skinny lily-white legs poking out the ends, his short hair drenched in sweat. 'How're you going with the heat, Josh?' I asked.

'Too warm!' he replied.

'How was your first flight with Gordon and Paul?'

'Yeah, it was good.'

'He's not a virgin anymore,' commented Gordon.

'How'd you go with the bumps, did you feel air-sick?' I queried.

'No, I was fine. It was smoother than I expected,' he replied, a good sign for things to come.

'We had the sick-bags just in case,' Gordon added.

My brother-in-law, John Newman, was the superintendent for the Pilbara Region with the Fire and Emergency Services Authority of Western Australia (FESA), now known as the Department of Fire and Emergency Services (DFES). Earlier in the year he'd contacted Tony Stevenson from the DFES in Kununurra, who'd offered to help us out.

Tony was middle-aged, tanned —everyone had a tan in these parts—laid-back and an all-round lovely guy; generous with his time and interested in flying. He and his colleague, Graham Sears, were waiting for us as we landed with two 4WDs to take us to our accommodation.

The intense heat was suffocating. I felt a touch guilty sitting in the air-conditioned 4WD, supervising, while the rest of the team packed the cars.

Tony and Graham dropped us off at the Kimberley Grande Hotel; it was an oasis in the dry red landscape and offered very big rooms. Gordon and I were excited about the huge accessible bathroom—a luxury. The hotel had donated a room and volunteers from the Kununurra Fire and Rescue had raised money to cover the rest of our accommodation costs and all the food during our stay. The folk in these parts are so generous, willing to help out people they've never heard of, let alone met.

Tony was very thoughtful; he figured we'd be tired so he made sure no one would bother us; but in truth, it would have been nice to meet a few locals.

STAGE TWO: KUNUNURRA

It was a very relaxed night. Tony met us at the bar and grill for a drink, and a mate of Bob's from his army days plus a few of their friends joined us for the meal.

It was off to bed early again for a four a.m. start to head to Derby the next day, although dodgy weather was on its way.

Flying time: 2.6 hours.

Sitting outside in the afternoon heat I watched Paul, Michael and Josh race in the cool swimming pool, Bob the starter for each race. Linda was in our room talking to Base Support, reorganising accommodation for the next few days, while Gordon was having a lie-down. The day hadn't worked out the way we'd planned—we were back in Kununurra.

'Weatherman, what's the forecast for today?' I'd asked Michael at our morning briefing.

'It's shit, but we are good to go.'

A long rain-band had developed while we were in Darwin, stretching from out to sea at Broome and inland to central Australia. Over the last few days it had moved further north, slowly getting weaker but blocking our path around the coast where it was heavier. It was very unseasonal. 'Yeah, the weather's a bit strange this year,' said the locals. 'It should be sunny and blue skies.'

'Are we going or staying?' I asked the pilots.

They agreed to go, but I could sense some apprehension—which is natural when conditions are not ideal.

Initially, we'd intended to refuel at Truscott, a remote airfield in the northwest Kimberley that's used to fly helicopters to the gas rigs off the coast; but with a $600 landing fee per aircraft, this option was dismissed. Our only alternative was Kalumburu, the northernmost settlement in Western Australia, formerly known as Drysdale River Mission.

My podcast episode on *Plane Crazy Down Under* was getting airplay even in the far north. As I was getting ready to depart, the three crew from Air North dropped by for a chat—pilots Trent and Tim, and the lovely Sami, the flight attendant. Their job was to fly executives into the Argyle mine in the morning and back to Kununurra in the afternoon; not a bad job. There's obviously a lot of money in diamonds.

I was eager to get going as the clouds were building in the heat and the weather would only get worse. We said our goodbyes to Tony and Graham, assuming we'd never see them again.

Departing at 8.30 a.m., we tracked direct to Kalumburu. A thunderstorm band was south of the settlement, but we were confident we'd manage to avoid it by tracking further north to the coast. Into the distance the cloud was getting more consistent as we gained height over the Kimberley Plateau, reaching around 1500 feet above sea level (ASL).

Thirty minutes out of Kununurra Michael came over the radio. 'I have a revised weather report for Kalumburu. A SIGMET (Significant Meteorological Information) has been issued. Thunderstorms and significant rain ahead,' he reported.

Paul consulted the weather radar on his iPad. 'It looks nasty!' he reported.

Our flight path that day offered few airstrips to land at if the weather closed in. It was a no-brainer. 'OK, let's head back to Kununurra,' I radioed. 'Michael, please ask Linda to call Tony and see if he can help us again.'

We turned our aircrafts 180 degrees and headed back to Kununurra for the night. It was déjà vu for Tony as he again met us at the airport and took us to the motel.

Over dinner, we discussed our options for the following day, which depended on the weather. The choices were: our originally planned coastal route up to Kalumburu then around the coast to

Derby; tracking straight to Derby despite being tight on fuel if we had headwinds; or inland to Halls Creek, then to Derby. I wanted to stick to our original plan and do coastal if we could. I didn't want to compromise if we weren't forced to, given this was the point of the flight around (the coast of) Australia.

Dave Coulston worked at Virgin and knew it wasn't looking good for us so, to give us a better chance, he asked one of their meteorologists to provide an expert forecast for the next day. It looked like the heavy rain was out at sea with light to moderate showers on the coast and some cloud inland. It gave us some hope that we'd get out the following day. We agreed to decide in the morning after receiving the latest forecast.

It was early to bed as I had to be up at three a.m. to ensure an early start before the heat, clouds and rain.

Flying time: 1.4 hours.

28

CHANGE OF PLAN AND HAPPY BIRTHDAY

A little after six a.m. Paul and Michael knocked on the door, ready to discuss the day's weather. 'What's it look like, Michael?' I asked.

'Truscott has rain and possible thunderstorms. Over the mountains there's low cloud,' he reported.

'Yeah, that's not too good.'

'If we go inland to Halls Creek then Derby, we'll have fuel and alternates on the way if the cloud gets low,' Paul suggested.

Maybe we should stay one more day, I thought as I tried to avoid the inevitable. Disappointment churned in my gut as an inland route seemed the only realistic option. But even if we did stay another day, there was no guarantee we'd get out and the way the weather was looking, it might be a few days or even a week before we could go the coastal route.

Also weighing on my mind were the implications of delays: we'd likely lose accommodation, requiring more money than I'd budgeted for. If we spent another day— or two, or three—in the hope of clearer weather, and were then delayed down south (which was likely with winter approaching), we were screwed.

Again, it was a no-brainer. I agreed with Paul and Michael to go to Halls Creek as it was the safest route. I knew it was the right decision, but I still felt immensely disappointed—as if I'd failed in a way. The route via Halls Creek wasn't any shorter so, from a distance and flying-time perspective, my achievement would be the same. I guess I felt that since we had gone coastal for most of the flight, not to do so was akin to giving in. Also, I'd been looking forward to flying around the northwest section of coast for so long; missing it was such a disappointment.

We should always be true to our goals, but at times it's necessary to be open-minded enough to adjust a little in order to achieve the larger goal, especially when the risk of failure is increased by doggedly sticking to the original plan. The larger goal was to get around Australia, so it was the right decision to change our path.

Reading many of the comments from followers on the blog put my disappointment into perspective. In essence, many said: *Stop being an idiot and enjoy the spectacular scenery.* It was good advice, and I had to stop being so hard on myself.

'Hopefully we won't see you again, Tony,' I yelled from the cockpit, giving him a wave as Josh closed the door.

Although we had to duck under, over and around a lot of cloud as we tracked south between 2500 to 3500 feet, following the Northern Highway towards Halls Creek, I was compelled by the striking scenery. Off my left wing the mirrored waters of Lake Argyle reflected the painted textures of cloud and the morning sun. The mountains and gorges, eroded over eons, resembled a Monet painting; in the distance, the rugged landscape appeared a vibrant green but up close, sparse trees clung to the red rock surfaces. I realised that the decision to come inland was a blessing in disguise; it was breathtakingly beautiful.

After refueling and a lunch of sandwiches with flies at Halls Creek, it was an uneventful flight to Derby. Passing Fitzroy Crossing, the cloud dissipated into a clear sky and upon arrival I was greeted by a few of the locals and tourists. 'We heard you on the radio this morning and thought we'd come down for a chat,' said one lady. I'd been interviewed on ABC Kimberley at 5.30 that morning and was surprised anyone had been listening; I felt like a rock star.

'I'd love to do your trip, sounds like a great holiday you're having,' said one of the blokes who I guessed was a tourist.

God, if only these people knew!

While I was chatting, one lovely local woman approached and said, 'If you need a car you can borrow one of ours while you're here.'

'I really appreciate that, but we've organized a lift,' I said, indicating Kim Maldon from DFES who was waiting for the team to put the planes to bed. Kim was based in Broome but also serviced Derby over 200 kilometres away. He'd driven all the way from Broome to pick us up from Derby airport and cart us to DFES headquarters in Derby to shower and relax. Linda and I felt really bad because the day before, he'd driven most of the way from Broome to Derby before we could notify him that we'd been delayed another day.

'Who wants to play cards?' Josh asked, casually shuffling the deck he'd found. Paul, Michael and Bob were keen so they settled in for a few rounds of Texas Hold'em over a few beers and rum. Gordon watched on, drinking his bottle of red, while Kim cooked spaghetti bolognaise, chicken in a tomato sauce and veggies with garlic bread. It was one of our best meals.

We had bypassed most of the unsettled weather, but I felt physically and mentally exhausted. It was another leg of the flight down, bringing us that much closer to home.

Flying time: 4.3 hours.

'Linda, who's out the front making all that racket?' I asked as Josh got me into my wheelchair at 5.30 a.m.

'I think it's the ladies from the Country Women's Association,' she said as half a dozen woman were preparing for Australia's Biggest Morning Tea to raise money for cancer.

Last night we'd stayed at the CWA house in Derby, which they'd generously made available to us. It was an old weatherboard with crocheted doilies, eclectic furniture—some from the turn of the century—and books from the 1940s. The musty mothball and old timber smell reminded me of my nana's house.

With a big flying day to Karratha ahead—I was excited to see my sister Marg, who lives there—Kim promptly picked us up at seven a.m., shuttling us to the airport for an early departure.

'Aw, not again,' I remarked as Josh looked quizzically at the flat tyre on the Jab, the same one that had gone down in Cooktown.

There was no problem getting it fixed; it was more a question of how long it would take, as we couldn't leave too late and risk running out of daylight.

Josh placed the toolbox next to the wheel. 'I guess we take this off first,' he said, tapping the top of the wheel cover.

'You need to take the inside bolts off first,' advised Michael.

Josh poked his head around the back to find the bolts, rummaged in the toolbox to find a socket, then lay down under the plane and started taking off the rear bolts, following Michael's guidance.

While Michael and Josh worked together, quickly pulling off the wheel spat and bolts, Bob found two empty 44-gallon drums, a block of wood and, with Linda's now-worn yoga mat, the plane was jacked up.

Fortunately, Kim hadn't left for Broome yet and was glad to drive Bob into town, where Bridgestone Service Centre expedited the job to minimise our delay.

With the tyre fixed and planes packed we had a special team briefing: today was Bob's seventieth birthday—not a bad effort for someone his age to be flying around Australia. 'Here Bob, happy birthday,' Gordon said, handing him a present: a stubby-holder containing a can of beer with a tag attached to the ring-pull that read, *Remove before flight*. It's an in-joke for pilots.

'I might fly better with this,' he commented with a chuckle.

'Happy birthday, Bob,' said Linda, then gave him a kiss on the cheek and handed him a card.

'What's this?' he asked.

'Michael's going to get a haircut in Karratha,' I said with a smirk.

He laughed as a nose-ring slid out of the card. 'Not a chance!' he replied, holding it up to his nose.

Throughout the trip, Bob had been stirring Michael to get a haircut and said that if he did, he would get a nose-ring.

Although we were two and a half hours late, we were in the air by eleven a.m., giving us enough time to get to Karratha well before last light, providing there wasn't a headwind.

As my plane climbed over the bay, I peered down to glimpse the mudflats that stretched out a long way with the low tide. I'd been anticipating seeing the huge tides that occur in this part of the world. If we'd been able to follow the Kalumburu route, we would have flown over the Horizontal Waterfall north of Derby that offers an impressive demonstration of these tides. From the air, the massive amount of water rushing from a lagoon through a small gap between two land masses makes it look like a waterfall—but it is horizontal. I was disappointed not to see it—for another adventure, perhaps.

Heading past Broome, the Indian Ocean looked like it was filled with Harpic toilet-cleaner; the iridescent blue against the white beaches was quite breathtaking.

Arriving at Port Hedland, our refuel and lunch stop, three hours later took me back twenty-three years. I had flown into Port Hedland on a commercial flight two years after my accident to visit Marg and John, who'd been living there; I'd had to get out of the plane on a pallet using a fork-lift. The pallet itself wasn't so bad, but looking down without side-rails one storey up made me a little uncomfortable as the fork-lift jerked and rocked while it backed away from the plane. At the time, I'd never imagined in my wildest dreams that I would eventually pilot my own plane, let alone fly into Port Hedland.

Now pushing daylight, we had a quick lunch at the Port Hedland international terminal building before heading off. I expected I'd be sick of sandwiches by then, but with Josh's creativity—which grew weirder by the day—I never knew what I would get. The most bizarre was grapes with cheese, but funnily enough, it tasted pretty good. The most important consideration was to avoid anything that would make the bread go soggy, as Josh and Michael often made the sandwiches either in the morning or the night before.

Departing just after 3.30 p.m. was the latest we'd ever started our last leg for the day, but it was only around one hour of flying from Port Hedland to Karratha.

It was a magical time to fly, floating down the coast on silky smooth air, the softer light drawing purples, oranges and reds out of the landscape, with shadows reaching from the hills as two gold spheres converged on the mirrored ocean.

We'd originally planned to land at Roebourne, 20 NM from Karratha. But when I'd called in the morning to check the condition of the strip, I was told that it was now restricted as it had been taken over by a skydiving company. This was news to me as I'd confirmed our arrival a few months before. With no other options, Michael chatted with the air-traffic controllers at Karratha airport and gained permission for me to fly, in-company again, so we could land there. All the air-traffic controllers we'd come across on the flight had been tremendously accommodating, allowing us to come in with just a phone call. This made the flight so much easier and took the pressure off me when it really mattered. A very big thanks to them.

Although it was a change to our plan, it turned out to be a blessing as there was available fuel and Marg and John didn't have to travel to pick us up. I'd always been a little uncomfortable about leaving our planes unattended at Roebourne, as a few people had told me, 'You won't have much of a plane left when you get back!' Apparently, there was a high crime rate.

Karratha's operations manager had told me, 'Karratha is the third-busiest airport in Australia'—and he wasn't wrong. Listening on the radio, I discovered that many aircraft were at different stages of approach and departure, and I sensed the tension in the air-traffic controller's voice as he shuffled the incoming traffic—737 passenger jets, helicopters and us. It seemed to take forever to get on the ground as we had to do huge circuits, flying to each turning point the air-traffic controller instructed as the light began to fade.

With the planes tied down and our luggage on a trolley, we met Marg and John outside the security fence. 'You made it, well done to you all!' congratulated Marg as I introduced the team.

'We thought you might get stuck up north, Davo,' John remarked.

'We probably would have if we hadn't gone to Halls Creek,' I answered.

'Good decision. The storms in that area can be pretty big. A few planes have come to grief in those parts,' he commented, diminishing my regret.

Marg had arranged all our accommodation. Linda, Josh and I would stay at their place with Erin, my eighteen-year-old niece. Gordon and Paul were with Phil and Michelle, friends of Marg's; while Bob and Michael stayed at the Bay Village workers' accommodation, which offered a nice discount. The staff at Marg's workplace, Karratha Glass Service, had donated $200 to help cover our remaining accommodation costs.

After settling in, we met at Marg's place for a barbeque and celebrated Bob's birthday. He looked very dapper in his dark-grey pressed suit that he'd carefully carted all the way around the country, and beamed as Marg brought out a chocolate cake she'd made. 'How about a poem, Bob?' Linda said.

Of course, the bush poet couldn't help himself. 'Yeah, righto,' he responded, thinking for a moment before clearing his throat.

'Up, up in the air with a wing and a chair
From Derby to Karratha, a great trip I did share
When we finally land the place will hum
'Cos in the back of the plane is a bottle of rum
There'll be food and wine, we will stay up late
Not every day you turn forty-eight!'

It was such a fun night, and being with family, with Marg taking care of everything, allowed me and Linda to really relax. After a couple of wines, we could hardly keep our eyes open so went to bed early. As for the rest of the team—some had a pretty big night.

Flying time: 4.6 hours.

It was another rest day so Josh foraged for tomorrow's lunch in Karratha while Gordon, Paul, Michael and Bob played with the planes and couldn't turn down another chance to visit the airport control tower.

On what felt like a special occasion, Linda and I borrowed Marg's car and looked around town. Apart from Darwin, we'd never had the opportunity to see anything together in the towns we'd visited so, on Marg's recommendation, we went to the shopping centre, relishing the opportunity to be alone and to simply enjoy a good coffee at a café. I was pleasantly surprised to get a coffee that rivalled one of Melbourne's—I am a coffee snob!

On the way back, we dropped into the chemist to fill a script that Dr Tom, our team's base doctor, had sent through for me. To my surprise, the pharmacy staff had heard of our flight, but what blew me away was news of actor Samuel Johnson. He'd recently passed through town on his epic trip riding a unicycle around Australia to raise money for breast cancer. He finished the ride in February the following year (2014)—such an impressive feat; it's a hell of a long way.

When we got back, my only scheduled appointment was an interview with Gautam Lewis. He was the founder of UK-based Freedom in the Air, an organisation that supports people with disabilities to learn to fly. There was, and is, a lot going on in the UK and Europe, compared to Australia, for people with physical disabilities. There are clubs with planes fitted with hand-controls that are available for hire and instructors offering tuition, making flying much more accessible.

In Australia, apart from Wheelies with Wings, which provides flying scholarships for people with physical disabilities, there is little else, which is unfortunate. It is usually cost-prohibitive for many people to get into flying, as it is expensive to buy and modify a plane, let alone find and pay for an instructor.

Linda was having withdrawal symptoms from Zeus, our Border Collie, so Dexter, Marg and John's dog, received heaps of attention. And Marg made her famous lasagna, which is definitely the best on the western seaboard, if not Australia. Spending time with family in their home was a welcome change from motels; it would have been nice to spend longer with them.

The rest in Darwin had been a much-needed recharge for everyone. Coupled with knowing we'd broken the back of the flight, and with good weather forecasts down the west coast promising easy and enjoyable flying, the team exuded more confidence and enthusiasm as we embarked on the next leg.

With 27 days down and only six more flying days to go, providing we weren't delayed, the team was eager to get moving. We were another step closer to getting this mission done and dusted.

Each morning was a new start with a new goal to work towards—reaching that day's destination. To achieve this flight—daunting when contemplated—we had to break down the huge goal into smaller, more achievable ones. It was a matter of taking one step at a time and sticking at it. This was how I'd lived my life since the accident—setting one small goal, working towards it, achieving it, and then setting the next one, each time progressing to a more ambitious goal.

The boys' eyes lit up when Michael opened the present Marg gave the team—a Texas Hold'em card-game kit. 'Now you can play properly and don't have to use M&M's,' she said—the lollies used as gambling chips never lasted the duration of the game. The game would get a lot of use over the next week or so.

The logistics of transporting our luggage to the planes parked a good distance from the entry at Karratha airport would be tricky. But then we received an email from Andrew Gray and Michael Ardagh from Karratha Flying Services (KFS), who helped us get our luggage through the gates and to our planes, making our lives a lot easier. They also provided OWC with a generous $500 donation.

Fuel was unavailable between Karratha and Carnarvon, our next overnight stop. Although I could have made it on one tank, I would've got low and didn't want to take unnecessary risks as anything could happen—such as changed weather or having to divert due to an airfield closing. For minimal inconvenience and peace of mind, I strapped two 20 L jerry-cans into the passenger seat for the trip to Onslow, where I planned to top up my tanks.

Before take-off, I chatted to the very helpful air-traffic controller to clarify the departure procedure—the calls to make and position reports—which was straightforward.

With a stiff breeze blowing down the huge runway, lifting off was within meters, which the air-traffic controllers weren't used to as

Spectacular rivers on a barren canvas resembling vines or trees: the deep green trunks snaking into the distance, estuaries shooting off like branches, mangroves for leaves. South of Weipa, Qld. *Photo: Linda Sands*

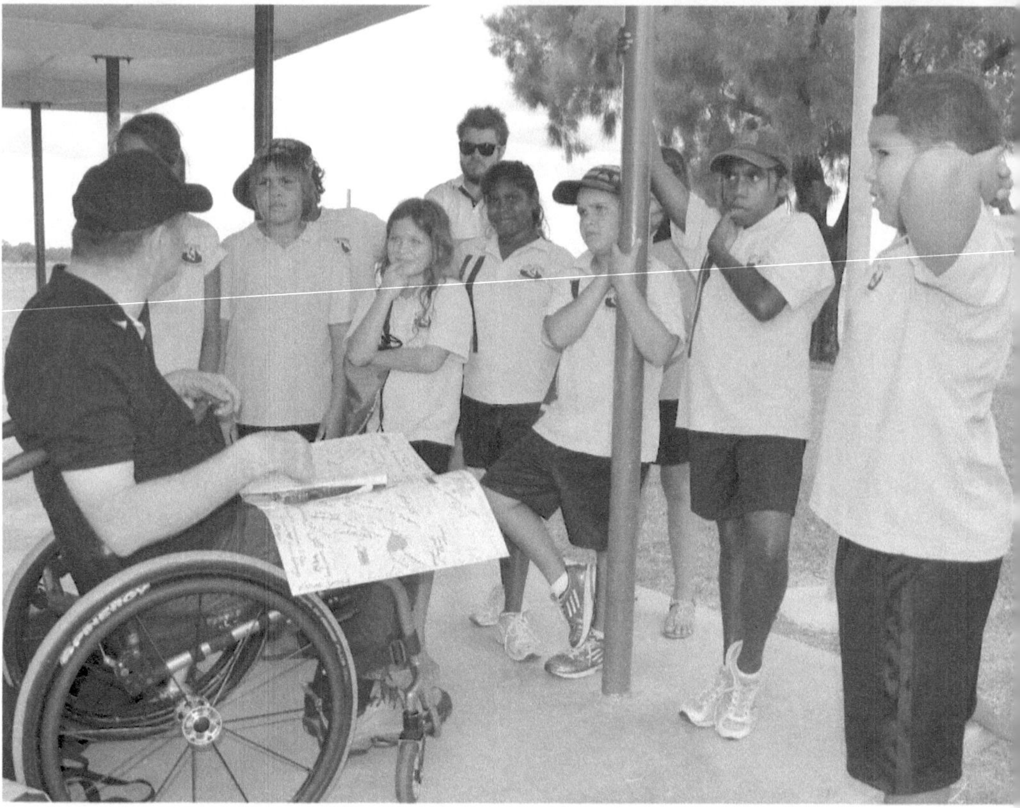

A highlight of our journey was meeting the Burketown State School kids. They showed an infectious joy and I felt privileged to receive gifts of chocolate biscuits, wonderful drawings and messages of support. *Photo: Linda Sands*

Above: Our rooms in Arnhem Village workers accommodation in Nhulunbuy, NT. We had great wheelchair-accessible rooms. *Photo: Gordon McCaw*

Left: One of the awesome pictures drawn by the Burketown State School kids. *Photo: Linda Sands*

The endless coastline of mangroves and mudflats stretched into the distance towards Borroloola, NT.

Enjoying our first rest day in Darwin, joined by our new member Josh, with Bob, Linda, Michael and myself. We relaxed in the afternoon heat at an outside bar drinking cold beer, eating tapas and telling tall stories.

We had begun our second part of the epic flight landing at Kununurra, WA. We were met by Tony Stevenson (right) and Graham Sears (middle) from DFES who generously helped us out during our stay. *Photo: Linda Sands*

It was a blessing in disguise having to divert inland to avoid dodgy weather. We got to experience the magnificent beauty of the Kimberley. *Photo: Linda Sands*

Above: Bob's birthday present opening ceremony before we headed off from Derby and onto Karratha, WA. *Photo: Linda Sands*

Left: Kim Maldon from DFES picked us up from the airport and prepared a delicious feast for the hungry team in Derby, WA. *Photo: Linda Sands*

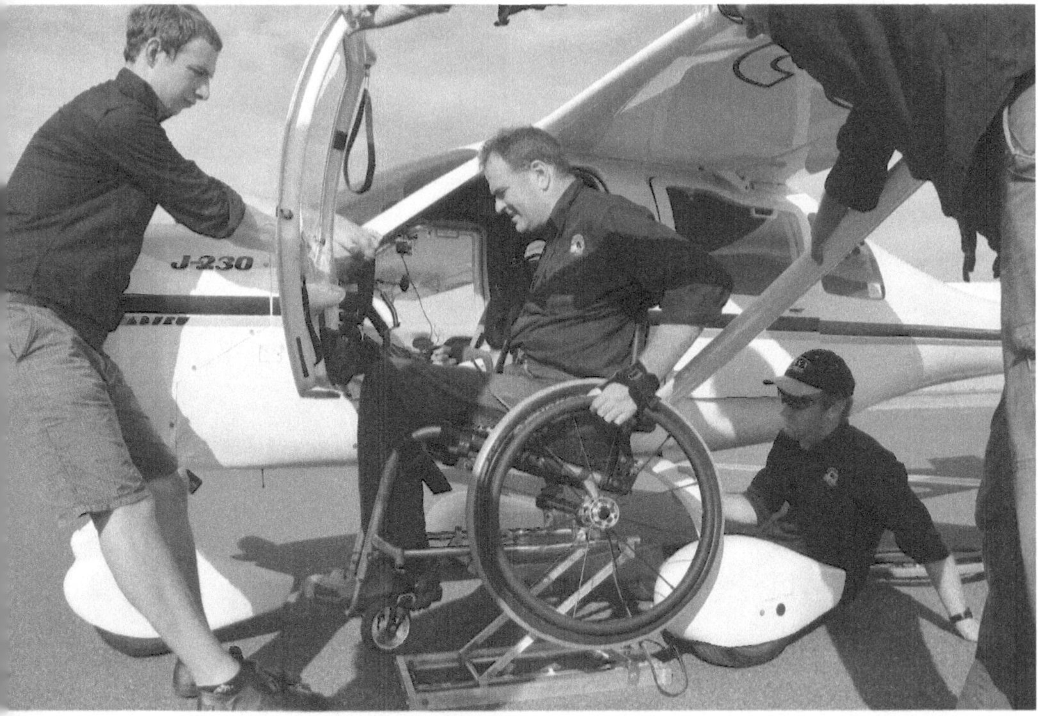

A team effort loading and unloading me from the plane. *Photo: Linda Sands*

Flying down the coast of Western Australia, somewhere between Broome and Port Hedland. The Indian Ocean's iridescent blue was breathtaking.

It was great to catch up with my sister Marg and partner John in Karratha, WA. *Photo: Linda Sands*

Marg made Bob a chocolate cake to celebrate his 70th birthday. *Photo: Linda Sands*

The rugged coast and salt stockpiles north of Carnarvon, WA.
Photo: Linda Sands

Day 28 we crossed our fourth and final milestone, Australia's most westerly point, Steep Point, WA. *Photo: Linda Sands*

I began to sweat and feel a little unwell as I tracked along the cliffs and barren landscape that stretched into the distance towards Geraldton, WA.

The boys' smiles say it all after Denise Bess, captain of the Midwest Aeroclub, took them up for some aerobatic manoeuvres in her Super Decathlon.
Photo: Linda Sands

I felt like a RAAF Roulette leading the two Moonie aircraft towards Fremantle. *Photo: Gordon McCaw*

Passing Fremantle docks heading towards our overnight stop at Mandurah, south of Perth.

The vibrant green landscape at Albany, WA, was a dramatic contrast with the dry west coast.
Photo: Linda Sands

Gordon takes cover under my wing as we wait for the rain to pass over Esperance airport.
Photo: Linda Sands

Moisture in my GoPro gave the cliffs along the Great Australia Bight a hazy Doris Day look.

Nullarbor Hotel, SA, with its long orange dirt airstrip on the remote and sparse Nullarbor plain. *Photo: Linda Sands*

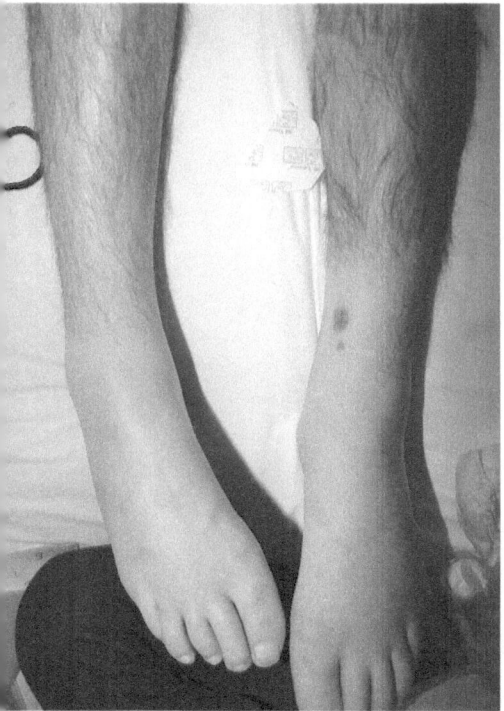

The nasty red burn on my leg took seven months to heal. *Photo: Linda Sands*

Postie man riding through the puddle at Caiguna Roadhouse airstrip testing the surface. *Photo: Linda Sands*

We had become confident, seasoned adventurers. About to head off from the Nullarbor Hotel to Port Lincoln, SA. *Photo: Linda Sands*

Mick Hart off my left wing escorting me into Port Lincoln, SA.

Mick Hart's incredible Barnstormers Inn, full of boys' toys.
Photo: Linda Sands

Another delay, the blanket of fog wouldn't let us out over the hills, having to spend another night at Aldinga, SA. *Photo: Linda Sands*

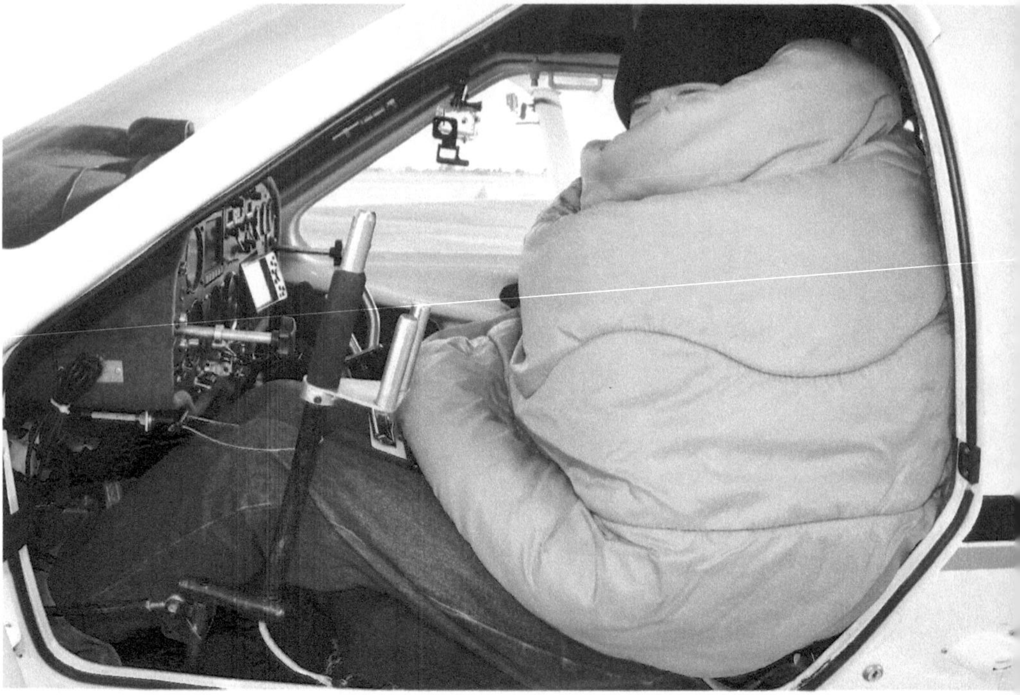

Wrapped up in Michael's sleeping bag to keep me warm from the bitter cold, we waited and hoped for the wall of fog to lift at Kingston SE.
Photo: Linda Sands

Day 38, we finally made it back to Tooradin. We were greeted by friends and family and a lot of yellow balloons.

Arriving home, I felt a little overwhelmed with all our supporters and the media. *Photo: Linda Sands*

Above: I was so happy to have completed my ultimate goal and flown solo around Australia. *Photo: Rudy Van Donkelaar*

Left: Brian and Roberta (Dad and Mum) our incredible Base Support who were relieved to have us home. *Photo: Linda Sands*

It was a tremendous achievement for the team and I felt honoured to have experienced it with them.

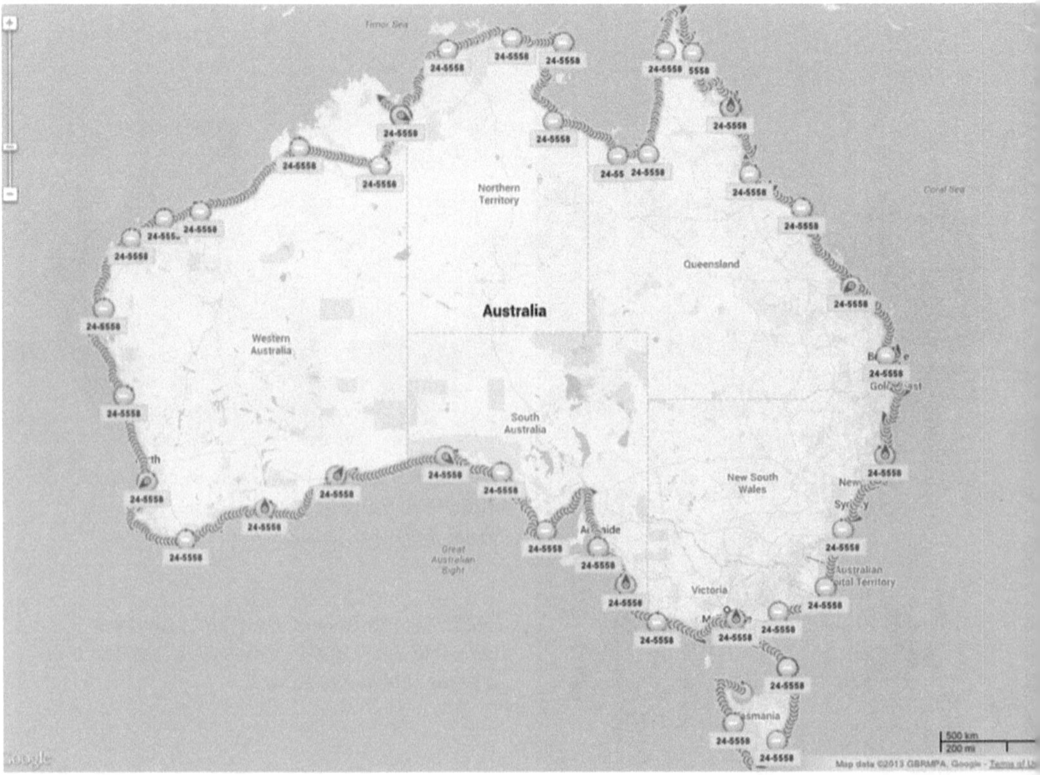

Spidertracks completed flight track around Australia.

jets take up most of the bitumen. I turned right and headed down the coast toward Onslow. Climbing to 2500 feet, the air smoothed out and I found a nice 20-knot tailwind and made good time.

Onslow was easy to spot with piles of white salt emerging against the orange landscape. There wasn't much there apart from a couple of site-sheds joined by a large semicircle structure with shade-sail over the top; this was the terminal building. Adjacent was a family living in a caravan, two young kids running around in shorts, barefooted, faces grimy with dirt.

'What'd you put in the wrap, Josh, it tastes strange?' I queried. I was a little worried about the answer, as he and Michael had been drinking when making lunch the night before.

'I think it's pesto,' he said uncertainly.

Drawing on his hiking adventures, Josh bought instant noodles with dried fragments of multicoloured MSG to accompany our sandwiches; it too became a staple.

Bob emptied the two jerries into my wing tanks and we got going again not long after noon, heading for Carnarvon.

I fly around 215km/hr (115 knots air speed), and within an hour or so as I headed south along the coast the landscape transformed surprisingly quickly from multicoloured reds, browns and greens to steep rugged cliffs rising from the sea—a natural barricade to potential invaders.

'I can't guarantee we'll be there at three, but we'll do our best,' I heard Linda say as I opened the door to my plane at Carnarvon airport. She was talking to our contact south of Perth where we were to stop the following day for two nights. The person had generously offered to cover some accommodation costs, provide discounted fuel, organise transport, and introduce some local dignitaries when we arrived, amongst other things.

However, our contact was insistent that we arrive by three p.m.—which wasn't possible—and wouldn't accept our realistic estimate of between 3.30 and 4.30 p.m.

'If you leave earlier, you can make it by three p.m.,' came the suggestion.

'No, we can't. Dave already gets up at four a.m. We can't get there any earlier.'

Back and forth the argument went. In the end, he was just too unreasonable, unwilling to consider our challenges, so with no choice, Linda told him to cancel everything.

Throughout the journey, this was the only time we'd come across anyone who was difficult or put demands on us, especially ones we couldn't meet. The rest of the time we received only the utmost support from people who were willing to help us out any way they could.

Each time we stopped overnight there was someone to help us—like the Caboolture Rotary Club who provided a house, cars and a fridge full of food; the team lunch in Weipa provided by Snoddy's wife; Andrew Daken, the pilot who offered a bed at Groote Eylandt; and even a stranger in Derby who offered us their car. Later in the flight, in Perth, Adrian Van Schouwen, a CFI from Cloud Dancer Sport Aircraft, helped me after I told him I couldn't get to Jandakot airport, 60 kilometres from our accommodation, to pick up a spare tyre, tubes and oil for the Jab.

'Where are you staying?' he asked.

'Mandurah.'

'Leave it with me. I will get it to you today,' he answered.

He didn't know me from a bar of soap, but he caught a train and dropped the parts at his parents' place, who then dropped them off at our motel.

Those people and many others strengthened my belief that there are a lot of kind and generous people in this world willing to help someone if they can. It was those people who helped make the OWC flight viable.

A young reporter strutted across the tarmac at Canarvon airport dressed in a frock and heels better suited to the Melbourne Cup. 'I was at another function and heard you'd arrived, so I came down as quickly as I could,' she said, tinkering with her camera.

Following a short interview and photos for a story in the local paper, we were again met by DFES, who helped us out: Tim Dalwood had organised everything. Gary and Nita, retiree SES members, provided transport and the Fascine Lodge offered three rooms free of charge. All we needed was the pub.

Flying time: 3.4 hours.

29

HOMEWARD BOUND

Day 28 would be a long but monumental day, presenting our fourth and last milestone: Steep Point, the westernmost point of Australia. This thought made it much easier to drag myself out of bed at four a.m.

Although the conditions were perfect, I was in the habit of getting Josh to secure my feet with the bungee straps. 'Make sure the metal hooks aren't against my skin,' I warned. I didn't want to risk getting pressure sores.

We were excited to be crossing Steep Point that morning; the first three milestones—South East Cape, Cape Byron and Cape York—seemed so long ago. Each day blurred into the last; I could barely remember what had happened a week ago, let alone a month.

Turning right at Long Point, tracking west over the bay, I felt so much more relaxed over water, having spent most of my time off the coast; the engine hadn't missed a beat. Passing Monkey Mia, a favourite tourist destination for swimming with the dolphins, the desolate Steep Point came into view.

From my vantage point, the little outcrop of land extending from the mainland resembled an arthritic finger. There were cliffs on all sides, small bushes attempted to cover the sandy earth and 4WD tracks wove across the landscape like veins in a leaf. The lone white light beacon stared out at the empty ocean.

'Done it!' I said aloud as I crossed the tip. It was a euphoric moment: a mixture of excitement, team pride and satisfaction that we'd accomplished it. I think it felt extra special because we were now on our way home.

As I orbited this remote point at 1000 feet, the air was smooth enough for me to snap a few photos and videos on my GoPros. As with every other milestone, the Lance got into position and Linda took some great shots of me rounding the tip.

Over the radio Simon and Garfunkel's 'Homeward Bound' filled my headset; Paul was transmitting it from the Archer on our chat channel. It was the perfect song for the moment, giving me goose bumps. As I followed the coast south to Geraldton, our lunch stop, I sang along to the chorus, so happy to be heading for home.

It was only one hour into the flight but for some reason I was starting to sweat, which meant I was dysreflexing. As I'm unable to feel pain on most parts of my body, I usually go through a process of elimination to work out the problem. I had peed recently so a full bladder wasn't the issue, I'd had a crap that morning so that was out, and my feet and legs seemed in the correct position. The only thing I could think of was my bum, which was a little sore but nothing unusual. My bum was usually fine for up to three hours sitting in the plane, but at times it would hurt for no reason, like now—a sort of phantom pain. Without another obvious cause, it seemed to be the likely explanation for my profuse sweating, which was getting worse. I couldn't do anything about it at 3500 feet with an hour and a half to Geraldton; I just had to put up with it.

South of Kalbarri, the isolated landscape began to change. Touches of civilisation marked by square fenced-off paddocks became more frequent, and many more tracks crisscrossed the landscape. Geraldton looked so green compared to the dry low bush landscape further north; from the air it appeared to be a neat and ordered town, the long wharf stretching out to the ocean.

When I landed I felt exhausted, my bum was sore and my whole body just didn't feel right. I hoped that a good break over lunch might sort me out.

Donna, an old friend from Melbourne, was waiting at the terminal gate. Even after so many years, she hadn't changed. Donna and her family had been following our journey on Facebook and had come down to the airfield when Linda posted our arrival time. Although it was a brief catch-up, it was special to see her and meet her family. I felt a bit like a celebrity with the girls wanting a photo of me and the plane.

Denise Bess, captain of the Midwest Aeroclub, had also been following our journey and made us very welcome in the club rooms, offering drinks and a place to relax for lunch. Denise was middle-aged, friendly, down-to-earth and very passionate about flying—which wasn't surprising given she was a competition aerobatic pilot in her Super Decathlon.

When she offered to take up Paul, Michael and Josh for a few loops and spins, they jumped at the chance. Denise took each of them up individually, giving them an aerobatic equivalent of a hamburger with the lot including pineapple and beetroot—she didn't hold back. There was no need to watch; the changing sounds of the engine revving high on the descents through to a flattening growl on the climbs told the story.

When they emerged from the back seat, Paul and Michael were beaming from ear to ear. I'd never seen such smiles from them before, and I think Michael was in love. But when Josh slithered from the back seat, he looked shaky and a little *green*, immediately lying on the tarmac for a few minutes.

'Are you OK, Josh?' I asked.

'Yeah fine, I just need a few minutes,' he said, then jumped up and ran to the rear of the building. I guess his sandwich didn't agree with him.

I still felt ordinary, and with time getting on we headed to Mandurah, our two-night stay. This final leg was only two hours in easy flying conditions with a good tailwind. As we flew further down the coast from Geraldton, white beaches stretched into the distance and evidence of civilisation increased. Bitumen roads with cars came into view and small towns and cleared farmland expanded into the distance. The sight seemed foreign given we'd seen nothing but remote and mostly untouched landscape since the east coast.

Luck was on our side: the restricted airspace along the coast to Perth had been de-activated, which made it easier to fly coastal all the way along the seaside suburbs of the city and down past Fremantle. I had been looking forward to this; it was going to be spectacular.

The faint city monoliths stood tall in the distance with sprawling suburbs radiating outwards. I remember thinking, *We are actually in Perth*. It didn't seem real, as it had been but a thought in my mind for the last six years.

Reaching Burns Beach, a suburb north of Perth, two Moonie aircraft flown by members of the Royal Aeroclub of Western Australia came out to meet us. After a few position calls, they spotted me, turned around and radioed, 'Keep it level and straight, Dave, we're coming up from behind.' It was really cool being the lead aircraft, with a plane on my left and right wings. They were formation flyers so they knew what they were doing, even if I didn't. I felt like an RAAF Roulette as we passed over the shipping docks at the mouth of the Swan River in Fremantle at 1000 feet; then they broke off and blasted ahead of me 10 miles from Murray Field airfield.

Touching down just after four p.m., I was low on blood sugar and felt a little weak. Linda grabbed some chocolate from my survival kit and shoved it in my mouth, whereupon I devoured it quicker than our dog Zeus eating his dinner, almost swallowing it whole. After the obligatory interview with a local journalist, I met a few of the aeroclub members who'd waited around for a chat.

Before the flight I'd been in contact with a distant relative, Robyn Jacka Hunt. She'd offered the team accommodation at her vineyard but I'd declined it, assuming our lodgings would be provided—which turned out not to be the case. Robyn was lovely, reminding me of an energetic socialite, and willing to help with anything. As always, I was disappointed not to have more time to chat with her.

Before leaving she gave me a gift, a book called *Hard Jacka* by Michael Lawriwsky. In it she'd inscribed: *You are living proof that Jacka men are trailblazers.* It struck a chord with me then, and still does.

The subject of the book, Albert Jacka, was my grandfather's cousin on my dad's side. He was the first Australian VC (Victoria Cross) recipient of WWI at Gallipoli, then received an MC (Military Cross) with a bar on the Western Front. Many people who served under him, as well as historians, say he should have received another VC for his gallant efforts in France. He was a man of selfless heroism and bravery, a great leader who stood up for what he believed in. Men lined up to be in Jacka's mob, and would willingly go into battle with him. After the war, he kept fighting for those who had served, especially during the depression when many were unemployed.

When he died in 1932 at the age of thirty-nine from kidney disease, more than 6000 people filed past his coffin as it lay in state and his funeral procession, flanked by thousands of onlookers, was led by over 1000 returned soldiers. There are very few people today who would command this type of respect, certainly not our current world leaders.

Since completing an assignment on 'Bert' in Year Nine, I'd always admired his traits. Especially salient for me was his leadership, his compassion and his example. He inspired those around him to do their best and even be willing make the ultimate sacrifice. I admired his courage and his steadfastness; often he butted heads with generals when holding to his convictions.

I was deeply moved by Robyn's message, and hoped I shared some of Bert's qualities.

Flying time: 5.3 hours.

30

WE'RE GOING COASTAL

I still felt a little off when I went to bed, as did Josh after his aerobatic adventure—he couldn't stomach the Chinese food we had for dinner. As Linda peeled off my pants that night, to my horror a red burn wound the size of a 10-cent piece just above my left ankle declared itself. The mystery of my sweats was thereby revealed; it looked nasty.

When Josh had fastened the bungee straps around my ankles, one of the metal hooks might have pressed against my skin, or had moved during flight and, without feeling, I was unaware. It had been a cool morning so I put the heater on, which blew hot air off the engine onto my feet, heating the metal hook like a branding iron. Put simply, the small spot on my ankle was effectively slow-roasted for three hours, resulting in a deep third-degree burn which would take seven months to heal.

As with all incidents, I took a lesson from it and from then on I placed a hand towel around my ankles.

'You sound pretty sexy, Dave,' said Linda as I croakily completed my fourth podcast with *Plane Crazy Down Under*. I certainly didn't feel sexy; I was tired and felt very ordinary.

Fortunately, the days were getting easier. Being better organised, we were getting more sleep, often in bed by ten p.m.

The rest day was again a very busy one. I tried to rest and keep warm while catching up on a few things, and Linda spent most of the day on the phone organising the days ahead. Without transport, Josh hired a car for the day so Bob, Josh, Michael and Paul headed to the airfield to service my plane for the last time, refuel it and shop for food and other supplies.

At that night's team meeting we expressed concern about the weather. This southern part of Australia, the Great Australian Bight, was always going to be a challenge and it seemed it wouldn't disappoint. A series of cold fronts were lined up, including one coming through that night. These would likely bring showers and possible thunderstorms; but we'd see how it looked in the morning.

'Would you consider cutting the corner and going inland?' Michael asked.

I felt anger well up inside me when he suggested it. It wasn't directed at Michael, but the thought of even considering such a compromise when it wasn't necessary was like a dentist poking a raw nerve in a tooth.

'I'm going coastal,' I said curtly.

Inland may have avoided some of the weather but would have cut off the southwest corner of Western Australia. If we were to cut off the corner now, why not just fly straight home?

Of course, I would never endanger the team by taking an unnecessary risk, but I also wasn't going to compromise one of the goals of this flight which was to fly coastal unless it was absolutely necessary to go inland, as had been the case up north in the Kimberley.

'Looking at the charts, if we go coastal there are a lot of ALAs (aircraft landing airfields) so if the weather deteriorates, we'll have plenty of places to put down,' Paul remarked.

Paul is very practical, level-headed, and looks at things objectively, which is a great asset when making decisions, especially when emotions and personal fears are in play. All heads nodded, with some grunts of agreement.

'How about going coastal and if we can't get through, we can turn inland and avoid the weather,' I proposed.

'Sounds good,' was the consensus.

31

THE GREAT AUSTRALIAN BIGHT

Six months ago to the day, on 28 November 2012, Linda and I were in a beautiful resort in Thailand for our wedding. Today I was sitting in a dodgy motel with a shower that changed from Antarctic cold to lobster-scalding in a nano-second, depending on who turned a tap on in a unit ten doors up, and outside it was bloody cold.

With everything we'd encountered since, it was a credit to our relationship that Linda and I were still together. What helped us, I think, was that we were (and remain) like two pillars: we are separate but stand together, on the same path in life.

We each have our personal goals and aspirations that we individually work towards, but then we come together to share our experiences, offer each other support and do the things that connect us and bring us closer.

Our different interests give us the independence and space we need to be who we are, and not feel as though we are compromising our personal goals in being together. But this can also be a double-edged sword. If left unchecked we can become too focused on our personal goals and forget about nurturing the relationship, which causes us to drift apart. We try to be mindful of this.

For Linda and me, the flight had been a job. Being goal-focused helped us deal with the stresses and frustrations we experienced as we worked together; our shared priority was for the project to succeed, which minimised disagreement between us.

Further, both of us dislike confrontation. When something starts to annoy us, we'll eventually raise the issue and talk about it to resolve the problem. But sometimes the remedy is a little space, and often a walk to de-stress does the trick.

Puddles of water dotted the black tarmac. In the distance, thin, broken low-level cloud sat on the horizon, telltale remnants of the front that had passed during the night. It promised to be a good day: the amount of blue sky increased to the south where we were heading, then we'd follow the coastline east to Albany, finishing in Esperance.

With a good sleep under my belt, I was more energised and my leg hadn't gone septic. Knowing we were on the home straight, the light at the end of the tunnel was growing brighter.

It was Day 30 and if all went to plan, we'd be home in six days. This would be the longest number of days flying in a row, and some of the longest legs. There was a lot of coastline to cover in four days of flying, with a one-day stopover in Aldinga, South Australia; then one more day to reach our start-point, Tooradin. It would be a hard slog but everyone was looking forward to it.

'Weatherman?' I prompted Michael at our team briefing.

'Albany will be nice, but that front seems to be between Albany and Esperance—more towards Esperance, which explains the reduced vis (visibility) and thunderstorms and stuff. By 0600 (UTC—Coordinated Universal Time, two p.m.), which is in five hours, that front will be to the east of Esperance.'

'OK, so it will take us more than five hours, so we should be good, right?' I asked.

More grunts of agreement from the pilots.

'You going right around or cutting the corner?' Bob asked cheekily.

'Nope, right around, Bob. You're only ripping yourself off,' I shot back.

Josh split up the lunches; today it was Subway as he forgot to get to the supermarket yesterday before it closed. It was a nice change from his mystery packages that a forensic scientist would struggle to identify.

'Make sure we have them in our plane; you know how grumpy a girl can get when hungry,' Linda joked. Everyone laughed but I didn't; I knew she wasn't joking.

Tracking south left us without a tailwind, one of the few occasions during the trip. Passing Margaret River reminded me of how far I'd come since I was there last, just after rehab. I had come to Perth for a holiday in 1990 with Janine—a nurse who'd become a close friend—to forget about my abruptly altered life and do something different from the usual hospital scene. We hired a small Ford Laser without air-conditioning to save money and drove south in the stifling summer heat to visit some of the wineries at Margaret River. Drinking a few glasses of white port from Redgate Winery each evening was a wonderful and much-needed change for me.

Given the perfect weather, there was no need for the ALAs (aircraft landing airfields), but I kept track of them in case of any issues—standard practice.

Remnants of the weather front started to build as we approached Albany airfield. The landscape was so green it looked like deep-green icing on a cake with two wide licorice straps for runways. Perhaps it was so noticeable because I hadn't seen so much green for a while.

The leg had taken longer than expected and when I landed, I was hungry and cold; we were also running short on time to get to Esperance. While I did a quick interview with the local TV GWN7, the team downed the Subways and the customary Cup-A-Soups and noodles. Now well-practiced with the media—mainly because they asked the same questions: Why are you doing the flight? What is your disability? How do you fly the plane?—I gave them my well-rehearsed spiel. That night I had to laugh when I saw the segment, as most of the flying footage was taken from my videos of flying over the Flinders Ranges a couple of years ago, and not of the current flight.

'I just spoke to the forecaster and he said the front has moved past Esperance,' Michael said over lunch. 'We'll probably get a few scattered showers.' This was welcome news and would give us a relatively easy run.

But once in the air, I started to question the forecaster's information as at times I had to drop to 500 feet, my track resembling a winding river as I dodged the constant showers. This began to play on my mind as we were using up precious time needed to get to Esperance airport to refuel, then take off and head to our overnight accommodation.

'It looks pretty ordinary toward the airport,' Bob said over the radio.

I wasn't expecting this.

As the Lance flew further and approached the town, passing the remnants of the front, Bob radioed again to let us know that it was all clear to the airport. I was still 20 minutes behind, and was hoping to beat the rain-band in. I had plenty of fuel and could orbit behind the rain-band to let it pass if needed, but time was on my mind. I wanted to avoid getting delayed so decided to give it a shot.

Ten minutes later, the rain-band was dead ahead. How can I describe it? It looked really crap! In front of my windscreen was a dark-grey mass of cloud and a wall of water reaching the ground between me and the town on the east side. The water wall had now moved closer, but I was unsure how close it was to the airport.

The bright-yellow glow of the low afternoon sun reflected off the west side of the cloud, making it look like a golden pavlova, but rounding the east side it was depressingly gloomy—which was where I was heading.

Lining up the airfield on the GPS, I pushed in the throttle to get a few more revs out of the engine and waited for the last 7 NM to slowly tick down as the weather approached. I was confident I would make it.

With the wall of water only a mile or so away, I circled over the airfield to position myself to join circuit, banked the plane around, lined up the nose with the runway and smoothly touched down. As I backtracked the runway to the parking area, the cascade of water enveloped me; it was like stepping into another world through the Stargate.

David Ford, whose place we were staying at that night, and a few Esperance Aeroclub members ran over in the rain to say 'Hi.' I sat in the cockpit chatting while the rain bucketed down, Gordon huddling under the wing to avoid most of it. As quickly as it came it passed, leaving a spectacular double rainbow glowing brightly against the dark backdrop. It was a really beautiful moment.

'What a small world,' I thought as I glanced out my window and recognised a face I'd never expected to see out there. Joe, a former colleague at Melbourne Water, was walking over with a mate in a wheelchair. After the 'What the hell are you doing here?' chat and introductions of the team, I realised they'd been waiting in the cold for quite a while just to meet me. I felt bad that I couldn't talk longer as we were now really pushed for time to refuel, get going and then land before running out of daylight.

To the west the setting sun glistened on the wet tarmac; to the southeast the black clouds slowly moved away. I wished I could have sat and absorbed the moment for a little longer, but we had to leave for David Ford's property 8 NM to the southeast, to land on an unsealed red gravel strip that crossed into his neighbour's property.

Andy Burns generously donated the Avgas (aviation fuel) for all three planes, and once refuelled we quickly got going, following David Ford in his Cessna.

Being unfamiliar with the area, I put the coordinates of the airfield in my GPS and followed the distant strobe-light on the tail of David's plane. David gave his call to turn base; I looked down but for the life of me I couldn't see the strip; it was all dark. Following the flashing beacon, I kept my eyes on it as it turned final and then, drawing an imaginary line ahead of the aircraft, I finally located the airstrip, a slightly different-coloured dark shape below.

Turning onto final, the setting sun in my face made it difficult to see ahead and judge the distance to the ground. The only sign of the strip was a break in the line of trees, and by looking out my left window I could just make out my height. When I was at an estimated few feet from the ground, I pulled off the power and dropped onto the deck, feeling relieved to be on the ground. The Archer came in next, then the Lance.

Taxiing to the huge hangar, I berated myself. Although it wasn't yet last light, we were landing late at an unfamiliar airfield and in the direction of the setting sun, which made it very hard to see. These were rookie mistakes that we'd been warned about in training, and I was making them; I should have known better. If we'd been a little later, and didn't have David to follow in, the outcome could have been very different.

David and Jen Ford's place was wonderfully spacious, to say the least. The house was effectively a big shed: high ceilings, open-plan areas with big windows and polished concrete floors; it had the feel of a luxury house. David had a degenerative physical disability, and although he could walk at the time, the house had been future-proofed and was wheelchair accessible.

Jen hosted a great dinner and a few of the aeroclub members joined us. It was so nice to meet some of the locals over a glass of red before turning to our night's work.

Flying time: 5.7 hours.

As the first rays of the rising sun beamed through the bedroom window, I felt hopeful that we'd have an easy flying day with good weather. It was to be five hours in the air and we needed to leave early. Not only was it a long day, but we'd also lose 1.5 hours when we entered South Australia.

The forecast looked pretty good, just some cloud off the coast with thunderstorms. We were confident the light northwesterly would keep the bad weather south of us; although, during breakfast, the morning fog started to roll in and our departure time of seven a.m. began to look shaky.

During my usual aircraft check, I noticed a bolt was missing on the wheel cover. Not that this was a critical piece of equipment, but it was best not to have anything loose during flight as it could potentially cause damage. But just at that moment Dave Wohling landed in his cool red and white RV 6, and surprisingly had an assortment of bolts on board, including one that fitted.

When the sun broke through, the fog slowly lifted, exposing an entirely different view from the previous evening. We managed to get in the air at eight a.m.

The clear skies at Esperance soon turned cloudy and I was forced to drop from 3500 feet to only 1500 feet as the sheer cliffs of the Great Australian Bight came into view. The photographs I had seen never quite captured the immense beauty of this coastline, with the deep-green Southern Ocean slapping at the base of the vertical cliff faces, slowly eroding them over the millennia. It was indeed spectacular, and I felt privileged to view the sight as I flew past. I tried to capture the moment with the GoPro on the wing, but annoyingly it was full of moisture and gave the photo a hazy Doris

Day look.

Caiguna Roadhouse was the only place we could get fuel on our way to the Nullarbor Hotel, our overnight stop. Before we left Esperance, I called the roadhouse to check the condition of the strip. In her nasal outback drawl, a woman said, 'A bloke landed a few days ago, said it was a bit soft … Oh yeah, it's got a big puddle in the middle.'

'Oh, a big puddle. How big is the puddle?' I asked.

'Aww … not that big, maybe a quarter way across. We haven't had any rain for a few days, so it should be better than when he flew in.'

The soggy strip was a bit of a worry, in particular for the Lance, which was much heavier than the Archer or my plane, but we didn't have any other options for fuel—this was it.

The Lance arrived first, Michael doing a few low passes for a closer look, but he was apprehensive about going in first. Gordon and Paul in the Archer arrived next, checked it out and decided that it looked OK to land. They touched down with no problems, landing to the left to avoid the puddle in the middle. Being the lightest, my aircraft also had no issues.

The Lance continued to circle above. Gordon and I radioed Michael confirming that the surface was good and if he went left of the puddle he'd be okay, but he was still concerned about giving it a go.

When the Archer and I pulled up at the fuel bowser, it looked like a scene from the film *Priscilla Queen of the Desert*. An old bus sat in the dusty landscape, then a dishevelled guy on an old, iconic red 80cc postie bike arrived; he was a local pilot.

After giving him a rundown of the situation, he said, 'The strip should be fine but I can take a look at the condition if you like.'

'Yeah, that'd be great,' we replied, and he rode off at full throttle, kicking up dust as he headed down the dirt track.

Postie man rode up and down the dirt runway and through the puddle a number of times before returning to us. 'The surface is good. If your mate goes left of the puddle, there won't be a problem,' he said.

Gordon relayed the message to the Lance and Michael turned the aircraft onto final approach. On his last radio call before landing he said, 'Full stop, maybe!' It was one of Michael's most impressive landings. Nothing like a little bit of pressure to bring out the best.

With a quick lunch, refuel and no problem taking off, we headed to our overnight stop following the Eyre Highway. The cloud soon disappeared and for a change I decided to climb to my highest flight level, 5500 feet, for the entire journey. I found a nice 15-knot tailwind, sat back, relaxed and enjoyed the scenery of sorts.

The Nullarbor Plain is very flat and there isn't much out there except for the low-lying salt bush which looked relatively green from the air. At ground level though, it resembles a desert. As the name suggests—Nulla-arbor = no tree—there are no trees.

Along the Eyre Highway there is nothing. The highway continues in a straight line into the horizon, seemingly forever. The section between Balladonia and Caiguna includes the longest straight stretch of tarred road in Australia and one of the longest in the world at 146.6 kilometres. It's signposted as the '90 Mile Straight.'

As I contemplated the remoteness of the area, and why anyone would want to live out here, a small settlement came into view, standing out like the Dalai Lama at a Chinese Communist Party convention. It was the long orange dirt airstrip of the Nullarbor Hotel.

Staying at the hotel was another highlight of the journey. The novelty of parking our planes at the back of our hotel rooms was pretty cool—well, for the pilots at least! The only other place I'd done this was in central Australia in 2010 when I flew up as a training run to prepare for the around-Australia flight. I landed at the historic Noccundra Hotel in Queensland, the last remnant of the township, taxied to the front door, went inside for a beer and stayed the night in a donga (a basic shed).

As the door of the plane swung open, a gust of wind delivered a face full of dust and a horde of ferocious flies dug into my ears, nose, mouth and eyes; it was horrible! The flies in the city are far more courteous.

Nothing was wheelchair accessible, but with only one step into the hotel room and a wide shower, it was fine. The room was basic—worn '80s décor and a musty smell—but it was clean and the hot high-pressure shower that could have stripped paint was heaven.

With another day down and another day closer to home, the team headed to the bar for a few beers. Josh, Michael and Paul had made themselves comfortable at the pool table, starting a play-off to see who'd be the next OWC champion.

Flying time: 5.4 hours.

I was invigorated by the crisp desert air seeping through my fleecy jumper and onto my shoulders. A gentle calm filled my body as the morning's orange and gold glow penetrated the blackness and distant clouds hovered on the edge of the horizon. It was wonderful to sit and enjoy the moment without having to rush to the airport.

'Your bacon and egg toasted sandwich is ready,' Linda called from the room a few metres away.

I couldn't help smiling. Ah, the start of a perfect morning!

I felt energised, a welcome change from my usual tiredness, and free of the effort of coordinating the team. I was also flying fit, accustomed to the daily routine. The early mornings, minimal sleep, uncomfortable beds, constant workload and long days had become easier.

Base Support had a question: 'Any thoughts about your welcome home dinner?' It made the imminent end of this journey feel real and motivated us to push on, knowing home was near.

Last night, as I was falling asleep, I had an uneasy sense that something could go wrong if we weren't careful. I felt compelled to share this at our morning team meeting.

As the team gathered around me in a semicircle near our planes, I said, 'Last night I was thinking about our landing at Esperance. We were in a big rush to refuel and get going, pushing last light. Even yesterday we were in a rush to get here.

'We've come so far and only have a couple of days to go; this is when we risk becoming a bit too relaxed and slack because we're getting tired with so much flying. Let's remember that we want to end this trip well. Let's keep up our concentration and have our eyes on the ball.

'I know myself: if I start to feel too comfortable and think we're almost there, that's when things could go wrong. When we pushed last light, we took a silly risk. Let's be sure to avoid that. Any comments?'

Everyone nodded in agreement. I hadn't said anything new, but it was worth a reminder. Each day there was a level of risk, but these were calculated, and all being equal, the risk of catastrophe was relatively low. I didn't want any of us not to make it home because we'd been a little careless or pushed it once too often.

The sparse desert was a good backdrop for a quick team photo before we took off. We looked so different from when we first started. Our bold expressions said it all—we were proud, seasoned adventurers exuding an air of battle-hardened confidence.

With the short flying time of around four hours, a tailwind and perfect conditions, we made great time scooting at 138 knots along the coast from the Nullarbor Hotel. I was lucky to glimpse a whale further out to sea, a common occurrence in these parts. The desert soon gave way to an abstract landscape of greens and browns towards the small coastal town of Ceduna where we refuelled our stomachs and our planes; then on to our overnight stop at Port Lincoln.

Approaching Coffin Bay, three aircraft radioed asking my location. Mick Hart, Kym Roach and Lyall Jaensch from Port Lincoln Flying Club had set out to escort us in. With Mick in his RV-6 off my left wing and below a line of rotating wind turbines perched atop the eroded cliffs, it was a memorable sight. Kym and Lyall followed as I went the scenic coastal route down south to West Point before heading back up to Port Lincoln. It was a magical moment and I felt privileged to have these guys flying with me.

On the ground, we were met by Barry Besold, the captain of the Port Lincoln Aeroclub, and his wife Pamela—both genuine and fun people. Barry was once a pilot in the US Air Force and an instructor, having flown some of the big transporters, including 747s.

Pam was a vivacious and very social person. She had multiple sclerosis (MS) but was still very mobile, getting around using a crutch. She had met Barry, the Silver Fox as she called him, when he flew, and I could see why they hit it off: both had a thirst for adventure.

They had arranged for people with disabilities to come down to meet us, and once I got my blood sugar levels up with chocolate from the diminishing supplies in my survival kit, I gave my talk. It was the biggest turnout we'd had on the trip, and it was fun to share our adventure and chat with the locals—of course showing the adaptations on my plane and demonstrating how I flew.

The aeroclub looked after us so well, providing transport to the luxurious Port Lincoln Hotel and covering the costs. A few members joined us for dinner; it was great to chat with Barry about his experiences and those of the other members, and to enjoy one of the restaurant's signature dishes—peppered tuna steak.

When flying in over the bay, I'd noticed large round cages

floating on the surface. Later I learned they were full of tuna being farmed for market. Although I'm now aware of the detrimental effects of tuna farming on the environment, at the time we couldn't refuse the succulent steaks straight out of the bay.

Flying time: 4.2 hours.

32

STUCK AGAIN

I'd always anticipated the southern coast would be one of the most difficult sections to get through, especially with the onset of winter weather. With a big low crossing South Australia and Victoria, it was starting to live up to my expectations.

As a large thunderstorm rolled over us during the night, I lay in bed hoping the weather would pass and allow for reasonable flying conditions.

Arriving at the airfield at nine a.m., the sky resembled a dark-grey blanket hanging above our heads. Nevertheless, pilots are generally an optimistic breed so we prepped the planes, checked weather sources and planned to wait in case a window opened up for our flight to Aldinga, three hours away. The plan was to fly north past Whyalla, cut across the bay, then south to Aldinga, doing a big U.

Michael called a few aeroclubs at airfields along our flight path to determine the weather in each location, but with rain and thunderstorms to the north and rain in Adelaide, the only other option was to fly out to sea over the bay to avoid the restricted areas, which I wasn't comfortable with given the deteriorating weather. So, to our frustration, we decided to call it a day.

Originally, we'd planned one night at Port Lincoln, two nights at Aldinga, and then back to Tooradin on Sunday 2 June. I was really hoping to make that date as various things were planned for our arrival. A few pilots from Tooradin had planned to meet us at Aldinga the following day and fly back with us on Sunday, where a lunch was planned at the aeroclub. Sofia had arranged media and, being a Sunday, we expected there'd be quite a few people to welcome us back. With this delay, we planned to shorten the stay in Aldinga to one night and hopefully still make it back on Sunday.

Fortunately, we could get the same rooms at the hotel with a discount, but they wouldn't be ready until two p.m. so to fill in the time Barry and Pam took us on a sightseeing tour of Port Lincoln, the highlight being Mick Hart's Skypark. This is a property with two airstrips, a hangar and a barn full of boys' toys. Michael was drooling at the assortment of aircraft and Bob was like a paparazzi snapping photos of everything.

The Barnstormers Inn, as Mick named it, is more like a museum showcasing planes, jeeps, bottles, guns, advertising signs, an old '50s caravan, and even an ornithopter (replica of the Flintstones' flying machine), all meticulously arranged. Mick fired up the vintage 1905 single-cylinder ornithopter; it cussed and spat in disgust, wings flapping. He momentarily put it into gear whereupon it jerked forward like a startled bull, scaring the crap out of us. I had visions of it careering out of control.

Against a wall I noticed a framed map of Australia with a flying route marked around the mainland. It was Mick's route from 2011 when he flew around mainland Australia in fourteen days, including three rest days, in his fast RV-6 with two other planes. He said he'd had perfect weather all the way and even got to Truscott in the far northwest where they landed momentarily. The manager threatened them with a hefty $600 landing fee if they didn't take off immediately. That was all the encouragement they needed.

Looking at the map, I was revisited by regret that I'd missed the bit up near Truscott, but on the plus side, I'd made it to Tassie.

With some unscheduled free time, I caught up on my growing mass of emails and blog comments. It was encouraging and inspiring to know that so many people were supporting our journey, collectively willing the weather to improve and boosting our spirits when things became hard. The longer the trip, the more people followed us, many eagerly awaiting the next update, not wanting it to end. *Love it, especially the blogs, photos and videos. Saddened the trip will end soon. Hope the weather slows you down! Only joking*, was one such message.

Although said in jest, the wish for bad weather became reality: the forecast for the next day was even worse. Disappointing as it was, we called a rest day: another night in Port Lincoln. Our plans to get back by Sunday had evaporated.

What the …? was my initial reaction as Gordon dropped a huge bombshell at the team meeting. He was leaving?! I was as shocked as the rest of the team.

He said he had a medical condition and had been chatting with his doctor to keep it under control, but it had reached a point where he could no longer manage it and needed to head back to Griffith to get it sorted.

After the meeting, I had a private word with Gordon, catching him at the elevator. Gordon being Gordon, the conversation was brief.

'I've had this condition for a while. I thought I could manage it but it's got worse.'

I'd had no idea he had a medical problem. 'Is there anything we can do to help?' I asked.

'No, I need to get back to Griffith and see the doctor.'

'Oh, OK. When are you thinking of leaving?' I asked.

'I'm checking out commercial flights and might leave in the

morning, but I'll see everyone before I leave.'

It was the last time I spoke with him on the flight. He left very early the following morning.

I later found out that his medical condition was caused by an undiagnosed tumor attached to his small bowel. He ended up having it removed, twice, before it went to his liver where thankfully, with ongoing treatment, it is being managed.

Gordon is a private person. He never let on that anything was wrong, and was always very matter-of-fact; but I imagine inside he would have been absolutely gutted.

Nevertheless, I was disappointed that Gordon hadn't been open with me or the team. In Ingham, I'd hoped that by being honest about how I was faring, the team would have felt encouraged to share any of their own troubling issues so we could manage them—but this wasn't Gordon. He was fiercely independent and wouldn't accept help from anyone. I kept thinking that if he had been upfront and shared his problem, there might have been something we could have done earlier to prevent it becoming unmanageable. I know it was his personal obstacle, but we were a team and his situation affected us all.

More than anything, though, I felt sad that he couldn't complete his personal goal for the flight—and it being so close, just two flying days short of our grand finale, made it even more disappointing.

Gordon had been a central member from the start, being the first person to put up his hand for the flight, and instrumental in getting Bob on board. He could cook a mean beef stew and always delivered what he'd promised. Paul would now fly the Archer with Josh the rest of the way, but it wouldn't be the same flying into Tooradin without one of our comrades.

With a luxurious sleep-in to nine a.m. that morning, it was a good opportunity to keep my shoes off for the day as my heels were getting red, which was becoming a concern, particularly given the small blister on my right heel. The bungee straps had caused more than one problem: first there was the blister caused by the hook that had heated up and roasted my leg; now I'd discovered that the bungee was putting extra pressure on my heels. There was nothing I could do but keep my shoes off as much as possible to avoid it turning into a pressure sore, and Josh would cover them when we got going again.

By 5.30 p.m., we'd received tomorrow's weather forecast so we gathered for our team meeting. Holding our breath, a sigh of relief drifted across the room as Michael gave the rundown: 'It's going to be cloudy with scattered showers, but it looks OK.' We would attempt to get out tomorrow.

Having caught up on most things, for once Linda and I had time for a drink with the team at the hotel sports bar. Everyone was relaxed and in good spirits—maybe from having a few spirits. Michael decided to play a joke on me. 'Dave, copy what I do, but if you stuff up you owe me ten dollars.'

'So, if I don't stuff up, you give me ten, right?' I asked.

The others looked on with amusement as he'd probably done the same trick on them. Michael turned his beer glass clockwise; I turned my wineglass clockwise. He lifted his up and put it on a coaster, I did the same. He picked up his glass, took a sip then put it down on the table. I picked mine up and copied. He smiled at me, leaned forward and dribbled the sip of beer from his mouth back into the glass.

'You owe me ten dollars,' he said, leaning back in the seat with a big grin, thinking he'd got me.

I smiled, pursed my lips, and in a perfect narrow stream, shot the wine out of my mouth onto Michael's chest.

His eyes bulged with surprise as we burst into laughter, tears streaming down our faces.

33

PARTY, FOG AND FRUSTRATIONS

Three nights in Port Lincoln would have been great had we been tourists, but with flying on our minds and champing at the bit to get home, it had been difficult to think of anything else.

We took off around noon, the later start giving the weather time to improve, then tracked north, climbing to 2500 feet, as high as I could go with the blanket of cloud. The grey bleakness intensified the filth of the steel mill on the coast at Whyalla; it looked like a black and white photograph.

Isolated showers dotted our way ahead. Paul and Josh in the Archer were to my right in the distance as we moved in company towards the coast to track past Adelaide, as our original route behind the mountains was too dangerous given the cloud.

The Lance, with Michael, Bob and Linda, flew well ahead and to their delight were directed to take a scenic route over Adelaide to avoid the busy traffic into Adelaide airport.

'Sierra Delta Whiskey and in company, this is Adelaide Centre,' came a stern female voice over the radio.

'Adelaide Centre, Sierra Delta Whiskey,' said Paul on the radio.

'Sierra Delta Whiskey, you are in a restricted area, exit to the east immediately, Adelaide Centre.'

'Exiting to the east, Sierra Delta Whiskey,' replied Paul, finishing the call.

'Get that, Dave?'

'Roger that,' I said.

How did that happen? I thought. There were numerous restricted areas on the route, with most de-activated. We had thought this area was also de-activated, however we'd inadvertently gone to the right of Port Wakefield Road instead of to the left, just clipping the edge of a restricted area. After we got back, Paul and I received a call from our respective authorities, giving us slaps on the wrists.

Adelaide sprawled from the coast to the base of the mountains in the distance. Compared to Melbourne it looked more like a big country town, the small city centre populated with relatively low high-rise buildings. The last time I was in Adelaide was 1994, when I competed in a wheelchair rugby tournament. The most memorable part of the trip was getting an eye-full in the room I was sharing with one of the players when his attractive girlfriend unashamedly got out of bed to adjust the curtains while naked.

Aldinga Airfield, south of Adelaide, is surrounded by farms and some well-known vineyards, with the McLaren Vale winery just down the road. The narrow black strip stood out from the green fields, calling me in. Two more landings to go, I thought as the wheels gripped the bitumen.

Evan John, the president, and other members of the Aldinga Aeroclub, as well as 5DME, a group of professional flying nerds promoting aviation, met us as we pulled up. They'd patiently waited the last few days for our arrival, the aeroclub ready to help with transport and anything else we needed.

I had no idea how many followers we had on the blog and Facebook. As the trip progressed, some of our cyber friends became a little friendlier, offering opinions and encouragement as I shared my experiences. With some, it felt like a weird long-distance relationship.

PARTY, FOG AND FRUSTRATIONS

When I met Mary, one of my avid followers, I saw it for what it was. She came up to me with a huge smile, gave me a hug, a kiss on the cheek and presented me with Amelia Bearheart, a stuffed bear dressed like an aviator with goggles, hat and jacket. 'I'm so proud of you, thank you,' she said.

To be honest, I was a little taken aback with the attention, but it made me realise that people were experiencing the flight with us, riding the highs, the lows, the fun times and the scary moments. They were getting something out of it, whether it was motivation, inspiration, entertainment or just a good laugh; they were part of it.

Due to delays, the original accommodation had fallen through so Neil and Linda Geddes donated a beautiful Victorian-style house for Josh, Paul, Michael and Bob while Linda and I stayed in a wheelchair-accessible motel.

The weather forecast looked pretty good for tomorrow apart from some fog, so this was to be our last night together. Josh went shopping and organised a dinner of gastronomic delight at the house. Conveniently, the house was only 300 metres from the motel so Linda and I walked around, rugged up in the cold winter air.

The house was bustling: Michael in charge of the kangaroo and lamb on the barbeque, Josh sorting the salads and setting the table while Bob coordinated in front of the TV with a beer. It was our own little party, a night to celebrate, reflect and appreciate all the experiences we'd had—from the cold and rain on the Tassie west coast, to the scary moments at Airlie Beach, getting stuck at Dunk Island, meeting the delightful Burketown schoolkids, the banquet of food at Nhulunbuy, the fun at Monsoons, Josh's weird sandwich fillings, and of course all the wonderful people we'd met along the way.

I had a lousy sleep that night but with the anticipation of getting home, I was ready for the long day ahead. We intended to stop at Portland to refuel, then on to Tooradin: around five hours' flying.

The club members, Evan and Phil John and David Ellis, picked us up and delivered us to the airfield just after seven a.m. There was a little fog in the South Mount Lofty Ranges, but it didn't look too bad. The cloud was quite high and our southern track didn't seem too bad either.

I felt confident we would get out, and at 8.08 a.m., with the last goodbye, I was in the air heading south and following the coast towards Cape Jervis. At 7 NM out from Aldinga Airfield, my confidence evaporated as a large bank of fog loomed in the distance. Beyond that, another wall of fog was sweeping to my right while on my left low cloud and fog blocked the tops of the mountain range.

If I kept going, I knew what would happen—I would fly down a tunnel, the walls slowly narrowing, and eventually I would be trapped. I'd been there before: it's a scary place and I never wanted to experience it again.

A few years earlier, when flying with my carer back from Mungo Lodge in NSW to Tooradin, the weather deteriorated the closer we got to Ballarat. With the ground getting higher and the cloud lower, we ran into a wall of cloud and rain that blocked our path ahead, left and right. With nowhere to go, I instinctively turned around to head back the way we'd come, but when I saw what was ahead, my heart stopped. The way out had closed behind us and we were trapped in every direction.

Feeling very stressed, I looked down and to my relief Ballarat airport was directly below. We were saved.

We spent the night at a motel, making it back home safely the next day. I have made a few mistakes, maybe pushed things a little too much at times, but I always learn from them. The trick is not to make one that costs you your life.

All paths had closed so, as disappointing as it was, the only option was back to Aldinga. I radioed to the Archer and Lance and we headed back.

This wasn't the first time any of us had had to turn around, and we still had some optimism left given it was early morning. Fog usually lifts with the warmth of the sun, so maybe we'd be in luck.

By 10.30 a.m., it was evident that the fog was getting worse, so reaching Tooradin that day had become impossible. We changed our goal for the day and decided to try for Portland or Warrnambool instead. As the minutes, then hours, slowly and painfully passed, conditions slightly improved but then got worse. I sat in the middle of the taxiway scouring the sky and hoping it would miraculously lift and clear. If I were religious, I would have prayed. The thick wall of fog just sat on top of the mountain range like a lid on a jar.

Each day Sofia had to contact the media outlets to let them know when we would get into Tooradin, but she would first call Linda to see how we were travelling.

'What time will you be arriving today?' asked Sofia.

'We're still waiting for the fog to lift and the pilots think we'll only get to Portland today—if we get up at all,' Linda reported.

'Oh, OK, will you be back tomorrow?'

'Ahh … maybe, but we don't know.'

'Oh, when will you know?'

'Don't know, maybe tomorrow.'

'Really?'

'Yep, really.'

One thing people find hard to understand, although not unexpectedly, is that we weren't like a commercial plane, able to fly in more demanding conditions. We flew fair-weather aircraft, limited to VFR, which basically meant we had to be able to see where we were flying.

Paul opened his iPad to check the weather. 'Portland's got moderate rain and cloud down to 800 feet and Warrnambool's got drizzle.' We'd run out of time, run out of luck and run out of options.

'OK, looks like we're staying here again,' I said to the team sitting around the table in the flying club.

Unloading and tying down the planes, I felt flat and the rest of the team also seemed drained of energy. Bob moved slowly; he looked like he was stooping as he dragged his feet around the Lance, unpacking it.

The day had started with the excitement and anticipation of getting home for the grand finale. Now everyone was quiet and went about their tasks without the usual chatter. The fog, our impenetrable barrier, had swept away our hope of making it home.

But this is what challenges are all about. By definition, they are hard, things don't go to plan and sometimes you don't even attain your goal. It is about rolling with the punches and adjusting the plan when circumstances change—as had happened in the Kimberley. Sticking to the plan too rigidly can be disastrous, leading to unnecessary risks.

We were on an emotional roller coaster, experiencing the highs and lows such as the boredom and uncertainty waiting on the airfield. These moments are the real challenge that test your resolve to maintain focus and keep going.

Flying isn't so much a physical challenge, but a psychological one. Flying in small planes is highly dependent on weather conditions and, of course, the pilot's skill. This means you must decide each day whether weather conditions are favourable. When the weather is good, decisions are easy, but when conditions are changeable and uncertain, you never know if your choice is the right one. Making these decisions daily over a long period of time eventually wears you down—as was evident that afternoon.

Linda quickly got to work to sort out where we would stay and, fortunately, we could return to the same accommodation. Evan, Phil and David shipped us back to our temporary home.

PARTY, FOG AND FRUSTRATIONS

There was no party that night.
Flying time: 0.5 hours.

34

WORTH THE FISH 'N' CHIPS

'One flying day to go!' We'd been saying this for two days. Today had to be it.

The golden orb of the low morning sun shone through high white stratus cloud, translucent wispy edges merging to a soft blue. To the south a low layer of grey cloud and fog hung above the rural landscape, obscuring the top of the mountain range.

The track south around Cape Jervis was blocked, but the route to the east directly across the mountains to Victor Harbor looked open. This was our way out.

With planes packed and goodbyes to Evan and the crew—they were no doubt hoping this was it—we were in the air by eight a.m.

Banking left, circling over the airfield and gaining height to line up with Victor Harbor, a wave of relief swept through me as I spotted the coast on the other side. My heart rate picked up with the thought, *We're on our way home!*

'It looks good, guys!' I radioed to the others as I headed over the mountains. With the cloud around 1000 feet above the highest peak, the view resembled the Hand of God: beams of light penetrating the grey and white cloud like fingers. It was one of those scenes you might imagine but rarely see.

We had finally escaped our frustrating imprisonment; we were over the wall and sprinting across the open field to freedom, not daring to look back, focused only on following the coast home.

As the Murray River mouth near Goolwa drifted by, I reflected on how different it looked now compared to last January when we flew through here on the trial flight: the skies had been cloudless and the summer heat horrific. It made me shudder just thinking about it. I didn't know it at the time, but where the Murray River mouth meets the ocean would be the final goal of another adventure, three years later—kayaking the 2226-kilometre length of the Murray River.

At 2500 feet, the coastline stretched into the distance. Past Younghusband Peninsula toward Salt Creek, the cloud-base started to get lower, forcing me to descend to 1500 feet. The occasional low wispy cloud became more frequent, which wasn't a good sign.

Within minutes, a large fog bank came into view, stretching from far inland out to sea. 'Sierra Delta Whiskey, Jabiru 5558, what's your position?' I radioed.

'Two miles south of Kingston. Cloud's down to the ground, we're turning around,' Paul replied.

'Affirm, I'm gonna try a little east. Will let you know how I go,' I replied.

Heading east a few miles inland, it became apparent there was no possible way through. Our short bid for freedom was over; the meteorological prison guards had cornered us once again. Banking to my left, Kingston SE airfield came into view, offering a nice bitumen strip where we could land and wait for the fog to pass.

For the next one and a half hours, I sat in my aircraft, sipping pre-mixed cappuccino and waiting to see if a passage through the cloud and fog would open up. The bitter Antarctic wind was like a deep freeze; I couldn't stop shivering, so Bob grabbed me a beanie and rugged me up in Michael's green sleeping bag to keep warm.

Another plane landed while we waited. A pilot in his thirties got out and chatted with Michael and Paul, then took off on a scud run (flying very low to the ground in marginal visibility) through the fog to get home.

When you're so focused on reaching your destination, a common condition known in the flying world as Get-there-itis can set in. *Maybe I could get through if I go a little lower. Just take it easy. I'm sure the fog won't go too far*, you tell yourself. The little voice in your head tries to persuade your better sense of judgement. It is so tempting to push it.

I wondered whether he got through, but we weren't about to risk it. We were virtually in our backyard and so close to the end. We'd been going for 37 days, six days longer than planned. The excitement of the adventure was mostly in the past: moving from place to place, eating out and being uncertain of where we would end up each day had lost its gloss. Also, the boys' wallets were a lot lighter after all the pubs they'd patronised.

Everyone had put their life on hold for this trip. Bob, Michael and Paul had jobs to get back to and lives to live in Griffith, while Josh had to return to his studies. For Linda and me—well, we just looked forward to doing nothing for a while. The flight and preparation had consumed our lives, and it would be a relief not to think about blogs or Facebook, forward planning, team organisation—or anything else to do with the flight. But most of all, I wanted my bed so I could get a good night's sleep and Linda was missing our dog, Zeus.

So yes, we were focused on our mission but were not about to take stupid risks. As the old saying goes, 'There are old pilots and bold pilots. But no old, bold pilots.'

The weather seemed a little better so once again we saddled up: the Archer and I took off first to head home. After taking off to the north, climbing to 1500 feet, I turned to track south, but all I could see in the distance were banks of low cloud reaching the ground. The last option—heading east inland around the fog bank—was equally futile.

Paul was up in the air and radioed to the Lance on the ground that it was a no-go. Grounded again. We parked the planes and I got out.

I was freezing, and not looking forward to sitting in the cold. Auspiciously, Brian Harris, a local flyer from the Kingston Flying Club arrived, opened up the clubhouse for us and got the heaters going to warm me up.

We chatted to Brian about his big adventure: flying solo in a Drifter (a slow, docile rag and tube ultralight) through central Australia, experiencing all weather conditions and the goodwill of local people who invited him in. This was in the '80s when ultralights were new on the scene and not very reliable.

It was now another waiting game—the worst bit. With nothing to do, all we could think about was getting going. Every ten minutes, one of us would venture outside hoping to see a change in the weather. It was frustration to the point of delirium. If the conditions didn't improve in a couple of hours, the day would be over.

Word had got around that we were temporarily stuck. Leon Brice in Naracoorte, some 42 NM to the east of Kingston SE, cajoled his sister Susan, who lived in Kingston SE, to drop in and see if she could help us.

Leon had first contacted me in 2010 after reading an article about my flying. At the time, his son Charles was still in the Adelaide hospital following a motorbike accident that left him with quadriplegia, a level similar to mine. My article opened their minds to the possibilities and gave the family a little hope for the future, which was in short supply at the time. This was one of the reasons why the *On a Wing & a Chair Around Australia Flight* was so important to me, and why I had to do it properly. Apart from changing attitudes of society to be more open, accepting and supportive of people with disabilities, it was about showing people that a disability does not define who you are or limit what you can achieve. What really limits a person is their mindset, what they *believe* they can do. With an open mind and perseverance, impossibilities can become possibilities.

Susan made our day by bringing her sandwich toaster to revive our cold soggy sandwiches, but our excitement levels peaked when Bob and Josh came back with fish and chips for lunch. Maybe it was the cold and hunger, but at the time they tasted like the best meal in the world and almost worth the delay. Needless to say, we didn't eat the sandwiches.

By two p.m., things weren't improving. Michael took my Jab up for a quick inspection of the conditions. There were showers down along the coast to the south towards Mount Gambier but to the east, in the direction of Naracoorte, it looked OK.

'We could go to Naracoorte and get some fuel,' Michael said, toying with the idea.

'Naracoorte gets fog at this time of year,' Brian Harris remarked.

'We can go to Naracoorte for fuel, but I'll be flying back to the coast in the morning,' I said to emphasise the goal of the flight.

Michael checked with the weather forecaster, confirming that tomorrow was likely to be better with only a five percent chance of fog. This was the clincher. We'd stay in Kingston SE tonight and head off early tomorrow morning for our 'one flying day to go'—hopefully!

Without delay, Base Support arranged our motel accommodation in the town. Fortunately, they had a van and picked us up, along with our gear. There was also a damn good heater.

Linda and I knocked out the blog and updated social media in record time, then went to the pub for dinner and drinks with the team.

Knocking off our chicken parmigianas, we wondered if we would actually get home tomorrow. We'd expected to have this flight done three days ago, but each time the weather gods had decided to ground us. I had anticipated the south coast would be a challenge, but I hadn't expected this.

Flying time: 1.7 hours.

35

WELCOME HOME DAVE AND TEAM

'Damn it's cold, I'm bloody freezing,' I moaned as I sat in my chair and vigorously shrugged my shoulders up and down in a vain attempt to keep warm as the bitter Antarctic wind blew across the airfield, penetrating my clothes like needles. At seven a.m., the sun was dull in an overcast sky. *At least there's no fog*, I thought.

'Try this on,' said Bob, wrapping Michael's lime-green sleeping bag around me.

'Thanks Bob ... Aww, piss off!' I yelled in annoyance, jerking my head from whatever ice-cold object he'd put against my neck in an attempt to be funny.

'What's wrong with ya? You're getting soft!' he said.

'You're what's wrong,' I said, cracking a smile.

'God, aren't you cold in that shirt, Josh?'

'No, I don't feel the cold,' he said as he tightened the oil cap on my plane.

'I can't last out here much longer, Josh,' I said. 'Hurry up, I've gotta get in.'

A high-pressure system was passing over us, producing plenty of wind, which meant no fog. I'd checked the weather forecast at six a.m. which indicated good weather and cloud around 3500 feet. We had a good chance of getting home today—but that's what we'd thought the last two times, and each time we were delayed. We weren't about to get too excited just yet. We knew that if we didn't get through today, we could be delayed for another week as more crappy weather was coming up fast behind us.

My body felt as stiff as a semi-frozen chicken as Josh bent my legs around the small door to get them into the tight cockpit. Already freezing, I wasn't sure how I would cope today and hoped the heater would warm me enough to at least avoid hypothermia.

My inability to control my body temperature is one of the most difficult things I have to deal with, given my level of disability. With a tolerable temperature range limited to 20–28 degrees, functioning outside the controlled environment is that much harder. Extremes just suck, with cold being the worst because it takes so long to warm up. The way I felt, I'd be lucky to warm up by the end of the day, even if I stayed out of the cold.

With the added motivation of escaping the deep freeze, and the clear possibility of getting home, it was the fastest pack and prep ever. We were in the air at eight a.m.

Climbing through 2500 feet, it was pure joy with the smooth air and a fantastic tailwind of about 23 knots giving me a ground speed of 138 knots—I was really flying!

People had been messaging us for our ETA so they could be at Tooradin when we landed. Once in the air, Linda texted Sofia so she could contact Channel Seven and shot off a Facebook post to let our followers know we were in the air and hoping to make Tooradin. She would provide an update at Portland to confirm our ETA.

Without available fuel at Kingston SE airport, we headed for our original planned refuel stop of Portland, over the border in Victoria.

According to the weather forecast, the wind would be gusting to 25 knots at Portland, a little challenging if it was a crosswind. Overflying the airport to take a look at the windsock, I was pleased to see the sock only slightly up (30 degrees or so from the vertical), indicating the wind was light and straight down the strip, making for an easy landing.

With teeth still chattering, the team rushed me out of the aircraft and into the Portland Aero Club house. While I blasted my face and shoulders with my trusty blow-heater, I consumed pea and ham Cup-A-Soup and MSG-laden hot noodles for the next one and a half hours as my body slowly thawed.

Peter Tapscott, the club's president, got us sorted and generously donated a tank of fuel for my plane. While we were waiting, he contacted the local reporter but they didn't show up until I was about to leave, which was annoying. Linda had just let the world know we'd be touching down at Tooradin at 1.30 p.m., which meant I had to be in the air by 11.30. It was going to be tight.

Quickly spewing out what I knew they needed, I got in the air just in time—my quickest interview and photo shoot of the trip.

With the tailwind still behind me, I rocketed toward home, passing Warrnambool, the Twelve Apostles and on towards Cape Otway. This was my backyard, and each minute my excitement grew.

I knew the strong northerly would generate rotor off the Cape Otway Mountains, which would make for rough flying, so I decided to fly out wide over the ocean to avoid the worst of it. Tightening my seat belt a little more, and checking to ensure my feet were strapped down, I waited.

Rounding the southern tip, the buffeting began. Only small bumps at first, but I dropped the engine revs to slow the plane's speed and make the ride a little smoother.

With my comfort level steadily decreasing, I braced my left arm against the window and locked my left hand into the rudder-lever to keep balance, then let the aircraft find its own way and ride the airwaves as it saw fit. I didn't fight the controls, gave just enough input to keep it heading in the right direction.

I noticed my altitude dropping so I put on more revs to gain height, not wanting to get too low over the ocean as my little plane swayed, rocked and rolled like a cork on a stormy sea. If I were able to clench my bum-cheeks, I could've cracked walnuts as flashbacks to Shute Harbour filled my mind.

As the faint township of Torquay grew clearer in the distance, it was the most beautiful sight I had seen for so long. Even in the turbulence, I relaxed a little, knowing what was to come.

The air soon smoothed out, as did my nerves, and I could see the familiar local landmarks ahead.

During this last short leg, both support aircrafts stuck with me. Just after crossing the heads of Port Phillip Bay towards Rosebud, the familiar voices of Tooradin aircraft traffic crackled on the radio. We were almost home.

Approaching French Island, I gave a call: 'Tooradin Traffic Jabiru 5558 and two in-company aircraft inbound 10 miles southwest, descending through 2700, estimating circuit at 35, Tooradin.'

'Welcome back, Dave,' said Dan, one of Tooradin's instructors.

I let the aircraft in the area know of our intensions for a low-level pass. I had no idea if anyone would be there; it was just something I'd been wanting to do ever since Day 1 when I did the first pass, which seemed so long ago.

Three miles out I gave a radio call of my intentions and lined up for my approach. In the distance, against the gloomy overcast sky, I could see yellow specks to the left of the runway. *Was it a sectioned-off area, a crashed plane with yellow markers?* I thought. Coming closer, I realised that the yellow dots were balloons people were holding as I blasted overhead. Yeah, baby, woohoo!

With a sense of purpose, the engine roared as I blew on my sip/puff tube, climbed to 1000 feet, banked right and joined downwind on Runway 04 to come in for my final landing for the *On a Wing & a Chair Around Australia Flight.* A little bit of turbulence near the hangars buffeted me around before settling down in the familiar manner just before the wheels touched.

With the customary little squeak and rumble as the wheels grabbed the bitumen, an immense sense of relief washed over me.

As I turned off the runway onto the mid taxiway, someone came on the radio: 'Jabiru, can you backtrack runway 04?' The Channel Seven film crew wanted to get a shot of me taxiing down the runway, so I had to do a 180 and taxi back towards the camera.

Turning off the runway, I glanced out my right window to see a bunch of yellow balloons lifting into the air, the cheers drowned out by the engine.

Flicking off the 'Mag' switches, the engine stopped, and … silence. I breathed a colossal sigh of relief. In a sense, the sigh released the last six years of holding my breath, never knowing whether I'd achieve my ultimate goal.

On 5 June 2013, after 38 days, 94 hours of flying, travelling a distance of around 18,000km, equivalent to flying from Melbourne to London, I achieved a world first: I was the first person with quadriplegia to fly solo around Australia. I had done it!

The wave of people hesitantly drifted over to my plane. First came the photographers from the *Herald Sun* and Channel Seven who scampered around, vying for a decent shot. In the crowd I noticed Lida and Gordon's wife, Bronwynne, many friends, my family and a lot of faces I didn't know. Some were my Facebook friends whom I'd soon meet.

A white sheet strung on the side of the hangar caught my eye: 'Welcome back Dave & Team,' read the black spray-painted lettering.

It was surreal; I felt almost in a daze. As I swung the door open, photographers clicked away as the crowd circled me.

'Well done, Dave!'

'Congratulations!'

I wasn't sure what to do as I had to wait for Josh and Paul to land before I could get out.

'G'day, how's it going?' I figured a bit of small talk wouldn't hurt. The crowd laughed.

Mum came over and gave me a big hug. 'Congratulations, I'm so proud of you!' she said.

I felt a little emotional—just for a moment.

'Give us a hand up,' yelled a photographer, snapping away furiously.

'Open your eyes,' said the other.

Dad shook my hand. 'Tremendous, Dave, magnificent, really, really tremendous! Roberta and I can now get some sleep,' he added. This was as massive a relief for them as it was for me.

'I finally made it!' I yelled, the crowd cheering and laughing; I think they couldn't believe we were finally home either.

Josh and Paul soon arrived and helped me from my cocoon. Following a second round of photos in my wheelchair and with Linda, an interview for Channel Seven and *Plane Crazy Down Under*, I could finally catch my breath and try to chat with everyone. I felt a little self-conscious and awkward, but at the same time so grateful that people were interested enough to see the team arrive. I tried to greet everyone and have a chat but it was a whirlwind, my head spinning with people coming up to shake my hand and give me hugs, ask questions and request photos. A couple of people said, 'I loved your blogs, but now I have nothing to look forward to each night.' It made all the late nights worth it.

With the team sorting out gear and putting the planes to bed, I saw Dr Tom eyeing off my leg.

'Let me take a look at your leg, Dave,' he said, opening up his toolkit of patches, swabs and disinfectant.

Dr Tom was our go-to doctor for the flight if we needed help; he was the husband of a good friend of mine, Deb, whom I had known for almost twenty-five years. She'd been one of my carers in the early days. Dr Tom was very unassuming, with thinning blond hair and silver wire-rim glasses. His compassionate and genuine persona often gave way to a mischievous smile, like a young boy being naughty.

When he pulled the patch off the burn, it was red, deep and nasty.

'How's it looking?' I asked.

'I don't think we'll need to amputate just yet,' he said with a grin.

Dr Tom gave the wound a good hard clean to remove the dead tissue and muck. I was so glad I couldn't feel it; just looking at it made me feel queasy.

With the planes put away, the crowd drifted off. We packed the cars and headed to Mum and Dad's place, giving a phone interview to the *Herald Sun* on the way. We were tired and I think the final delays had drained at least some of the excitement.

Sipping champagne, we toasted the success of the flight, our safe arrival back and the afternoon at Monsoons—because Bob will never forget it. Bob also suggested, 'Let's toast our fallen man, Gordon.'

Bronwynne had tears in her eyes. I think she felt the disappointment about Gordon having to leave the flight early. Given his paraplegia, the flight was a challenge for Gordon, doing everything for himself, on top of which was his medical issue—the strength with which he handled it was a credit to his remarkable tenacity, skill and independence.

I may have succeeded in flying solo around Australia, but it was only possible because of my team; I can never repay them for their invaluable assistance and commitment. The team allowed each of us to achieve something that would have been impossible as individuals. The flight was a once in a lifetime adventure, allowing us to see parts of the country that very few would. Then, everyone went back home and picked up their lives.

For Bob, however, the flight stirred his adventurous spirit. A month later he was on the phone asking, 'When's the next adventure?'

After a failed attempt in 2014 due to poor weather, in 2017 Bob, Linda and I crossed eight deserts and flew along the coastline of the northwest Kimberley which we'd missed in 2013. The *8 Deserts Run* gave us a chance to experience one of the most spectacular parts of Australia; another unforgettable experience.

For Michael, I think the adventure boosted his confidence in his pilot abilities and skills. He later followed his dream and got a job flying for a commercial airline in the USA.

When I returned to work, I looked around at everyone sitting in the same chairs, at the same desks, doing the same jobs as when I'd left. This was the moment I realised that I no longer fitted into the same mould; I had changed, I was different.

I found it hard to put my finger on what was different, mainly because it wasn't just one thing. Inner confidence in my capabilities had grown, whether in managing and leading a team, in my skills as a pilot, or in the now firm belief that despite the challenges of a situation, I knew I could work through them. My world of possibilities had expanded.

The goals we find the hardest—those we struggle with, that take immense effort to accomplish—are the ones that generate the most personal growth and add value to our lives. By working through the highs, lows and challenges over the six years of preparation and during the flight, especially the times when I wanted to give up, I had learned so much about myself.

Working through seemingly formidable challenges has consolidated my belief that by 'doing it differently'—having an open mind to possibilities and finding creative solutions, combined with the courage to push through our fears, doggedly persevering and drawing upon the support of the right people, we can achieve far more than we think is possible.

The OWC flight pushed me mentally and physically, at times way beyond my comfort zone. Because of this, the most surprising thing I learnt about myself on this flight was that I hadn't reached my limits. I began to wonder: what is my true potential? Where do my limits lie? Indeed, where do *anyone's* limits lie?

This was what I needed to find out.

36

AFTER THE FLIGHT

The silence of the house closed in on me. The frenzied activity of flight planning, organising, leading, social media, stress, excitement—all of it had suddenly disappeared. The world had screeched to a halt with a deafening silence.

In the immediate aftermath of the flight, I just wanted to crawl into a hole and switch off from everything for a while. I felt exhausted—physically, mentally and emotionally shattered. I didn't have the energy to see people or think about anything more than directing my carers and deciding what I needed for breakfast. I was so happy to sleep in my own bed, to get up when I wanted, to have time to myself as well as quality time with Linda, and to do nothing. I also had to allow time for my leg to recover from the nasty burn; it took seven months to heal.

But it wasn't long before I felt at a loose end, a little lost. My sense of purpose for the last six years had come to an abrupt end and I struggled to readjust to normal life. I still had plenty to keep me busy—in particular, distributing $10,000 the flight had raised, which we donated to two charities, the Able Management Group and the Australian Quadriplegic Association (Victoria), both of which provide support to people with disabilities.

The flight and our mission caught the imagination of the

public. I was awarded the Victoria Pride of Australia Medal, but the most humbling was being nominated as a Victorian Finalist for Australian of the Year 2014. I could never have dreamed of being worthy of such a nomination, let alone to be in the same league as the other recipients. Topping it all off, I was awarded an Order of Australia Medal in 2015 for my contribution to people with a disability through sport.

The most satisfying aspect of these experiences was meeting so many amazing people. Each of them inspired me to do even more. They weren't overpaid actors, rich businesspeople or self-important celebrities. They were the many unassuming Australians who dedicate years to helping their communities and making a difference in peoples' lives. They don't do it for wealth, fame or ego; they do it because they want to contribute to the betterment of our world. These are the true unsung heroes of our society.

The question I ask myself is: Did we make a difference? And my answer is, 'yes.' By how much? Well, who knows. For some, hopefully a lot; for others, perhaps we might have planted a small seed, an idea, that over time and with the right conditions can flourish. The degree doesn't really matter. Anything positive was worth the effort.

Our aim was to raise the public's expectation of what people with disabilities are capable of.

In addition, I hope that, by example, we encouraged people—whether with a disability or without—to consider, even question, their true potential and what they could ultimately achieve in life.

In the following years, I've received emails from people around the world, and locals would say to me in person, 'If you can fly around Australia, I can do … (whatever their dream is).'

A young guy who'd heard one of my talks emailed me the following message: *You have inspired me to follow my dream. A lot of people say I can't do it, but seeing you fly means I can.*

His dream was base-jumping. I hope he is OK!

One of the most touching emails I received was from one of the kids we met from Burketown State School:

My name's Latreya and I know you wouldn't remember me.

But I have always remembered you and the day you flew into Burketown and spoke to the kids from my school when I was in Year Five.

And I just wanted to tell you, I am in Year Nine now and your story touched my heart and ever since that day you have always been my inspiration.

EPILOGUE

A few weeks after the flight, I began to feel restless. I needed another project, but this time I wanted a personal adventure to see how far I could push myself, to truly test my physical and mental limits and capabilities.

On 1 March 2016, my support team and I set off on the Paddle Wheel Murray River Expedition for my world-first attempt to paddle 2,226 kilometres down the Murray River from Lake Hume, NSW, to the sea at Goolwa (Murray Mouth) in South Australia. I was in a modified kayak, my hands taped to the paddle.

Over eighty-nine grueling days, I experienced extreme heat, exhaustion, cold, rain, no river flow, infected hands, blue-green algae, spectacular scenery, diverse wildlife, the sinking of our punt and equipment, getting lost and much more. It was one hell of an adventure … but that's another story!

ACKNOWLEDGEMENTS

Many people helped get the *On a Wing & a Chair Around Australia Flight* off the ground. Each person involved owns a part of our success, and I hope they feel proud. I am so grateful for your support.

There are a number of people who played key roles in the project that I want to single out and thank:

Firstly, my wife, Linda Sands, who not only met but married me during the project—despite the Bangkok incident! Thank you from the bottom of my heart for your love and unreserved support, for dedicating yourself entirely to the project, working tirelessly with minimal sleep and doing so much more than I could cover in this book.

To my parents, Brian and Roberta Jacka: you did so much more than fulfil the role of Base Support. You were with me from the very beginning of this journey, through all my struggles and triumphs, supporting me when I needed a rock to lean on and talk things through. You always made yourselves available to help with whatever you could to take the pressure off me, Linda and others. You are the most wonderful and generous people; I am so proud and love you both.

The Magnificent Seven flight team—my gratitude goes to Bob Frauenfelder and Gordon McCaw for piloting and supplying your aircraft and fuel; to Michael Prince and Paul McCaw for your technical knowledge, pilot skills and keeping Bob and Gordon on the straight and narrow. Huge thanks to Lida Paunova and Josh Foote for assisting me as personal support. Thank you all for your friendship, support and for being part of our adventure. You are incredible people and it was due to your individual skills, knowledge and inner strength that we made it around the country in one piece.

I thank the OWC executive team, Arlee Hatfield, Nick Fenwick and Louise Alexander, for your friendship, willingness to help me get OWC off the ground and your assistance and support during the project. It was a long haul but we got there in the end! Thanks also to Matt McInnes for your valued assistance and advice with the website and social media platform.

To Sofia Dedes from Will & Word Communications: a huge thanks for providing pro-bono your time, skills and networks; for sourcing tons of media that gave OWC incredible national exposure, ensuring our message was heard.

A massive thanks to the incredible Karen Rumley from I.D. Yours for donating your amazing talents to designing the OWC website, logos, banners, business cards, the map in this book and anything else I could dream up for you. Also, I greatly appreciate all the pro-bono work you've done for my ongoing adventures.

I can't forget the families, partners and employers who supported those involved in the project, enabling them to make a difference in our small patch of the world—thank you!

A huge thanks to those who donated money to OWC; all proceeds were distributed to two worthy charities, AQA (Victoria) and AMG, which support people with disabilities. Also, a big thanks to the kids at Trinity Primary School for their generous donation and letters of support.

Many other people generously provided information, equipment, uniforms, accommodation, transport, food, good company, conversations, friendships and assistance. Thanks, in particular, to the following (in no particular order):

ACKNOWLEDGEMENTS

Tooradin Flying School, Ian Loveridge
Punkin Head Air Sports (aircraft cover)
Matt Browne, Rosbert International
Chris Dixon, Thompson aviation
Telstra
Electro Cut Signs (aircraft stickers)
John Kidon
Craig Fraser and The Legends of GOFPOS, Signal X,
Neil Wise and The Night Before Tomorrow
Wynyard Aeroclub
Dale Triffett, Island Air Maintenance
ParaQuad Association of Tasmania
East Gippsland Aeroclub
Frogs Hollow Aeroclub
Illawarra Flyers
Candy Anderson, Terralong Terrace Apartments
Hastings District Flying Club
Rotary Club of Caboolture
Airlie Beach Hotel, Airlie Beach
Whitsunday Aeroclub
Compass Whitsundays
Peter Bond, owner of Dunk Island
Tropixx Motel, Ingham
Michael Coates, XCOM Avionics
Jill Williams, Endeavour Lions Club, Cooktown
Tony Likiss, Cooktown Shire Council
Seaview Motel, Cooktown
Trevor and Pam Snodgrass
Weipa State Emergency Service Unit
Albatros Bay Resort, Weipa
Anchorage caravan park, Weipa
Gove Operations Pacific Aluminium (Rio Tinto)

Scott Barlow
Top End Flying Club
Darwin Central Hotel, Darwin
Tony Stevenson and Kim Maldon and the Department of Fire and Emergency Services (DFES)
Kimberley Grande Hotel, Kununurra
Kununurra Fire & Rescue
Dave Coulston, Virgin Australia
Country Women's Association of WA (Inc), Derby
Marg Jacka and Jon Newman
Bay Village workers accommodation, Karratha
Karratha Flying Services
Adrian Van Schouwen, Cloud Dancer Sport Aircraft
Carnarvon State Emergency Service Unit
Fascine Lodge, Carnarvon
Midwest Aeroclub
Royal Aeroclub of Western Australia
Curtin Flying Club
David and Jen Ford, Andy Burns, and Esperance Aeroclub
Barry and Pamela Besold, Mick Hart, Kym Roach, Lyall Jaensch and Port Lincoln Flying Club
Port Lincoln Passenger Service
Port Lincoln Hotel, Port Lincoln
Aldinga Aeroclub
Neil and Linda Geddes
Leon and Susan Brice
Portland Aero Club
Air Traffic Controllers around Australia

ACKNOWLEDGEMENTS

A special thanks to Darrell Pitt for mentoring me during my writing journey, assisting with this book as well as my first, *Six Percent*. I greatly appreciate you sharing your experience and ideas that helped me persevere when it was hard-going.

Thank you to my dad, Brian Jacka, for straightening out my tenses, grammar and paragraph structure in an early draft. And for adding your perspective on specific moments in the flight.

A big thanks to Tanya Carter for your help during the project, but also recently in reviewing this book and providing valuable feedback—especially from a non-flyer's perspective. Also, thanks to Andrew Raszevski for working your magic on my photos; they look so much better.

Finally, many thanks to Nadine Davidoff. You are a literary archeologist, chipping away at the mass of material to reveal a hidden treasure. Your skilled copy-editing has once again made my story shine even brighter.

www.ingramcontent.com/pod-product-compliance
Lightning Source LLC
Chambersburg PA
CBHW020315010526
44107CB00054B/1856